W9-BJU-235

BHAGWAN SHREE RAJNEESH

THE BOOK
OF
THE SECRETS-I

Discourses on "Vigyana Bhairava Tantra"

COMPILATION:

Ma Yoga Astha

EDITORS:

Ma Ananda Prem
Swami Ananda Teerth

HARPER COLOPHON BOOKS
Harper & Row, Publishers
New York, Hagerstown, San Francisco, London

The sutras quoted in this book are taken from "Centering" in *Zen Flesh, Zen Bones* (Anchor Books edition, 1972 reprint), transcribed and compiled by Paul Reps, and are printed with the kind permission of the author.

A hardcover edition of this book is published by Harper & Row, Publishers, Inc.

THE BOOK OF THE SECRETS—I. Copyright © 1974 by Rajneesh Foundation, Poona, India. All rights reserved. Printed in the United States of America. No part of this book may be used or reproduced in any manner whatsoever without written permission except in the case of brief quotations embodied in critical articles and reviews. For information address Harper & Row, Publishers, Inc., 10 East 53d Street, New York, N.Y. 10022.

First HARPER COLOPHON edition published 1977

ISBN: 0–06–090564–6

77 78 79 80 81 10 9 8 7 6 5 4 3 2

The Book Of The Secrets—I

Eighty discourses on "Vigyana Bhairava Tantra"
(Lord Shiva's 112 Methods of meditation)
in five volumes

Given by
Bhagwan Shree Rajneesh

From October 1972 to November 1973
in Bombay, India

Contents

1
The World Of Tantra

October 1, 1972, Bombay, India

SUTRA:

Devi asks:

Oh Shiva, what is your reality?
What is this wonder-filled universe?
What constitutes seed?
Who centers the universal wheel?
What is this life beyond form pervading forms?
How may we enter it fully, above space and time, names and descriptions?
Let my doubts be cleared!

Some introductory points. First, the world of "Vigyana Bhairava Tantra" is not intellectual; it is not philosophical. Doctrine is meaningless to it. It is concerned with method, with technique — not with principles at all. The word "tantra" means technique, the method, the path. So it is not philosophical: note this. It is not concerned with intellectual problems and inquiries. It is not concerned with the "why" of things: it is concerned with "how" — not with what is Truth, but how the Truth can be attained.

"Tantra" means technique. So this treatise is a scientific one. Science is not concerned with "why": science is concerned with "how". That is the basic difference between philosophy and science. Philosophy asks, "Why this existence?" Science asks, "How this existence?" The moment you ask the question "How?" method, technique, become important. Theories become meaningless; experience becomes the center.

Tantra is science: tantra is not philosophy. To understand philosophy is easy because only your intellect is required. If you can understand language, if you can understand concept, you can understand philosophy. You need not change; you require no transformation. As you are, you can understand philosophy — but not tantra.

You will need a change; rather, a mutation. Unless YOU are different, tantra cannot be understood because tantra is not an intellectual proposition : it is an experience. Unless you are receptive, ready, vulnerable to the experience, it is not going to come to you.

Philosophy is concerned with the mind. Your head is enough; your totality is not required. Tantra needs you in your totality. It is a deeper challenge. You will have to be in it whole and sole. It is not fragmentary. A different approach, a different attitude, a different mind to receive it is required. Because of this, Devi is asking "apparently" philosophical questions. Tantra starts with Devi's questions. All the questions can be tackled philosophically.

Really, any question can be tackled in two ways: philosophically or totally, intellectually or existentially. For example, if someone asks, "What is love?" you can tackle it intellectually, you can discuss, you can propose theories, you can argue for a particular hypothesis. You can create a system, a doctrine — and you may not have known love at all.

To create a doctrine experience is not needed. Really, on the contrary, the less you know the better because then you can propose a system unhesitatingly. Only a blind man can easily define what light is. When you do not know you are bold. Ignorance is always bold; knowledge hesitates. And the more you know, the more you feel that the ground underneath is dissolving. The more you know, the more you feel how ignorant you are. And those who are really wise, they become ignorant. They become as simple as children or as simple as idiots.

The less you know, the better. To be philosophical, to be dogmatic, to be doctrinaire — this is easy. To tackle a problem intellectually is very easy. But to tackle a problem existentially — not just to think about it, but to live it through, to go through it, to allow yourself to be transformed through it — is difficult. That is, to know love one will have to be in love. That is dangerous because you will not remain the same. The experience is going to change you. The moment you enter love, you enter a different person. And when you come out you will not be able to recognize your old face. It will not belong to you. A discontinuity will have happened. Now there is a gap. The old man is dead and the new man has come. That is what is known as rebirth — being twice-born.

Tantra is non-philosophical and existential. So, of course, Devi asks questions which appear to be philosophical, but Shiva is not going to answer them that way. So it is better to understand it in the beginning; otherwise you will be puzzled because Shiva is not going to answer a single question. All the questions that Devi is asking, Shiva is not going to answer at all. And still he answers ! And, really, only he has answered them and no one else — but on a different plane.

Devi asks, "What is your reality, my Lord ?" He is not going to answer it. On the contrary, he will give a technique. And if Devi goes through this technique, she will know. So the answer is round-about; it is not direct. He is not going to answer "who am I". He will give a technique. Do it and you will know.

For tantra, doing is knowing, and there is no other knowing. Unless you do something, unless you change, unless you have a different perspective to look at, to look with, unless you move in an altogether different dimension than the intellect, there is no answer. Answers can be given: they are all lies. All philosophies are lies. You ask a question and the philosophy gives you an answer. It satisfies you or doesn't satisfy you. If it satisfies you, you become a convert to the philosophy, but you remain the same. If it doesn't satisfy you, you go on searching for some other philosophy to be converted to. But you remain the same; you are not touched at all; you are not changed.

So whether you are a Hindu or a Mohammedan or a Christian or a Jain, it makes no difference. The real person behind the facade of a Hindu or a Mohammedan or a Christian is the same. Only words differ, or clothes. The man who is going to the church or to the temple or to the mosque is the same man. Only faces differ, and they are faces which are false: they are masks. Behind the masks you will find the same man, the same anger, the same aggression, the same violence, the same greed, the same lust — everything the same. Is Mohammedan sexuality different from Hindu sexuality ? Is Christian violence different from

Hindu violence? It is the same! The reality remains the same; only clothes differ.

Tantra is not concerned with your clothes: tantra is concerned with you. If you ask a question it shows where you are. It shows also that wherever you are you cannot see; that is why the question. A blind man asks, "What is light?" Philosophy will start answering what is light. Tantra will know only this — that if a man is asking "What is light?" it shows only that he is blind. Tantra will start operating on the man, changing the man, so that he can see. Tantra will not say what is light. Tantra will tell how to attain insight, how to attain seeing, how to attain vision. When the vision is there, the answer will be there. Tantra will not give you the answer; tantra will give you the technique how to attain the answer.

Now this answer is not going to be intellectual. If you say something about light to a blind man, this is intellectual. If the blind man himself becomes capable of seeing, this is existential. This is what I mean when I say that tantra is existential. So Shiva is not going to answer Devi's questions. Still, he will answer — the first thing.

The second thing: this is a different type of language. You must know something about it before we enter into it. All the tantra treatises are dialogues between Shiva and Devi. Devi questions and Shiva answers. All the tantra treatises start that way. Why? Why this method? It is very significant. It is not a dialogue between a teacher and a disciple: it is a dialogue between two lovers. And tantra signifies through it a very meaningful thing: that the deeper teachings cannot be given unless there is love between the two — the disciple and the teacher. The disciple and teacher must become deep lovers. Only then can the higher, the beyond, be expressed.

So it is a language of love: the disciple must be in an attitude of love. But not only this, because friends can be lovers. Tantra says a disciple moves as receptivity. So the disciple must be in a feminine receptivity; only then is something possible. You need not be a woman to be a disciple, but you need to be in a feminine attitude of receptivity. Devi asks: it means the feminine attitude asks. Why this emphasis on feminine attitude?

Man and woman are not only physically different: they are psychologically different. Sex is not only a difference in the body. It is a difference in psychologies also. A feminine mind means receptivity — total receptivity, surrender, love. A disciple needs a feminine psychology; otherwise he will not be able to learn. You can ask, but if you are not open then you cannot be answered. You can ask a question and still remain closed. Then the answer cannot penetrate you. Your doors are closed; you are dead. You are not open.

A feminine receptivity means a womb-like receptivity in the inner depth so that you can receive. And not only that: much more is implied. A woman is not only receiving something. The moment she receives it, it becomes a part of her body. A child is received. A woman conceives. The moment there is conception, the child has become part of the feminine body. It is not alien, it is not foreign. It has been absorbed. Now the child will live not as something added to the mother, but just as a part, just as the mother. And the child is not only received: the feminine body becomes creative; the child begins to grow.

A disciple needs a womb-like receptivity. Whatsoever is received is not to be gathered as a dead knowledge. It must grow in you; it must become blood and bones in you. It must become a part now. It must grow! This growth will change you, will transform you — the receiver. That is why tantra uses this device. Every treatise starts with Devi asking a question and Shiva replying to it. Devi is Shiva's consort, his feminine part.

One thing more: now modern psychology, depth psychology particularly, says that man is both man and woman. No one is just male and no one is just female. Everyone is bi-sexual. Both sexes are there. This is a very recent research in the West, but for tantra this has been one of the most basic concepts for thousands of years. You must have seen some pictures of Shiva as *ardhanarishwar* — half man, half woman. This is the only concept like it in the whole history of man. Shiva is depicted as half man, half woman.

So Devi is not just a consort. She is Shiva's other half. And unless a disciple becomes the other half of the teacher, it is impossible to convey the higher teachings, the esoteric methods. When you become one then there is no doubt. When you are one with the teacher — so totally one, so deeply one — there is no argument, no logic, no reason. One simply absorbs; one becomes a womb. And then the teaching begins to grow in you and change you.

That is why tantra is written in love language. Something must also be understood about love language. There are two types of languages: logical language and love language. There are basic differences between the two.

Logical language is aggressive, argumentative, violent. If I use logical language, I become aggressive upon your mind. I try to convince you, to convert you, to make a puppet of you. My argument is "right" and you are "wrong". Logical language is egocentric : "I am right and you are wrong, so I must prove that I am right and you are wrong." I am not concerned with you. I am concerned with my ego. My ego is "always right".

Love language is totally different. I am not concerned with my ego; I am concerned with you. I am not concerned to prove something, to strengthen my ego. I am concerned to help you. It is a compassion to help you to grow, to help you to transform, to help you to be reborn.

Secondly, logic will always be intellectual. Concepts and principles will be significant. Arguments will be significant. With love language what is said is not so significant; rather, it is the way it is said. The container, the word, is not important. The content, the message, is more important. It is a heart-to-heart talk, not a mind-to-mind discussion. It is not a debate: it is a communion.

So this is rare: Parvati is sitting in the lap of Shiva and asking, and Shiva answers. It is a love dialogue — no conflict, as if Shiva is speaking to himself. Why this emphasis on love — love language ? Because if you are in love with your teacher, then the whole gestalt changes: it becomes different. Then you are not hearing his words. Then you are drinking him. Then words are irrelevant. Really, the silence between the words becomes more significant. What he is saying may be meaningful or it may not be meaningful — but it is his eyes, his gestures, his compassion, his love.

That is why tantra has a fixed device, a structure. Every treatise starts with Devi asking and Shiva answering. No argument is going to be there, no wastage of words. There are very simple statements of fact, telegraphic messages with no view to convince, but just to relate.

If you encounter Shiva with a question, with a closed mind, he will not answer you in this way. First your closing has to be broken. Then he will have to be aggressive. Then your prejudices, then your preconceptions — they have to be destroyed. Unless you are cleared completely of your past, nothing can be given to you. But this is not so with his consort Devi: with Devi there is no past.

Remember, when you are deeply in love your mind ceases to be. There is no past; only the present moment becomes everything. When you are in love the present is the only time. The now is all — no past, no future.

So Devi is just open. There is no defense — nothing to be cleared, nothing to be destroyed. The ground is ready. Only a seed has to be dropped. The ground is not only ready, but welcoming, receptive, asking to be impregnated.

So all these sayings that we are going to discuss will be telegraphic. They are just sutras. But each sutra, each telegraphic message given by Shiva, is worth a Veda, worth a Bible, worth a Koran. Each single sentence can become the base of a great scripture. Scriptures are logical: you have to propose, defend, argue. Here there is no argument: just simple statements of love.

Thirdly, the very words "Vigyana Bhairava Tantra" mean the technique of going beyond consciousness. "Vigyana" means consciousness, *"Bhairava"* means the state which is beyond consciousness and "tantra" means the method — the method of going beyond consciousness. This is the supreme doctrine — without any doctrine.

We are unconscious, so all the religious teachings are concerned with how to go beyond unconsciousness, how to be conscious. For example, Krishnamurti, Zen, they are all concerned with how to create more consciousness, because we are unconscious. So how to be more aware, alert? From unconsciousness, how to move toward consciousness? But tantra says that this is a duality — unconscious and conscious. If you move from unconsciousness to consciousness, you are moving from one duality to another. Move beyond both! Unless you move beyond both, you can never reach the Ultimate. So be neither the unconscious nor the conscious: just go beyond, just be. Be neither the conscious nor the unconscious: just BE! This is going beyond yoga, going beyond Zen, going beyond all teachings.

"Vigyana" means consciousness and "Bhairava" is a specific term, a tantra term, for one who has gone beyond. That is why Shiva is known as Bhairava and Devi is known as Bhairavi — those who have gone beyond the dualities.

In our experience only love can give a glimpse. That is why love becomes the very basic device to impart tantra wisdom. In our experience we can say that only love is something which goes beyond duality. When two persons are in love, the deeper they move in it, the less and less they are two, the more and more they become one. And a point comes and a peak is reached when only "apparently" they are two : inwardly they are one; the duality is transcended.

Only in this sense does Jesus' saying that "God is love" become meaningful; otherwise not. In our experience love is nearest to God. It is not that God is loving as Christians go on interpreting — that God has a fatherly love for you. Nonsense ! "God is love" is a tantric statement. It means love is the only reality in our experience which reaches nearest to God, to the

Divine. Why ? Because in love oneness is felt. Bodies remain two, but something beyond the bodies merge and become one.

That is why there is so much hankering after sex. The real hankering is after oneness, but that oneness is not sexual. In sex two bodies have only a deceptive feeling of becoming one, but they are not one. They are only joined together. But for a single moment two bodies forget themselves in each other, and a certain physical oneness is felt. This hankering is not bad, but to stop at it is dangerous. This hankering shows a deeper urge to feel oneness.

In love, on a higher plane, the inner one moves, merges into the other, and there is a feeling of oneness. Duality dissolves. Only in this non-dual love can we have a glimpse of what is the state of a *Bhairava*. We may say that the state of a *Bhairava* is absolute love with no coming back. From the peak of love there is no falling back. It is remaining on the peak.

We have made Shiva's abode on Kailash. That is simply symbolic: it is the highest peak, the holiest peak. We have made it Shiva's abode. We can go there, but we will have to come down. It cannot be our abode. We can go on a pilgrimage. It is a *Teerthyatra* — a pilgrimage, a journey. We can touch for a single moment the highest peak; then we will have to come back.

In love this holy pilgrimage happens, but not for all because almost no one moves beyond sex. So we go on living in the valley, the dark valley. Sometimes someone moves to the peak of love, but then he falls back because it is so dizzying. It is so high, and you are so low. And it is so difficult to live there. Those who have loved, they know how difficult it is to be constantly in love. One has to come back again and again. It is Shiva's abode. He lives there; it is his home.

A *Bhairava* lives in love; that is his abode. When I say that is his abode, I mean now he is not even aware of love — because if you live on Kailash, you will not be aware that this is Kailash, this is a peak. The peak becomes a plain. Shiva is not aware of love. We are aware of love because we live in non-love. And because of the contrast we feel love. Shiva IS love. The state of

11

"*Bhairava*" means that one has become love, not loving: one has become LOVE, one lives on the peak. The peak has become his abode.

How to make this highest peak possible, beyond duality, beyond unconsciousness, beyond consciousness, beyond the body and beyond the soul, beyond the world and beyond the so-called *Moksha* (Liberation)? How to reach this peak? The technique is "tantra". But tantra is pure technique, so it is going to be difficult to understand. First let us understand the questions — what Devi is asking.

"Oh Shiva, what is your reality?" Why this question? You can also ask this question, but it will not carry the same meaning. So try to understand why Devi asks, "What is your reality?" Devi is in deep love. When you are in deep love, for the first time you encounter the inner reality. Then Shiva is not the form, then Shiva is not the body. When you are in love, the body of the beloved falls, disappears. The form is no more and the formless is revealed. You are facing an abyss. That is why we are so afraid of love. We can face a body, we can face a face, we can face a form. But we are afraid of facing an abyss.

If you love someone, if you really love, his body is bound to disappear. In some moments of climax, of peak, the form will dissolve, and through the beloved you will enter the formless. That is why we are afraid : it is falling into a bottomless abyss. So this question is not just a simple curiosity: "Oh Shiva, what is your reality?"

Devi must have fallen in love with the form. Things start that way. She must have loved this man as man, and now when the love has come of age, when the love has flowered, this man has disappeared. He has become formless. Now he is to be found nowhere. "Oh Shiva, what is your reality?" It is a question asked in a very intense love moment. And when questions are raised, they become different according to the mind in which they are asked.

So create the situation, the milieu of the question in your mind. Parvati must be at a loss. Devi must be at a loss. Shiva has disappeared. When love reaches its peak the lover disappears. Why does this happen? This happens because, really, everyone is formless. You are not a body. You move as a body, you live as a body, but you are not a body. When we see someone from the outside, he is a body. Love penetrates within. Then we are not seeing the person from the outside. Love can see a person as the person can see himself from within. Then the form disappears.

A Zen monk, Rinzai, attained his Enlightenment, and the first thing he asserted was, "Where is my body? Where has my body gone?" And he began to search. He called his disciples and said, "Go and find out where my body is. I have lost my body."

He had entered the Formless. You are also a formless existence, but you know yourself not directly, but from other's eyes. You know through the mirror. Sometime, while looking in the mirror, close your eyes and then think, meditate: If there was no mirror, how could you have known your face? If there was no mirror, there would have been no face. You do not have a face : mirrors give you faces. Think of a world where there are no mirrors. You are alone — no mirror at all, not even others' eyes working as mirrors. You are alone on a lonely island; nothing can mirror you. Then will you have any face? Or will you have any body? You cannot have one. You are not having one at all. We know ourselves only through others, and the others can only know the outer form. That is why we become identified with it.

Another Zen mystic, Hui-Hai, used to say to his disciples, "When you have lost your head meditating, come immediately to me. When you lose your head, come immediately to me. When you begin to feel there is no head, do not be afraid; come immediately to me. This is the right moment. Now something can be taught to you." With a head, no teaching is possible. The head always comes in between.

Parvati, Devi, asks Shiva, "Oh Shiva, what is your reality? Who are you?" The form has disappeared; hence, the question. In love you enter the other as himself. It is not you answering.

You become one, and for the first time you know an abyss — a formless presence.

That is why, for centuries together, centuries and centuries, we were not making any sculpture, any picture of Shiva. We were only making "Shivalinga" — the symbol. The "Shivalinga is just a formless form. When you love someone, when you enter someone, he becomes just a luminous presence. The Shivalinga is just a luminous presence, just an aura of light.

That is why Devi asks, "What is your reality ? What is this wonder-filled universe ?" We know the universe, but we never know it as wonder-filled. Children know, lovers know. Sometimes poets and madmen know. We do not know that the world is wonder-filled. Everything is just repetitive — no wonder, no poetry — just flat prose. It doesn't create a song in you; it doesn't create a dance in you; it doesn't give birth to the poetry inside. The whole universe looks mechanical. Children look at it with wonder-filled eyes. When the eyes are wonder-filled, the universe is wonder-filled.

When you are in love, you again become like children. Jesus says, "Only those who are like children will enter my Kingdom of God." Why ? Because if the universe is not a wonder, you cannot be religious. The universe can be explained : then your approach is scientific. The universe is known or unknown, but that which is unknown can be known any day. It is not "UN-KNOWABLE". The universe becomes unknowable, a mystery, only when your eyes are wonder-filled.

Devi says, "What is this wonder-filled universe ?" And suddenly there is the jump from a personal question to a very impersonal one. She was asking, "What is your reality ?" and then suddenly, "What is this wonder-filled universe ?"

When form disappears, your beloved becomes the universe, the Formless, the Infinite. Suddenly Devi becomes aware that she is not asking a question about Shiva: she is asking a question about the whole universe. Now Shiva has become the whole universe. Now all the stars are moving in him, and the whole firmament and the whole space is surrounded by him. Now he

is the great engulfing factor, "the Great Encompassing." Karl
Jaspers has defined God as "the Great Encompassing".

When you enter into love, into a deep intimate world of love,
the person disappears, the form disappears, and the lover becomes just a door to the universe. Your curiosity can be a scientific one. Then you have to approach through logic. Then you
must not think of the Formless. Then beware of the Formless.
Then remain content with the form. So science is always concerned with the form. If anything formless is proposed to a
scientific mind, he will cut it into form; unless it takes a form
it is "meaningless". First give it "a form — a definite form".
Only then does the inquiry start.

In love, if there is form, then there is no end to it. Dissolve
the form ! When things become formless, dizzy, without boundaries, every thing entering another, the whole universe
becoming a Oneness, then only is it a wonder-filled universe.

"What constitutes seed ?" Then Devi goes on: from the universe she goes on to ask, "What constitutes seed ? This formless,
wonder-filled universe, from where does it come ? From where
does it originate ? Or, does it NOT originate ? What is the seed ?
"Who centers the universal wheel ?" (asks Devi). This wheel
goes on moving and moving — this great change, this constant
flux. But who centers this wheel ? Where is the axis, the center,
the unmoving center ?

She doesn't stop for any answer. She goes on asking as if she
is not asking anyone, as if talking to herself: "What is this life
beyond form pervading forms ? How may we enter it fully above
space and time, names and description ? Let my doubts be
cleared." The emphasis is not on questions but on doubts : "Let
my doubts be cleared." This is very significant. If you are asking
an intellectual question, you are asking for a definite answer so
that your problem is solved. But Devi says, "Let my doubts be
cleared." She is not really asking about answers. She is asking
for a transformation of her mind, because a doubting mind will
remain a doubting mind whatsoever answers are given. Note
it: a doubting mind will remain a doubting mind. Answers are

irrelevant. If I give you one answer and you have a doubting mind, you will doubt it. If I give you another answer, you will doubt that also. You have a doubting mind. A doubting mind means you will put a question mark to anything.

So answers are useless. You ask me, "Who created the world? and I tell you A created the world. Then you are bound to ask who created A. So the real problem is not how to answer questions. The real problem is how to change the doubting mind, how to create a mind which is not doubting — or, which is trustful. So Devi says, "Let my doubts be cleared."

Two or three things more. When you ask a question, you may be asking for many reasons. One may be just this, that you want a confirmation. You already know the answer; you have the answer. You just want it to be confirmed that your answer is right. Then your question is false, pseudo. It is not a question. You may be asking a question not because you are ready to change yourself, but just as a curiosity.

The mind goes on questioning. In the mind questions come as leaves come on a tree. That is the very nature of the mind — to question. So it goes on questioning. It matters not what you are questioning. With anything given to the mind it will create a question. It is a grinding machine to create questions. So give it anything: it will cut it into pieces and create many questions. One question answered, and the mind will create many questions from the answer. This has been the whole history of philosophy.

Bertrand Russell remembers when he was a child he thought that one day, when he will be mature enough to understand all philosophy, all questions will be answered. Then later, when he was eighty, he said that "Now I can say that my own questions are there standing, as they were standing when I was a child. No other questions have come up because of these theories of philosophy." So he said, "When I was young I used to say philosophy is an inquiry for ultimate answers. Now I cannot say it. It is an inquiry for endless questions."

So one question creates one answer and many questions. The

doubting mind is the problem. Parvati says, "Do not be concerned with my questions. I have asked so many things: "What is your reality? What is this wonder-filled universe? What constitutes seed? Who centers the universal wheel? What is life beyond form? How can we enter it fully above time and space? But do not be concerned with my questions. Let my doubts be cleared. I ask these qestions because they are in my mind. I ask them just to show you my mind, but do not pay much attention to them. Really, answers will not fulfill my need. My need is 'Let my doubts be cleared'."

But how can the doubts be cleared? Will any answer do? Is there any answer which will clear your doubts? Mind is the doubt. It is not that the mind doubts. Mind is the doubt! Unless the mind dissolves, doubts cannot be cleared.

Shiva will answer. His answers are techniques — the oldest, most ancient techniques. But you can call them the latest also because nothing can be added to them. They are complete — 112 techniques. They have taken in all the possibilities, all the ways of cleaning the mind, transcending the mind. Not a single method could be added to Shiva's 112 methods. And this book "Vigyana Bhairava Tantra" is 5,000 years old. Nothing can be added; there is no possibility to add anything. It is exhaustive, complete. It is the most ancient and yet the latest, yet the newest. Old like old hills, the methods seem eternal; and they are new like a dewdrop before the sun because they are so fresh.

These 112 methods of meditation constitute the whole science of transforming mind. We will enter them one by one. We will try to comprehend first intellectually. But use your intellect only as an instrument, not as a master. Use it as an instrument to understand something, but do not go on creating barriers with it. When we will be talking about these techniques, just put aside your past knowledge, your knowing, whatsoever information you have collected. Put them aside: they are just dust gathered on the road.

Encounter these methods with a fresh mind — with alertness, of course, but not with argumentation. And do not create the

17

fallacy that an argumentative mind is an alert mind. It is not, because the moment you move into arguments you have lost the awareness, you have lost the alertness. You are not here then.

These methods do not belong to any religion. Remember, they are not Hindu, just as the theory of relativity is not Jewish because Einstein conceived of it. And radio and television are not Christian. No one says, "Why are you using electricity? This is Christian, because a Christian mind conceived of it." Science doesn't belong to races and religions — and tantra is a science. So remember, this is not Hindu at all. These techniques were conceived by Hindus, but these techniques are not Hindu. That is why these techniques will not mention any religious ritual. No temple is needed. You are quite a temple yourself. You are the lab; the whole experiment is to go on within you. No belief is needed.

This is not religion: this is science. No belief is needed. It is not required to believe in the Koran or the Vedas or in Buddha or in Mahavir. No, no belief is needed. Only a daringness to experiment is enough, courage to experiment is enough; that is the beauty. A Mohammedan can practise and he will reach to the deeper meanings of the Koran. A Hindu can practise and he will for the first time know what the Vedas are. And a Jain can practise and a Buddhist can practise: they need not leave their religion. Tantra will fulfill them, wherever they are. Tantra will be helpful, whatsoever their chosen path.

So remember this, tantra is pure science. You may be a Hindu or a Mohammedan or a Parsi or whatsoever. Tantra doesn't touch your religion at all. Tantra says that religion is a social affair. So belong to any religion: it is irrelevant. But you can transform yourself, and that transformation needs a scientific methodology. When you are ill, when you have fallen ill or you have caught tuberculosis or anything, then whether you are a Hindu or a Mohammedan makes no difference. The tuberculosis remains indifferent to your Hinduism, to your Mohammedanism, to your beliefs — political, social or religious. Tuberculosis has to be treated scientifically. There is no Hindu tuberculosis, no Mohammedan tuberculosis.

You are ignorant, you are in conflict, you are asleep: this is a disease, a spiritual disease. This disease has to be treated by the tantra. You are irrelevant, your beliefs are irrelevant. It is just a coincidence that you are born somewhere and someone else is born somewhere else. This is just a coincidence. Your religion is a coincidence. So do not cling to it. Use some scientific methods to transform yourself.

Tantra is not very well known. Or even if known, it is very much misunderstood. There are reasons for it. The higher and purer a science, the less is the possibility that the masses will know of it. We have only heard the name of relativity, the theory of relativity. It used to be said that only twelve persons understood it when Einstein was alive. All over the world only one dozen minds could understand it. It was difficult even for Albert Einstein to make it understood to someone, to make it understandable, because it moves so high. It goes above your head. But it can be understood. A technical, mathematical, knowledge is needed, a training is needed, and it can be understood. But tantra is more difficult because no training will help. Only transformation can help.

That is why tantra could never become understood by the masses. And it always happens when you cannot understand a thing that at least you will misunderstand, because then you can feel, "Okay, I understand." You cannot simply remain in the vacuum.

Secondly, when you cannot understand a thing, you begin to abuse it because it insults you. You cannot understand it ! You ? YOU cannot understand it ? That is impossible ! Something must be wrong with the thing itself ! One begins to abuse. One begins to talk nonsense, and then he feels, "Now it is okay."

So tantra was not understood : tantra was misunderstood. It was so deep and so high that this was natural. Secondly, because tantra moves beyond duality the very standpoint is amoral. Please understand this word. Moral, immoral, amoral: we understand morality; we understand immorality. But it becomes difficult if something is amoral—beyond both.

Tantra is amoral. Look at it in this way. A medicine is amoral: it is neither moral nor immoral. If you give it to a thief it will help; if you give it to a saint it will help. It will make no difference between a thief and a saint. The medicine cannot say, "This is a thief so I am going to kill him and this is a saint so I am going to help him." A medicine is a scientific thing. Your being a thief or being a saint is irrelevant.

Tantra is amoral. Tantra says no morality is needed — no particular morality is needed. On the contrary, you are immoral because you have a very disturbed mind. So tantra cannot make a precondition that first you become moral, and then you can practise tantra. Tantra says this is absurd.

Someone is ill, feverish, and the doctor comes and says, "First bring down your fever; first be quite healthy. Only then can I give you the medicine." This is what is happening. One thief comes to a saint and he says, "I am a thief. Tell me how to meditate." He says, "First leave your profession. How can you meditate if you remain a thief?" One alcoholic comes and he says, "I am an alcoholic. How can I meditate?" The saint says, "The first condition is leave alcohol, and only then can you meditate." The conditions become suicidal. The man is alcoholic or a thief or immoral because he has a disturbed mind, an ill mind. These are the effects, the consequences of the diseased mind, and he is told, "First be well and then you can meditate." But then who needs meditation? Meditation is medicinal. It is a medicine.

Tantra is amoral. It doesn't ask you who you are. Your being a man is enough. Wherever you are, whatsoever you are, you are accepted.

Choose a technique which fits you, put your total energy into it, and you will not be the same again. Real, authentic techniques always will be like that. If I make preconditions, it shows I have a pseudo technique. I say, "First do this and first do not do that, and then..." And those are impossible conditions because a thief can change his objects, but he cannot become a non-thief.

A greedy man can change the objects of his greed, but he cannot become non-greedy. You can force him or he can force upon himself non-greed, but also only because of a certain greed. If heaven is promised he may even try to be non-greedy. But this is greed par excellence. Heaven, *Moksha* (Liberation), *Satchitananda* (Existence, Consciousness, Bliss), they will be the obects of his greed.

Tantra says you cannot change man unless you give him authentic techniques to change. Just by preaching nothing is changed. And you can see this all over the world: Whatsoever tantra says is written all over the world. So much preaching, so much moralizing, so many priests, preachers: the whole world is filled with them, yet everything is so ugly and so immoral.

Why is this happening ? The same will be the case if you give your hospitals to preachers. They will go there and they will start preaching. And they will make every ill man feel, "YOU are guilty ! You have created this disease; now change this disease." If preachers are given hospitals what will be the condition of hospitals ? The same as the condition of the whole world.

Preachers go on preaching. They go on telling people, "Don't be angry," without giving any technique. And we have heard this teaching for so long that we never even raise the question of "What are you telling ? I am angry and you simply say, 'Don't be angry.' How is this possible ? When I am angry it means 'I' am anger, and you just tell me. 'Don't be angry.' So I can only suppress myself."

But that will create more anger. That will create guilt — because if I try to change and cannot change myself, that creates inferiority. It gives me a feeling of guilt, that I am incapable. I cannot win over my anger; no one can win ! You need certain weapons, you need certain techniques, because your anger is just an indication of a disturbed mind. Change the disturbed mind and the indication will change. Anger is just showing what is within. Change the within and the without will change.

So tantra is not concerned with your so-called morality. Really, to emphasize morality is mean, degrading; it is inhuman. If someone comes to me and I say, "Leave anger first, leave sex first, leave this and that," then I am inhuman. What I am saying is impossible. And that impossibility will make that man feel inwardly mean. He will begin to feel inferior; he will be degraded inside in his own eyes. And if he tries the impossible he is going to be a failure. And when he is a failure he will be convinced that he is a sinner.

The preachers have convinced the whole world that "You are sinners". This is good for them, because unless you are convinced their profession cannot continue. You must be sinners: only then can churches, temples and mosques continue to prosper. Your being in sin is their "season". Your guilt is the base of all the highest churches. The more guilty you are, the more churches will go on rising higher and higher. They are built on your guilt, on your sin, on your inferiority complex. Thus, they have created an inferior humanity.

Tantra is not concerned with your so-called morality, your social formalities, etc. That doesn't mean that tantra says be immoral — no! Tantra is so much unconcerned with your morality that tantra cannot say be immoral. Tantra gives you scientific techniques for how to change the mind. And once the mind is different your character will be different. Once the basis of your structure changes, your whole edifice will be different. Because of this amoral attitude, tantra could not be tolerated by your so-called saints. They all went against it because if tantra succeeds, then all this nonsense which goes on in the name of religion will have to stop.

See this : Christianity fought very much against scientific progress. Why ? Only because if scientific progress is there in the material world, then the time is not very far off when in the psychological and in the spiritual world also science will penetrate. So Christianity started fighting scientific progress because once you know that you can change matter through technique the time is not very far off when you will come to know that you can change mind through techniques — because mind is nothing but subtle matter.

This is tantra's proposition, that mind is nothing but subtle matter; it can be changed. And once you have a different mind you have a different world, because you look through the mind. The world you are seeing, you are seeing because of a particular mind. Change the mind, and when you look there is a different world. And if there is no mind, that is the ultimate for tantra: to bring about a state where there is no mind. Then look at the world without a mediator. When the mediator is not, you are encountering the Real, because now no one is between you and the Real. Then nothing can be distorted.

So tantra says that when there is no mind that is the state of a Bhairava — a no-mind state. For the first time you look at the world — at that which is. If you have a mind, you go on CREATING a world; you go on imposing, projecting. So first change the mind; then change from mind to no-mind. And these 112 methods can help each and everyone. Any particular method may not be of use to you. That is why Shiva goes on relating many methods. Choose any one method which suits you. It is not difficult to know which suits you.

We will try to understand each method and how to choose for yourself one method which can change you and your mind. This understanding, this intellectual understanding, will be a basic necessity, but this is not the end. Whatsoever I talk about here, try it.

Really, when you try the right method it clicks immediately. So I will go on talking about methods here every day. You try them. Just play with them: go home and try. The right method, whenever you happen to it, just clicks. Something explodes in you, and you know that "This is the right method for me". But effort is needed, and you may be surprised that suddenly one day one method has gripped you.

So while I will be talking here, parallel to it go on playing with these methods. I say "playing" because you should not be too serious. Just play! Something may fit you. If it fits you, then be serious, and then go deep in it — intensely, honestly, with all your energy, with all your mind. But before that just play.

I have found that while you are playing your mind is more open. While you are serious your mind is not so open: it is closed. So just play. Do not be too serious: just play. And these methods are simple. You can just play with them.

Take one method: play with it for at least three days. If it gives you a certain feeling of affinity, if it gives you a certain feeling of well-being, if it gives you a certain feeling that this is for you, then be serious about it. Then forget the others: do not play with other methods. Stick to it — at least for three months. Miracles are possible. The only thing is that the technique must be for you. If the technique is not for you, then nothing happens. Then you may go on with it for lives together, but nothing will happen. If the method is for you, then even three minutes are enough.

So these 112 methods can be a miraculous experience for you or they may just be a listening. It depends on you. I will go on describing each method from as many angles as possible. If you feel any affinity with it, play with it for three days; then leave it. If you feel that it fits, that something clicks in you, continue it for three months. Life is a miracle. If you have not known its mystery, that only shows you do not know the technique for how to approach it.

Shiva proposes 112 methods. These are all the methods possible. If nothing clicks and nothing gives you the feeling that this is for you, then there is no method left for you: remember this. Then forget spirituality and be happy. Then it is not for you.

But these 112 methods are for the whole humanity — for all the ages that have passed and for all the ages that have yet to come. In no time has there ever been a single man, and there will never be one, who can say, "These 112 methods are all useless for me." Impossible! This is impossible!

Every type of mind has been taken into account. Every possible type of mind has been given a technique in tantra. There are many techniques for which no man exists yet; they are for the future. There are many techniques for which no man exists now: they are for the past. But do not be afraid. There are many methods which are for you. So we will start this journey from tomorrow.

2
The Path Of Yoga And The Path Of Tantra

October 2, 1972, Bombay, India

QUESTIONS:

1. The differences between yoga and tantra.
2. Surrender and techniques of meditation.
3. Indications of successful practice.

Many questions are there. The first: *"What is the difference between traditional yoga and tantra? Are they the same?"*

Tantra and yoga are basically different. They reach to the same goal. However, their paths are not only different, but contrary also. So this has to be understood very clearly.

The yoga process is also methodology; yoga is also technique. Yoga is not philosophy. Just like tantra, yoga depends on action, method, technique. Doing leads to being in yoga also, but the process is different. In yoga one has to fight: it is the path of the warrior. On the path of tantra one does not have to fight at all. Rather, on the contrary, one has to indulge — but WITH AWARENESS.

Yoga is suppression with awareness; tantra is indulgence with awareness. Tantra says that whatsoever you are the Ultimate is not opposite to it. It is a growth; you can grow to be the Ultimate. There is no opposition between you and the Reality. You are part of it. So no struggle, no conflict, no opposition to nature is needed. You have to use nature; you have to use whatsoever you are to go beyond.

In yoga you have to fight with yourself to go beyond. In yoga the world and the *Moksha* (Liberation) — you as you are and you as you can be — are two opposite things. Suppress, fight, dissolve that which you are so that you can attain that which you can be. Going beyond is a death in yoga. You must die for your real being to be born.

29

In the eyes of tantra yoga is a deep suicide. You must kill your natural self — your body, your instincts, your desires, everything. Tantra says accept yourself as you are. It is a deep acceptance. Do not create a gap between you and the Real, between the world and the Nirvana. Do not create any gap. There is no gap for tantra; no death is needed. For your rebirth, no death is needed: rather a transcendence. For this transcendence, use yourself.

For example, sex is there, the basic energy — the basic energy you are born through, born with. The basic cells of your being and of your body are sexual, so the human mind revolves around sex. For yoga you must fight with this energy. Through fight you create a different center in yourself. The more you fight, the more you become integrated in a different center. Then sex is not your center. Fighting with sex — of course, consciously — will create in you a new center of being, a new emphasis, a new crystallization. Then sex will not be your energy. You will create your energy fighting with sex. A different energy will come into being and a different center of existence.

For tantra you have to use the energy of sex. Do not fight with it: transform it. Do not think in terms of enmity: be friendly to it. It is your energy. It is not evil, it is not bad. Every energy is just natural. It can be used for you, it can be used against you. You can make a block of it, a barrier, or you can make it a step. It can be used! Rightly used, it becomes friendly; wrongly used, it becomes your enemy. But it is neither. Energy is just natural. As ordinary man is using sex, it becomes an enemy. It destroys him; he simply dissipates in it.

Yoga takes the opposite view — opposite to the ordinary mind. The ordinary mind is being destroyed by its own desires, so yoga says stop desiring; be desireless. Fight desire and create an integration in you which is desireless.

Tantra says be aware of the desire; do not create any fight. Move in desire with full consciousness, and when you move in desire with full consciousness you transcend it. You are in it and still you are not in it. You pass through it, but you remain an outsider.

Yoga appeals much because yoga is just opposite to the ordinary mind. So the ordinary mind can understand the language of yoga. You know how sex is destroying you — how it has destroyed you, how you go on revolving around it like a slave, like a puppet. You know this by your experience. So when yoga says fight it, you immediately understand the language. That is the appeal, the easy appeal, of yoga.

Tantra could not be so easily appealing. It seems difficult : How to move in desire without being overwhelmed by it ? How to be in the sex act consciously, with full awareness ? The ordinary mind becomes afraid. It seems dangerous. Not that it is dangerous: whatsoever you know about sex creates this danger for you. You know yourself, you know how you can deceive yourself. You know very well that your mind is cunning. You can move in desire, in sex, in everything, and you can deceive yourself that you are moving with full awareness. That is why you feel the danger.

The danger is not in tantra; it is in you. And the appeal of yoga is because of you, because of your ordinary mind, your sex-suppressed, sex-starved, sex-indulging mind. Because the ordinary mind is not healthy about sex, yoga has appeal. With a better humanity, with a healthy sex — natural, normal — the case would be different. We are not normal and natural. We are absolutely abnormal, unhealthy, really insane. But because everyone is like us, we never feel it.

Madness is so normal that NOT TO BE MAD may look abnormal. A Buddha is abnormal, a Jesus is abnormal amidst us. They do not belong to us. This "normalcy" is a disease. This "normal" mind has created the appeal of yoga. If you take sex naturally — with no philosophy around it, with no philosophy for or against; if you take sex as you take your hands, your eyes; if it is totally accepted as a natural thing; then tantra will have appeal. And only then can tantra be useful for many.

But the days of tantra are coming. Sooner or later tantra will explode for the first time on the masses, because for the first time the time is ripe — ripe to take sex naturally. It is possible that the explosion may come from the West, because Freud, Jung, Reich, they have prepared the background. They did not know anything about tantra, but they have made the basic ground for tantra to evolve. Western psychology has come to a conclusion that the basic human disease is somewhere around sex, the basic insanity of man is sex-oriented.

So unless this sex orientation is dissolved man cannot be natural, normal. Man has gone wrong only because of his attitudes about sex. No attitude is needed. Only then are you natural. What attitude have you about your eyes ? Are they evil or are they Divine ? Are you for your eyes or against them ? There is no attitude ! That is why your eyes are normal.

Take some attitude. Think that eyes are evil. Then seeing will become difficult. Then seeing will take the same problematic shape that sex has taken. Then you will want to see, you will desire and you will hanker to see. But when you see you will feel guilty. Whenever you see you will feel guilty that you have done something wrong, that you have sinned. You would like to kill your very instrument of seeing; you would like to destroy your eyes. And the more you want to destroy them, the more you will become eye centered. Then you will start a very absurd activity. You will want to see more and more, and simultaneously you will feel more and more guilty. The same has happened with the sex center.

Tantra says accept whatsoever you are. This is the basic note — total acceptance. And only through total acceptance can you grow. Then use every energy you have. How can you use them ? Accept them; then find out what these energies are, what is sex, what is this phenomenon. We are not acquainted with it. We know many things about sex taught by others. We may have passed through the sex act, but with a guilty mind, with a suppressive attitude, in haste, in a hurry. Something has to be done in order to become unburdened. The sex act is not a loving act.

You are not happy in it, but you cannot leave it. The more you try to leave it, the more attractive it becomes. The more you want to negate it, the more you feel invited.

You cannot negate it, but this attitude to negate, to destroy, destroys the very mind, the very awareness, the very sensitivity which can understand it. So sex goes on with no sensitivity in it. Then you cannot understand it. Only a deep sensitivity can understand anything; only a deep feeling, a deep moving in it, can understand anything. You can understand sex only if you move in it as a poet moves amidst flowers: ONLY then! If you feel guilty about flowers, you may pass through the garden, but you will pass with closed eyes. And you will be in a hurry, in a deep, mad haste. Somehow you have to go out of the garden. Then how can you be aware?

So tantra says accept whatsoever you are. You are a great mystery of many multi-dimensional energies: accept it, and move with every energy with deep sensitivity, with awareness, with love, with understanding. Move WITH it! Then every desire becomes a vehicle to go beyond it. Then every energy becomes a help. And then this very world is Nirvana, this very body is a temple — a holy temple, a holy place.

Yoga is negation; tantra is affirmation. Yoga thinks in terms of duality: that is why the word "yoga". It means to put two things together, to "yoke" two things together. But two things are there; the duality is there. Tantra says there is no duality. If there is duality, then you cannot put them together. And howsoever you try they will remain two. Howsoever put together they will remain two, and the fight will continue, the dualism will remain.

If the world and the Divine are two, then they cannot be put together. If really they are not two, if they are only appearing as two, only then can they be one. If your body and your soul are two, then they cannot be put together. If you and God are two, then there is no possibility of putting them together. They will remain two.

Tantra says there is no duality; it is only an appearance. So why help appearance to grow stronger ? Tantra asks why help this appearance of duality to grow stronger. Dissolve it this very moment ! Be one ! Through acceptance you become one, not through fight. Accept the world, accept the body, accept everything that is inherent in it. Do not create a different center in yourself, because for tantra that different center is nothing but the ego. For tantra, remember, it is nothing but the ego. Do not create an ego. Just be aware of what you are. If you fight, then the ego will be there.

So it is difficult to find a yogi who is not an egoist. It is difficult ! And yogis may go on talking about egolessness, but they cannot be egoless. Their very process creates the ego. The fight is the process. If you fight, you are bound to create an ego. And the more you fight, the more strengthened the ego will be. And if you win your fight, then you will achieve the supreme ego.

Tantra says no fight ! Then there is no possibility of the ego. If we understand tantra there will be many problems, because, for us, if there is no fight there is only indulgence. No fight means indulgence for us. Then we become afraid. We have indulged for lives together and we have reached nowhere. But for tantra indulgence is not "our" indulgence. Tantra says indulge, but BE AWARE.

You are angry : tantra will not say do not be angry. Tantra will say be angry wholeheartedly, but be aware. Tantra is not against anger. Tantra is only against spiritual sleepiness, spiritual unconsciousness. Be aware and be angry. And this is the secret of the method — that if you are aware anger is transformed: it becomes compassion. So tantra says anger is not your enemy. It is compassion in seed. The same anger, the same energy, will become compassion.

If you fight with it, then there will be no possibility for compassion. So if you succeed in fighting, in suppression, you will be a dead man. There will be no anger because you have suppressed it. There will be no compassion either because only anger can be transformed into compassion. If you succeed in your suppression (which is impossible) then there will be no sex, but no love either, because with sex dead there is no energy to grow into love. So you will be without sex, but you will also be without love. And then the whole point is missed, because without love there is no divineness, without love there is no liberation, and without love there is no freedom.

Tantra says that these same energies are to be transformed. It can be said in this way: if you are against the world, then there is no Nirvana — because this world itself is to be transformed into Nirvana. Then you are against the basic energies which are the source.

So tantric alchemy says do not fight: be friendly with all the energies that are given to you. Welcome them. Feel grateful that you have anger, that you have sex, that you have greed. Feel grateful because these are the hidden sources. And they can be transformed, they can be opened. And when sex is transformed, it becomes love. The poison is lost, the ugliness is lost.

The seed is ugly, but when it becomes alive it sprouts and flowers. Then there is beauty. Do not throw the seed because then you are also throwing the flowers in it. They are not there yet, not yet manifest so that you can see them. They are unmanifest, but they are there. Use this seed so that you can attain to flowers. So first let there be acceptance, a sensitive understanding and awareness. Then indulgence is allowed.

One thing more which is really very strange, but one of the deepest discoveries of tantra, and that is: whatsoever you take as your enemies — greed, anger, hate, sex, whatsoever — your attitude that they are enemies makes them your enemies. Take them as Divine gifts and approach them with a very grateful heart. For example, tantra has developed many techniques for the transformation of sex energy. Approach the sex act as if you are approaching the temple of the Divine. Approach the sexual act as if it is prayer, as if it is meditation. Feel the holiness of it.

That is why Khajuraho, in Puri, in Konark, every temple has *maithun* (intercourse) sculptures. The sex act on the walls of temples seems illogical, particularly for Christianity, for Islam, for Jainism. It seems inconceivable, contradictory. How is the temple connected with *maithun* pictures? On the outer walls of the Khajuraho temples, every conceivable type of sex act is pictured in stone. Why? In a temple it doesn't have any place, in our minds at least. Christianity cannot conceive of a church wall with Khajuraho pictures. Impossible!

Modern Hindus also feel guilty because the minds of modern Hindus are created by Christianity. They are "Hindu-Christians", and they are worse — because to be a Christian is good, but to be a Hindu-Christian is just weird. They feel guilty. One Hindu leader, Purshottamdas Tandon, even proposed that these temples should be destroyed, that they do not belong to us. Really, it looks like they do not belong to us because tantra has not been in our hearts for a long time, for centuries. It has not been the main current. Yoga has been the main current, and for yoga Khajuraho is inconceivable: it must be destroyed.

Tantra says approach the sex act as if you are entering a holy temple. That is why they have pictured the sex act on their holy temples. They have said approach sex as if you are entering a holy temple. Thus, when you enter a holy temple sex must be there in order that the two become conjoined in your mind, associated. Then you can feel that the world and the Divine are not two fighting elements, but one. They are not contradictory. They are just polar opposites helping each other. And they can exist only because of this polarity. If this polarity is lost, the whole world is lost. So see the deep oneness running through everything. Do not see only the polar points. See the inner running current which makes them one.

For tantra everything is holy. Remember this: for tantra EVERYTHING is holy; nothing is unholy. Look at it this way: for an irreligious person, everything is unholy; for so-called religious persons something is holy, something is unholy. For tantra, everything is holy.

THE PATH OF YOGA AND THE PATH OF TANTRA

One Christian missionary was with me some days before, and he said, "God created the world." So I asked him, "Who created sin ?" He said, "The Devil." Then I asked him, "Who created the Devil ?" Then he was at a loss. He said, "Of course, God created the Devil."

The Devil creates sin and God creates the Devil : then who is the real sinner — the Devil or God ? But the dualist conception always leads to such absurdities. For tantra God and the Devil are not two. Really, for tantra there is nothing that can be called "Devil": everything is Divine, everything is holy. And this seems to be the right standpoint, the deepest. If anything is unholy in this world, from where does it come and how can it be ?

So only two alternatives are there : first the alternative of the atheist who says everything is unholy. This attitude is okay: he is also a non-dualist; he sees no holiness in the world. Then there is the tantric's alternative: he says everything is holy. He is also a non-dualist. But between these two the so-called religious persons are not really religious. They are neither religious nor irreligious because they are always in a conflict. And their whole theology is just to make ends meet, and those ends cannot meet.

If a single cell, a single atom in this world is unholy, then the whole world becomes unholy, because how can that single atom exist in a holy world ? How can it be ? It is supported by everything; to be, it has to be supported by everything. And if the unholy element is supported by all the holy elements, then what is the difference between them ? So either the world is holy totally, unconditionally, or it is unholy; there is no middle path.

Tantra says everything is holy; that is why we cannot understand it. It is the deepest non-dual standpoint, if we can call it a standpoint. It is not, because any standpoint is bound to be dual. It is not against anything, so it is not any standpoint. It is a felt unity, a lived unity.

These are two paths, yoga and tantra. Tantra could not be so appealing because of our crippled minds. But whenever there is someone who is healthy inside, not a chaos, tantra has a beauty. Only he can understand what tantra is. Yoga has appeal, easy appeal, because of our disturbed minds.

Remember, it is ultimately your mind which makes anything attractive or unattractive. It is you who is the deciding factor. These approaches are different. I am not saying that one cannot reach through yoga. One can reach through yoga also, but not through the yoga which is prevalent. The yoga which is prevalent is not really yoga, but the interpretation of your diseased minds. Yoga can be authentically an approach toward the Ultimate, but that too is only possible when your mind is healthy, when your mind is not diseased and ill. Then yoga takes a different shape.

For example, Mahavir was on the path of yoga, but he was not really suppressing sex. He had known it, he had lived it, he was deeply acquainted with it. But it became useless to him, so it dropped. Buddha was on the path of yoga, but he had lived through the world, he was deeply acquainted with it. He was not fighting.

Once you know something you become free from it. It simply drops like dead leaves dropping from a tree. It is not renunciation; there is no fight involved at all. Look at Buddha's face: it doesn't look like the face of a fighter. He has not been fighting. He is so relaxed; his face is the very symbol of relaxation: no fight.

Look at your yogis: the fight is apparent on their faces. Deep down much turmoil is there. Just now they are sitting on volcanoes. You can look in their eyes, in their faces, and you will feel it. Deep down somewhere they have suppressed all their diseases; they have not gone beyond.

In a healthy world where everyone is living his life authentically, individually, not imitating others but living his own life in his own way, both are possible. He may learn the deep sensitivity which transcends desires; he may come to a point where all desires become futile and drop. Yoga can also lead to this, but to me yoga will lead to it in the same world where tantra can lead to it; remember this. We need a healthy mind, a natural man. In that world where natural man is, tantra will lead and yoga will also lead to transcendence of desires.

In our so-called ill society, neither yoga nor tantra can lead, because if we choose yoga we do not choose it because desires have become useless — no! They still meaningful; they are not dropping by themselves. We have to force them.

If we choose yoga, we choose it as a technique of suppression. If we choose tantra, we choose tantra as a cunningness, as a deep deception to indulge. So with an unhealthy mind neither yoga nor tantra can work. They will both lead to deceptions. A healthy mind, particularly a sexually healthy mind, is needed to start with. Then it is not very difficult to choose your path. You can choose yoga, you can choose tantra.

There are two types of persons — basically, male and female : I do not mean biologically, but psychologically. In those who are basically psychologically male — aggressive, violent, extrovert — yoga is their path. For those who are basically feminine, receptive, passive, non-violent — tantra is their path. So you may note it. For tantra, Mother, Kali, Tara, and so many *devis*, *bhairavis* (female deities), are very significant. In yoga you will never hear any name mentioned of a feminine deity. Tantra has feminine deities; yoga has male gods. Yoga is outgoing energy; tantra is energy moving inwards. So you can say in modern psychological terms that yoga is extrovert and tantra is introvert. So it depends on the personality. If you have an introverted personality, then fight is not for you. If you have an extroverted personality, then fight is for you.

But we are just confused; we are just in a mess. That is why nothing helps. On the contrary, everything disturbs. Yoga will disturb you, tantra will disturb you. Every medicine is going to create a new illness for you because the chosen is ill, diseased; his choice is ill, diseased. So I do not mean that through yoga you cannot reach. I emphasize tantra only because we are going to try to understand what tantra is.

Another question: *On the path of surrender, how does the seeker come to the right technique out of 112 methods?"*

On the path of will there are methods — these 112 methods. On the path of surrender, surrender itself is the method. There are no other methods, remember this. All methods are non-surrendering because a method means depending on yourself. You can do something : the technique is there, so you do it. On the path of surrender, you are no more, so you cannot do anything. You have done the ultimate, the last : you have surrendered. On the path of surrender, surrender is the only method.

All these 112 methods require a certain will; they require something to be done by you. You manipulate your energy, you balance your energy, you create a center in your chaos. You do something. Your effort is significant, basic, required. On the path of surrender only one thing is required : you surrender. We will go deep into these 112 methods, so it is good to say something about surrender because it has no method.

In these 112 methods there will be nothing for surrender. Why has Shiva not said anything about surrender ? Because nothing can be said. Bhairavi herself, Devi herself, has reached Shiva not through any method. She has simply surrendered. So this must be noted : she is asking these questions not for herself. These questions are asked for the whole humanity. She has attained Shiva. She is already in his lap; she is already embraced by him. She has become one with him, but still she is asking.

So remember one thing: she is not asking for herself; there is no need. She is asking for the whole humanity. But if she has attained, why is she asking Shiva ? Can she herself not speak to the humanity ? She has come through the path of surrender, so she doesn't know anything about method. She herself has come through love. Love is enough unto itself. Love doesn't need anything more. She has come through love, so she doesn't know anything about any methods, techniques. That is why she is asking.

So Shiva relates 112 methods. He also will not talk about surrender because surrender is not a method really. You surrender only when every method has become futile, when you cannot reach by any method. You have tried your best. You have knocked on every door, and no door opens and you have passed through all the routes and no route leads. You have done whatsoever you can do, and now you feel helpless. In that total helplessness surrender happens. So on the path of surrender there is no method. But what is surrender and how does it work? And if surrender works, then what is the need of 112 methods? Then why go into them unnecessarily the mind will ask.

Then okay! If surrender works, it is better to surrender. Why go hankering after methods. And who knows whether a particular method will suit you or not? And it may take lives to find out. So it is good to surrender, but it is difficult. It is good, but it is difficult. It is the most difficult thing in the world. Methods are not difficult. They are easy; you can train yourself. But for surrender you cannot train yourself. No training! You cannot ask how to surrender: the very question is absurd. How can you ask how to surrender? Can you ask how to love?

Either there is love or there is not, but you cannot ask how to love. And if someone tells you and teaches you how to love, remember, then you will never be capable of love. Once a technique is given to you for love, you will cling to the technique. That is why actors cannot love. They know so many techniques, so many methods, and we are all actors. Once you know the trick how to love, then love will not flower because you can create a facade, a deception. And with the deception you are out of it, not involved. You are secured.

Love is being totally open, vulnerable. It is dangerous. You become insecure. We cannot ask how to love; we cannot ask how to surrender. It happens! Love happens, surrender happens. Love and surrender are deeply one.

But what is it? And if we cannot know how to surrender, at least we can know how we are maintaining ourselves from surrendering, how we are resisting ourselves from surrendering. That can be known and that is helpful: How is it that you have not surrendered yet? What is your technique of non-surrendering? If you have not fallen in love yet, then the real problem is not how to love. The real problem is to dig deep to find out how you have lived without love, what is your trick, what is your technique, what is your structure — your defence structure, how you have lived without love. That can be understood, and that should be understood.

First thing : we live with the ego, in the ego, centered in the ego. "I" am without knowing who I am. I go on announcing, "I am." This "I-am-ness" is false, because I do not know who I am. And unless I know who I am, how can I say "I" ? This "I" is a false "I". This false "I" is the ego; this is the defence.

This protects you from surrendering. You cannot surrender, but you can become aware of this defence measure. If you have become aware of it, it dissolves. By and by, you are not strengthening it, and one day you come to feel, "I am not." The moment you come to feel "I am not", surrender happens. So try to find out whether you are. Really, is there any center in you that you can call "my I". Go deep down within yourself, go on trying to find out where is this "I", where is the abode of this ego.

Rinzai went to his teacher, his guru, and he said, "Give me freedom !" The teacher said, "Bring yourself. If YOU are, I will make you free. But if YOU are not, then how can I make you free ? You are already free. "And freedom," his guru said, "is not your freedom. Really, freedom is freedom FROM 'you'. So go and find out where this 'I' is, where you are, then come to me. This is the meditation. Go and meditate."

So the disciple Rinzai goes and meditates for weeks, months, and then he comes. Then he says, "I am not the body. Only this much I have found." So the guru says, "This much you have become free. Go again. Try to find out." Then he tries, meditates, and he finds that "I am not my mind, because I can observe my thoughts. So the observer is different from the observed : I am not my mind." He comes and says. "I am not mind." So his guru says, "Now you are three-fourths liberated. Now go again and find out who you are then."

So he was thinking, "I am not my body. I am not my mind." He had read, studied, he was well informed, so he was thinking, "I am not my body, not my mind, so I must be my soul, my *Atman*." But he meditated, and then he found that there is no *Atman* — no soul, because this *Atman*, this soul, is nothing but your mental information — just doctrines, words, philosophies.

So he came running one day and he said, "Now I am no more!" Then his guru said, "Am I now to teach you the methods for freedom?" Rinzai said, "I am free because I am no more. There is no one to be in bondage. I am just a wide emptiness, a nothingness."

Only nothingness can be free. If you are something, you will be in bondage. If you are, you will be in bondage. Only a void, a vacant space, can be free. Then you cannot bind it. Rinzai came running and said. "I am no more. Nowhere am I to be found." This is freedom. And for the first time he touched his guru's feet — for the first time! Not actually, because he had touched them many times before also. But the guru said, "For the first time you have touched my feet."

Rinzai asked, "Why do you say for the first time? I have touched your feet many times." The guru said, "But you were there, so how could you touch my feet while you were already there? While you are there how can you touch my feet?" The "I" can never touch anybody's feet. Even though it apparently looks like it touches somebody's feet, it is touching its own feet just in a round-about way. "You have touched my feet for the first time," the teacher said, "because now you are no more. And this is also the last time," the teacher said. "The first and the last."

Surrender happens when you are not, so you cannot surrender. That is why surrender cannot be a technique. You cannot surrender: you are the hindrance. When you are not, surrender is there. So you and surrender cannot cohabit, there is no coexistence between you and surrender. Either you are or surrender is. So find out where you are, who you are. This inquiry creates many, many surprising interpretations.

Raman Maharshi used to say, "Inquire 'Who am I?'" It was misunderstood. Even his nearest disciples have not understood the meaning of it. They think that this is an inquiry to find out really "Who am I?" It is not! if you go on inquiring "Who am I?" you are bound to come to the conclusion that you are not. This is not really an inquiry to find out "Who am I?" Really, this is an inquiry to dissolve.

I have given many this technique to inquire within "Who am I?" Then a month or two months later, they will come to me and say, "I have still not found 'Who am I?' The question is still the question. There is no answer."

So I tell them, "Continue. Someday the answer will come." And they hope that the answer will come. There is going to be no answer. It is only that the question will dissolve. There is not going to be an answer that "You are this". Only the question will dissolve. There will be no one to ask even "Who am I?" And then you know.

When the "I" is not, the real "I" opens. When the ego is not, you are for the first time encountering your being. That being is void. Then you can surrender; then you have surrendered. You are surrender now. So there can be no techniques, or only negative techniques like this inquiry into "Who am I?"

How does surrender work? If you surrender, what happens? How does it work? We will come to understand how methods work. We will go deep into methods, and we will come to know how they work. They have a scientific basis of working. How does surrender work?

When you surrender you become a valley; when you are an ego you are like a peak. Ego means you are above everyone else; you are somebody. The others may recognize you, may not recognize you: that is another thing. You recognize that you are above everyone: you are like a peak; nothing can enter you.

When one surrenders, one becomes like a valley. One becomes depth, not height. Then the whole Existence begins to pour into him from everywhere. The whole Existence begins to pour! He is just a vacuum, just a depth, an abyss, bottomless. The whole Existence begins to pour from everywhere. You can say

God runs from everywhere to him, enters him from every pore, fills him totally.

This surrender, this becoming a valley, an abyss, this surrendering, can be felt in many ways. There are minor surrenders; there are major surrenders. Even in minor surrenders you feel it. Surrendering to a guru is a minor surrender, but you begin to feel it because the guru begins to flow into you immediately. If you surrender to a teacher, suddenly you feel his energy flowing into you. If you cannot feel energy flowing into you, then know well you have not surrendered even in a minor way. You have NOT surrendered!

There are so many stories which have become meaningless for us because we do not know how they happened. Mahakashyap came to Buddha, and Buddha just touched his head with his hand, and the thing happened. And Mahakashyap began to dance. So Ananda asked Buddha, "What has happened to him ? And I have been for forty years with you ! Is he mad ? Or is he just fooling others ? What has happened to him ? And I have touched your feet thousands and thousands of times.

Of course, to Ananda, this Mahakashyap will look like he is either mad or as if he is just deceiving. He was with Buddha for forty years, but there was a problem. He was his elder brother — Buddha's elder brother: that was the problem. When Ananda came to Buddha forty years before, the first thing he said to Buddha was this: "I am your elder brother, and when you will initiate me, I will become your disciple. So give me three things before I become your disciple, because then I cannot demand. One, I will always be with you : Give me this promise. You will not say to me, 'Go somewhere else': I will follow you.

"Secondly, I will sleep in the same room where you sleep. You cannot say to me, 'Go out.' I will be with you like your shadow. And thirdly, if I bring anyone at any time, even at midnight, you will have to answer him. You cannot say, 'This is not the time.' And give me these three promises while I am still your elder brother, because once I become your disciple I will have to follow you. You are still younger than me, so give me these promises."

So Buddha promised, and this became the problem. This became the problem! For forty years Ananda was with Buddha, but he could never surrender, because this is not the spirit of surrender. Ananda asked many, many times, "When am I going to attain?" Buddha said, "Unless I die, you will not attain." And Ananda could attain only when Buddha died.

What happened to this Mahakashyap suddenly? Is Buddha partial — partial to Mahakashyap? He is not! He is flowing, constantly flowing. But you have to be a valley, a womb, to receive him. If you are above him, how can you receive? That flowing energy cannot come to you. It will miss you. So bow down. Even in a minor surrender with a guru, energy begins to flow. Suddenly, immediately, you become a vehicle of a great force. There are thousands and thousands of stories: just by a touch, just by a look, someone became Enlightened. They do not appear rational to us. How is this possible? This is possible! Even a look into your eyes will change your total being, but it can change only if your eyes are just vacant, valley-like. If you can absorb the look of the teacher immediately, you will be different.

So these are minor surrenders that happen before you surrender totally. And these minor surrenders prepare you for the total surrender. Once you have known that through surrender you receive something unknown, unbelievable, unexpected, never even dreamed of, then you are ready for a major surrender. And that is the work of guru — to help you in minor surrenders so that you can gather courage for a major surrender, for a total surrender.

One last question: *"What are the exact indications to know that the particular technique one is practising will lead to the Ultimate?"*

There are indications. One, you begin to feel a different identity within you. You are no more the same. If the technique fits you, immediately you are a different person. If you are a husband or a wife, you are never the same husband. If you are a shopkeeper, you are never again the same shopkeeper. Whatsoever you are, if the technique fits you, you are a different person that is the first meditation. So if you begin to feel strange about yourself, know that something is happening to you. If you remain the same and do not feel any strangeness, nothing is happening. This is the first indication of whether a technique fits you. If it fits, immediately you are transported, transformed into a different person. Suddenly this happens: you look at the world in a different way. Eyes are the same, but the looker behind them is different.

Secondly, all that creates tensions, conflicts, starts dropping. It is not that when you have practised the method for years, then your conflicts, anxieties, tensions will drop — no! If the method fits you, immediately they start dropping. You can feel an aliveness coming to you; you are being unburdened. You will begin to feel, if the technique fits you, that gravity has become reversed. Now the earth is not pulling you down. Rather, the sky is pulling you up. How do you feel when an aeroplane takes off? Everything is disturbed. Suddenly there is a jerk, and gravity becomes meaningless. Now the earth is not pulling you. You are going away from gravity.

The same jerk happens if a meditative technique fits you. Suddenly you take off. Suddenly you feel the earth has become meaningless; there is no gravity. It is not pulling you down. You are being pulled up. In religious terminology, this is called 'grace'. There are two forces — gravity and grace. "Grace" means you are being pulled upwards; "gravity" means you are being pulled downwards.

That is why in meditation many people suddenly feel they have no weight. That is why many people feel an inner levitation. So many have reported this to me when the technique fits them: "This is strange! We close our eyes and we feel that we are a little bit above the earth — one foot, two feet, even four feet above the earth. And when we open our eyes we are just on the ground; when we close our eyes we have levitated. So what is this? When we open our eyes we are just on the ground! We never levitated."

The body remains on the ground, but you levitate. This levitation is really a pull from the above. If the technique fits you have been pulled, because the working of the technique is to make available for you the upward pull. This is what the technique means: to make you available for the force which can pull you up. So if it fits, you know: you have become weightless.

Thirdly, whatsoever you will now do, whatsoever, howsoever trivial, will be different. You will walk in a different way, you will sit in a different way, you will eat in a different way. Everything will be different. This difference you will feel everywhere. Sometimes this strange experience of being different creates fear. One wants again to go back and be the same because one was so attuned with the old. It was a routine world, even boring, but you were efficient in it.

Now, everywhere you will feel a gap. You will feel that your efficiency is lost. You will feel that your utility is reduced. You will feel that everywhere you are an outsider. One has to pass through this period. You will become attuned again. You have changed, not the world. So you will not fit. So remember the third thing: When the technique fits you, you will not fit into the world. You will become unfit. Everywhere something is loose; some bolt is missing. Everywhere you will feel that there has been an earthquake. And everything has remained the same; only you, YOU, have become different. But you will be attuned again on a different plane, on a higher plane.

The disturbance is felt, just like when a child grows and becomes sexually mature. At the age of 14 or 15 every boy feels that he has become strange. A new force has entered — sex. It was not there — or it was, but it was hidden. Now, for the first time, he has become available for a new kind of force. That is why boys are very awkward: girls, boys, when they become sexually mature they are very awkward. They are nowhere. They are no longer children and they are not yet men, so they are in between, fitting nowhere. If they play with small children, they feel awkward: they have become men. If they start making friendships with men, they feel awkward: they are still children. They fit no one.

The same phenomenon happens when a technique fits you: a new energy source becomes available that is greater than sex. You are again in a transitory period. Now you cannot fit in this world of worldly men. You are not a child, and you cannot yet fit the world of saints. You are not yet "a man", so in between one feels awkward.

If a technique fits you these three things will come up, but you may not have expected that I should say these things. You may have expected that I would say you will become more silent, more quiet, and I am saying quite the contrary: you will become more disturbed. When the technique fits you will become more disturbed, not more silent. Silence will come later on. And if silence comes and not disturbance, know well that this is not a technique: this is just getting adjusted to the old pattern.

That is why more people go to a prayer than for meditation because prayer gives you a consolation: it fits you, adjusts you, into your world. Prayer was virtually doing the same thing that psychoanalysts are now doing. If you are disturbed, they will make you less disturbed, adjusted to the pattern, to the society, to the family. So by going to a psychoanalyst for one, two or three years you will not get better, but you will be more adjusted. Prayer does the same thing and priests do the same thing : they make you more adjusted.

Your child has died and you are disturbed, and you go to a priest. He says, "Do not be disturbed. Only those children die early whom God loves more. He calls them up." You feel satisfied. Your child has been "called up". God loves him more. Or, the priest says something else: "Do not be worried. The soul never dies. Your child is in heaven."

One woman was here just a few days before. Her husband had died just during the past month. She was disturbed. She came to me and she said, "Only assure me that he is reborn in a good place, and then everything will be okay. Just give me certainty that he has not gone to hell or he has not become an animal, that he is in heaven or he has become a god or some such thing. If you can just assure me of this, then everything is okay. Then I can bear it; otherwise I am miserable."

So the priest would say, "Okay! Your husband is born as a god in the seventh heaven, and he is very happy. And, he is waiting for you."

These prayers, they make you adjusted to the pattern. You feel better. Meditation is a science. It is not going to help you in adjustment. It is going to help you in transformation. That is why I say these three signs will be there as indications. Silence will come, but not as an adjustment. Silence will come as an inner flowering. Then silence will not be an adjustment with the society, with the family, the world, with the business — no! Then silence will be a real harmony with the universe — not with society, family, etc.

Then a deep harmony flowers between you and the Totality. Then there is silence, but that will come later. First you will get disturbed, first you will become mad, because YOU ARE MAD — only unaware.

If a technique fits, it will make you aware of everything that you are. Your anarchy, your mind, your madness, everything, will come to light. You are just a dark mess. When a technique fits, it is as if suddenly there is light and the whole mess becomes apparent. For the first time you will encounter yourself as you are. You would like to put the light off and go to sleep again. It is fearful. This is the point where the guru becomes helpful. He says, "Do not be afraid." This is just the beginning.

And do not escape from it. At first this light shows you what you are, and if you can go on and on, it transforms you toward what you can be.

Enough for today.

3
Breath—A Bridge To The Universe

October, 3, 1972, Bombay, India

SUTRAS:

Shiva replies:

1. *Radiant one, this experience may dawn between two breaths. After breath comes in (down) and just before turning up (out) — the beneficence.*

2. *As breath turns from down to up, and again as breath curves from up to down — through both these turns, Realize.*

3. *Or, whenever in-breath and out-breath fuse, at this instant touch the energy-less, energy-filled center.*

4. *Or, when breath is all out (up) and stopped of itself, or all in (down) and stopped — in such universal pause, one's small self vanishes. This is difficult only for the impure.*

Truth is always here. It is already the case. It is not something to be achieved in the future. YOU are the Truth just here and now. So it is not something which is to be created or something which is to be devised or something which is to be sought. Understand this very clearly; then these techniques will be easy to understand and also to do.

Mind is a mechanism of desiring. Mind is always in desire — always seeking something, asking for something. Always the object is in the future; mind is not concerned with the present at all. In this very movement, the mind cannot move: there is no space. The mind needs the future in order to move. It can move either in the past or in the future. It cannot move in the present; there is no space. The Truth is in the present, and mind is always in the future or in the past. So there is no meeting between mind and Truth.

When the mind is seeking worldly objects, it is not so difficult. The problem is not absurd; it can be solved. But when the mind starts seeking the Truth, the very effort becomes nonsense — because the Truth is here and now, and the mind is always then and there. There is no meeting. So understand the first thing: you cannot seek Truth. You can find it, but you cannot seek it. The very seeking is the hindrance.

The moment you start seeking you have moved away from the present, away from yourself, because YOU are always in the present. The seeker is always in the present and the seeking is in the future. You are not going to meet whatsoever you are seeking. Lao Tse says, "Seek not; otherwise you will miss. Seek not and find. Don't seek and find."

All these techniques of Shiva's are simply turning the mind from the future or the past to the present. That which you are seeking is already there. It is the case already. The mind has to be turned from seeking to non-seeking. It is difficult. If you think about it intellectually it is very difficult. How to turn the mind from seeking to non-seeking — because then the mind makes non-seeking itself the object! Then the mind says, "Don't seek." Then the mind says, " 'I' should not seek." Then the mind says, "Now non-seeking is my object. Now 'I' desire the state of desirelessness." The seeking has entered again. The desire has come again through the back door. That is why there are people who are seeking worldly objects, and there are people who think they are seeking non-worldly objects. All objects are wordly because "seeking" is the world.

So you cannot seek anything non-worldly. The moment you seek, it becomes the world. If you are seeking God, your God is part of the world. If you are seeking *Moksha* (Liberation) Nirvana, your Liberation is part of the world. Your Liberation is not something that transcends the world, because seeking is the world, desiring is the world. So you cannot desire Nirvana; you cannot desire NON-DESIRE. If you try to understand intellectually, it will become a puzzle.

Shiva says nothing about it. He immediately proceeds to give techniques. They are non-intellectual. He doesn't say to Devi, "The Truth is here. Don't seek it and you will find it." He immediately gives techniques. Those techniques are non-intellectual. Do them, and the mind turns. The turning is just a consequence, just a by-product — not an object. The turning is just a by-product.

If you do a technique, your mind will turn from its journey into the future or the past. Suddenly you will find yourself in the present. That is why Buddha has given techniques, Lao Tse has given techniques, Krishna has given techniques. But they always introduce their techniques with intellectual concepts. Only Shiva is different. He immediately gives techniques, and no intellectual understanding, no intellectual introduction, because he knows that the mind is tricky, the most cunning thing possible. It can turn anything into a problem. Non-seeking will become the problem.

There are people who come to me who ask how not to desire. They are DESIRING NON-DESIRE. Somebody has told them, or they have read somewhere, or they have heard spiritual gossip, that if you do not desire you will reach bliss, if you do not desire you will be free, if you do not desire there will be no suffering. Now their minds hanker to attain that state where there is no suffering, so they ask how not to desire. Their minds are playing tricks. They are still desiring: it is only that now the object has changed. They were desiring money; they were desiring fame; they were desiring prestige; they were desiring power. Now they are desiring non-desire. Only the object has changed, and they remain the same and their desiring remains the same. But now the desire has become more deceptive.

Because of this Shiva proceeds immediately with no introduction whatsoever. He immediately starts talking about techniques. Those techniques, if followed, suddenly turn your mind: it comes to the present. And when the mind comes to the present, it stops: it is no more. You cannot be a mind in the present. That is impossible. Just now, if you are here and now, how can you be a mind? Thoughts cease because they cannot move. The present has no space to move; you cannot think. If you are in this very moment, how can you move? Mind stops; you attain to no-mind.

So the real thing is how to be here and now. You can try, but effort may prove futile — because if you make it a point to be in the present, then this point has moved into the future. When you ask how to be in the present, again you are asking about the future. This moment is passing in the inquiry: "How to be present? How to be here and now?" This present moment is passing in the inquiry, and your mind will begin to weave and create dreams in the future: "Someday" you will be in a state of mind where there is "no movement, no motive, no seeking, and then there is bliss", so "How to be in the present?"

Shiva doesn't say anything about it. He simply gives a technique. You do it, and suddenly you find you are here and now. And your being here and now is the Truth, and your being here and now is the freedom, and your being here and now is the Nirvana.

The first nine techniques are concerned with breathing. So let us understand something about breathing, and then we will proceed to the techniques. We are breathing continuously from the moment of birth to the moment of death. Everything changes between these two points. Everything changes; nothing remains the same: only breathing is a constant thing between birth and death.

The child will become young; the youth will become old. He will be diseased, his body will become ugly — ill, everything will change. He will be happy, unhappy, in suffering: everything will go on changing. But whatsoever happens between these two points, one must breathe. Whether happy or unhappy, young or old, successful or unsuccessful, watsoever you are, it is irrelevant. One thing is certain: between these two points of birth and death you must breathe.

Breathing will be a continuous flow; no gap is possible. If even for a single moment you forget to breathe, you will be no more. That is why YOU are not required to breathe, because then it would be difficult. Someone might forget to breathe for a single moment, and then nothing could be done. So, really, YOU are not breathing, because YOU are not needed. You are fast asleep, and breathing goes on; you are unconscious, and breathing goes on; you are in a deep coma, and breathing goes on. YOU are not required: breathing is something which goes on in spite of you.

It is one of the constant factors in your personality — that is the first thing. It is something which is very essential and basic to life — that is the second thing. You cannot be alive without breath. So breath and life have become synonymous. Breathing is the mechanism of life, and life is deeply related with breathing. That is why in India we call it "prana". We have given one word for both. "Prana" means the vitality, the aliveness: your life is your breath.

Thirdly, your breath is a bridge between you and your body. Constantly, breath is bridging you to your body, connecting you, relating you to your body. Not only is the breath a bridge to your body. It is also a bridge between you and the universe. Body is just the universe which has come to you, which is nearer to you.

Your body is part of the universe. Everything in the body is part of the universe — every particle, every cell. It is the nearest approach to the universe. Your body is the NEAREST approach to the universe. Breath is the bridge. If the bridge is broken, you are no more in the body. If the bridge is broken, you are no more in the universe. You move into some unknown dimension; then you cannot be found in space and time. So, thirdly, breath is also the bridge between you, and space and time.

Breath, therefore, becomes very significant — the most significant thing, so the first nine techniques are concerned with breath. If you can do something with the breath, you will suddenly turn to the present. If you can do something with breath, you will attain to the source of life. If you can do something with breath, you can transcend time and space. If you can do something with breath, you will be in the world and also beyond it.

Breath has two points — one is where it touches the body and the universe, and another is where it touches you and that which transcends the universe. We know only one part of the breath. When it moves into the universe, into the body, we know it. But it is always moving from the body to the "no-body", from the "no-body" to the body. We do not know the other point. If you become aware of the other point, the other part of the bridge, the other pole of the bridge, suddenly you will be transformed, transplanted, into a different dimension.

But remember, what Shiva is going to say is not yoga: it is tantra. Yoga also works on breath, but the work of yoga and tantra is basically different. Yoga tries to systematize breathing. If you systematize your breathing, your health will improve. If you systematize your breathing, if you know the secrets of breathing, your life will become longer: you will be more healthy and you will live longer. You will be more strong, more filled with energy, more vital, alive, young, fresh.

But tantra is not concerned with that. Tantra is concerned not with any systematization of breath, but with using breath just as a technique to turn inward. One has not to practise a particular style of breathing, a particular system of breathing or a particular rhythm of breathing — no ! One has to take breathing as it is. One has just to become aware of certain points in the breathing.

There are certain points, but we are not aware of them. We have been breathing and we will go on breathing; we are born breathing and we will die breathing. But we are not aware of certain points. And this is strange. Man is searching, probing deep into space. Man is going to the moon; man is trying to reach farther, from earth into space, and man has not yet learned the nearest part of his life. There are certain points in breathing which you have never observed, and those points are the doors — the nearest doors to you from where you can enter into a different world, into a different being, into a different consciousness. But they are very subtle.

To observe a moon is not very difficult. Even to reach the moon is not very difficult: it is a gross journey. You need mechanization, you need technology, you need accumulated information, and then you can reach it. Breathing is the nearest thing to you, and the nearer a thing is, the more difficult it is to perceive it. The nearer it is, the more difficult; the more obvious it is, the more difficult. It is so near to you that again there is no space between you and your breathing. Or, there is such a small space that you will need a very minute observation.

Only then will you become aware of certain points. These points are the basis of these techniques.

So now I will take each technique: *"Shiva replied, 'Radiant one, this experience may dawn between two breaths. After breath comes in (down) and just before turning up (out) — the beneficence."* That is the technique: "Radiant one, this experience may dawn between two breaths." After breath comes in (that is down) and just before turning out (that is going up), "the beneficence." Be aware between these two points, and the happening. When your breath comes in, observe. When your breath comes in, OBSERVE. For a single moment or a thousandth part of a moment, there is no breathing — before it turns up, before it turns outward. One breath comes in; then there is a certain point and breathing stops. Then the breathing goes out. When the breath goes out, then again for a single moment, or a part of a moment, breathing stops. Then breathing comes in.

Before the breath is turning in or turning out, there is a moment when you are not breathing. In that moment the happening is possible, because when you are not breathing you are not in the world. Understand this: when you are not breathing you are dead : you are still, but dead. But the moment is of such a short duration, you never observe it.

For tantra, each outgoing breath is a birth and each new breath is a rebirth. Breath coming in is rebirth; breath going out is death. The outgoing breath is synonymous with death; the incoming breath is synonymous with life. So with each breath you are dying and being reborn. The gap between the two is of a very short duration, but keen, sincere observation and attention will make you feel the gap. If you can feel the gap, Shiva says, the beneficence. Then nothing else is needed. You are blessed. You have known; the thing has happened.

You are not to train the breath. Leave it just as it is. Why such a simple technique ? It looks so simple. Such a simple technique to know the Truth ? To know the Truth means to know that which is neither born nor dies, to know that eternal element which is always. You can know the breath going out, you can know the breath coming in, but you never know the gap between the two.

Try it. Suddenly you will get the point — and you can get it: it is already there. Nothing is to be added to you or to your structure: it is already there. Everything is already there except a certain awareness. So how to do this ? First, become aware of the breath coming in. Watch it. Forget everything: just watch breath coming in — the very passage. When the breath touches your nostrils feel it there. Then let the breath move in. Move with the breath fully conscious. When you are going down, down, down with the breath, do not miss the breath. Do not go ahead; do not follow behind. Just go with it. Remember this: do not go ahead; do not follow it like a shadow. Be simultaneous with it.

Breath and consciousness should become one. The breath goes in : you go in. Only then will it be possible to get the point which is between two breaths. It will not be easy.

Move in with the breath, then move out with the breath: in-out, in-out. Buddha tried particularly to use this method, so this method has become a Buddhist method. In Buddhist terminology it is known as "Anapanasati Yoga". And Buddha's Enlightenment was based on this technique — only this.

All the religions of the world, all the seers of the world, have reached through some technique or other, and all those techniques will be in these 112 techniques. This first one is a Buddhist technique. It has become known in the world as a Buddhist technique. It has become known in the world as a Buddhist technique because Buddha attained his Enlightenment through this technique. Buddha said, "Be aware of your breath as it is coming in, going out — coming in, going out." He never mentions the gap because there is no need. Buddha thought and felt that if you become concerned with the gap, the gap between two breaths, that concern may disturb your awareness. So he simply said, "Be aware: when the breath is going in move with it, and when the breath is going out move with it. Do simply this : going in, going out, with the breath." He never says anything about the latter part of the technique.

The reason is that Buddha was talking with very ordinary men, and even that might create a desire to attain the interval. That desire to attain the interval will become a barrier to awareness, because if you are desiring to get to the interval you will move ahead. Breath will be coming in, and you will move ahead because you are interested in the gap which is going to be in the future. Buddha never mentions it, so Buddha's technique is just half.

But the other half follows automatically. If you go on practising breath consciousness, breath awareness, suddenly, one day without knowing, you will come to the interval — because as your awareness will become keen and deep and intense, as your awareness will become bracketed (the whole world is bracketed out; only your breath coming in or going out is your world — the whole arena for your consciousness), suddenly you are bound to feel the gap in which there is no breath.

When you are moving with breath minutely, when there is no breath, how can you remain unaware? You will suddenly become aware that there is no breath, and the moment will come when you will feel that the breath is neither going out nor coming in. The breath has stopped completely. In that stopping, "the beneficence."

This one technique is enough for millions. The whole of Asia tried and lived with this technique for centuries. Tibet, China, Japan, Burma, Thailand (Siam), Ceylon, the whole of Asia except India, has tried this technique — only one technique — and thousands and thousands have attained Enlightenment through this technique. And this is only the first technique.

But, unfortunately, because the technique became associated with Buddha's name, Hindus have been trying to avoid it. Because it became more and more known as a Buddhist method, Hindus have completely forgotten it. And not only that : they have also tried to avoid it for another reason. Because this technique is the first technique mentioned by Shiva, many Buddhists have claimed that this book, "Vigyana Bhairava Tantra," is a Buddhist book, not a Hindu book.

It is neither Hindu nor Buddhist, and a technique is just a technique. Buddha used it, but it was there already to be used. Buddha became a Buddha (an Enlightened One) because of the technique. The technique preceded Buddha; the technique was already there. Try it. It is one of the most simple techniques — simple compared to other techniques: I am not saying simple for you. Other techniques will be more difficult. That is why it is mentioned as the first technique.

The second technique (all these nine techniques are concerned with breath: *"As breath turns from down to up, and again as breath curves from up to down — through both these turns, Realize."* It is the same, but with a slight difference. The emphasis is now not on the gap, but on the turning. The outgoing and ingoing breath make a circle. Remember, these are not two parallel lines. We always think of them as two parallel lines — breath going in and breath going out. Do you think that these are two parallel lines? They are not. Breath going in is half the circle; breath going out is the other half of the circle.

So understand this : first, breathing in and out creates a circle. They are not parallel lines, because parallel lines never meet anywhere. Secondly, the breath coming in and the breath going out are not two breaths. They are one breath. The same breath which comes in, goes out, so it must have a turn inside. It must turn somewhere. There must be a point where the incoming breath becomes outgoing.

Why put such emphasis upon turning? Because, Shiva says, "As breath turns from down to up and again as breath curves from up to down, through both these turns, Realize." Very simple, but he says realize the turns and you will Realize the Self.

Why the turn? If you know driving you know about gears. Each time you change the gear, you have to pass through the neutral gear which is not a gear at all. From the first gear you move to the second or from the second to the third, but always you have to move through the neutral gear. That neutral gear is a turning point. In that turning point the first gear becomes the sceond and the second becomes the third. When your breath goes in and turns out, it is in the neutral gear; otherwise it cannot turn out. It passes the neutral territory.

In that neutral territory you are neither a body nor a soul, neither physical nor mental, because the physical is a gear of your being and the mental is another gear of your being. You go on moving from gear to gear, but you must have a neutral gear where you are neither body nor mind. In that neutral gear you simply are: you are simply an existence — pure, simple unembodied, with no mind.

That is why the emphasis on the turn. Man is a machine — a large, very complicated machine. You have many gears in your body, many gears in the mind. You are not aware of your great mechanism, but you are a great machine. And it is good that you are not aware; otherwise you would go mad. The body is such a great machine that scientists say if we had to create a factory parallel to the human body, it would require four square miles of land. And the noise would be such that 100 square miles of land would be disturbed by it.

The body is a great mechanical device — the greatest. You have millions and millions of cells and each cell is alive. So you are a big city of seventy million cells: there are seventy million citizens inside you, and the whole city is running very silently, smoothly. Every moment the mechanism is working. It is very complicated. These techniques will be related at many points with the mechanism of your body and the mechanism of your mind. But always the emphasis will be on those points where suddenly you are not part of the mechanism : remember this. Suddenly you are not part of the mechanism. There are moments when you change gears.

For example, in the night when you drop into sleep you change gears because during the day you need a different mechanism for a waking consciousness. A different part of the mind functions. Then you drop into sleep, and that part becomes non-functioning. Another part of the mind begins to function, and there is a gap, an interval, a turning. A gear is changed. In the morning when you are again getting up, the gear is changed.

You are silently sitting, and suddenly someone says something and you get angry: you move into a different gear. That is why everything changes.

If you get angry, your breathing will suddenly change. Your breathing will become irritated, chaotic. A trembling will get into your breathing; you will feel suffocated. Your whole body would like to do something, shatter something. Only then can the suffocation disappear. Your breathing will change; your blood will take a different rhythm, a different movement. Different chemicals will have to be released in the body. The whole glandular system will have to change. You become a different man when you are angry.

A car is standing: you start it. Do not put it in any gear; let it be in neutral. It will go on pulling, vibrating, trembling, but it cannot move: it will get hot. That is why, when you are angry and you cannot do something, YOU will get hot. The mechanism is working to run and do something, and you are not doing: you will get hot. You are a mechanism, but, of course, not only a mechanism. You are more, but "the more" has to be found. When you get into a gear, everything changes inside. When you change the gear, there is a turning.

Shiva says, "As breath turns from down to up, and again as breath curves from up to down — through both these turns, Realize." Be aware at the turn. But it is a very short turn; very minute observation will be needed. And we are just without any observing capacity; we cannot observe anything. If I say to you, "Observe this flower: observe this flower which I give to you," you cannot observe it. For a single moment you will see it, and then you will begin to think of something else. It may be about the flower, but it will not be THE FLOWER. You may think ABOUT the flower — about how beautiful it is: then you have moved. Now the flower is no more in your observation. Your field has changed. You may say that it is red, it is blue, white : then you have moved. Observation means remaining with no word, within no verbalization, with no bubbling inside: just remaining "WITH". If you can remain with a flower for three minutes, completely, with no movement of the mind, the thing will happen — "the beneficence". You will Realize.

But we are not at all observers. We are not aware; we are not alert; we cannot pay attention to anything. We just go on jumping. This is part of our heritage — our monkey heritage. Our mind is just the growth of the monkey mind. So the monkey moves on. He goes on jumping from here to there. The monkey cannot sit still. That is why Buddha insisted so much on just sitting without any movement, because then the monkey mind is not allowed to go its way.

In Japan they have a particular type of meditation which they call Za-zen. The word "Za-zen" in Japan means just sitting, doing nothing. No movement is allowed. One is just sitting like a statue — dead, not moving at all. But there is no need to sit like a statue for years together. If you can observe the turn of your breath without any movement of the mind, you will enter. You will enter into yourself or into the beyond within.

Why are these turnings so important? They are important because on turning, the breath leaves you to move in a different direction. It was with you when it was coming in; it will be with you again when it goes out. But at the turning point it is not with you and you are not with it. In that moment the breath is different from you, and you are different from it. If breathing is life, then you are dead. If breathing is your body, then you are "no-body". If breathing is your mind, then you are "no-mind", in that moment.

I wonder whether you have observed it or not: if you stop your breath, the mind stops suddenly. If you stop your breath just now, your mind will stop suddenly; the mind cannot function. A sudden stoppage of breath and the mind stops. Why? Because they are disjoined. Only a moving breath is joined with the mind, with the body, and a non-moving breath is disjoined. Then you are in the neutral gear. The car is running; the power is running. The car is making a noise; it is ready to go forward. But it is not in the gear. So the body of the car and the mechan-

THE BOOK OF THE SECRETS

ism of the car are not joined. The car is divided into two. It is ready to move, but the moving mechanism is not joined with it.

The same happens when breath takes a turn. You are not joined with it. In that moment you can easily become aware of who you are. What is this "being"? What is this "to be"? Who is inside this house of the body? Who is the master? Am I just the house or is there some master also? Am I just the mechanism or does something else also penetrate this mechanism? In that turning gap, Shiva says, "Realize." He says, just be aware of the turning, and you become a Realized soul.

The third technique: *"Or whenever in-breath and out-breath fuse, at this instant touch the energy-less, energy-filled center."*

"Or whenever in-breath and out-breath fuse, at this instant touch the energy-less, energy-filled center": We are divided into the center and the periphery. The body is the periphery. We know the body, we know the periphery. We know the circumference, but we do not know where the center is. When the out-breath fuses with the in-breath, when they become one, when you cannot say whether it is the out-breath or the in-breath, when it is difficult to demarcate and define whether the breath is going out or coming in, when the breath has penetrated in and starts moving out, there is a moment of fusion. It is neither going out nor moving in. The breath is static. When it is moving out it is dynamic; when it is coming in it is dynamic. When it is neither, when it is silent, non-moving, you are near to the center. The fusion point of the in and outgoing breath is your center.

Look at it in this way: when the breath goes in, where does it go? It goes to your center. It touches your center. When it goes out, from where does it go out? It moves from your center. Your center has to be touched. That is why Taoist mystics and Zen mystics say that the head is not the center. The navel is your center. The breath goes to the navel, then it moves out. It goes to the center.

As I said, it is a bridge between you and your body. You know the body, but you do not know where your center is. The breath is constantly going to the center and moving out, but we are not taking enough breath. Thus, ordinarily, it does not really go to the center. Now at least, it is not going to the center. That is why everyone feels "decentralized"; everyone feels off center. In the whole modern world those who can think at all feel they are missing their center.

Look at a child sleeping. Observe his breath. The breath goes in; the abdomen comes up. The chest remains unaffected. That is why children have no chests, only abdomens — very dynamic abdomens. The breath goes in and the abdomen comes up; the breath goes out and the abdomen goes down. The abdomen moves. Children are in their center, at their center. That is why they are so happy, so bliss-filled, so energy-filled, never tired. overflowing, and always in the present moment with no past, no future.

A child can be angry: when he is angry, he is totally angry; he becomes the anger. Then his anger is also a beautiful thing. When one is totally angry, anger has a beauty of its own, because totality always has beauty.

You cannot be angry and beautiful. You will become ugly because partiality is always ugly. And not only with anger: when you love you are ugly because you are again partial, fragmentary. You are not total. Look at your face when you are loving to someone, making love. Make love before a mirror and look at your face: it will be ugly, animal-like. In love also your face becomes ugly? Why? Love is also a conflict. You are withholding something. You are giving very miserly. Even in your love you are not total. You do not give completely, wholly.

A child even in anger and violence is total. His face becomes radiant and beautiful; he is here and now. His anger is not something concerned with the past or something concerned with the future; he is not calculating. He is just angry. The child is at his center. When you are at your center you are always total. Whatsoever you do will be a total act. Good or bad, it will be total. When you are fragmentary, when you are off center, your every act is bound to be a fragment of yourself. Your totality is not responding — just a part. And the part is going against the total: that creates ugliness.

We all were children. Why is it that as we grow our breathing becomes shallow ? It never goes to the abdomen; it never touches the navel. If it would go down more and more, it would becomes less and less shallow. But it just touches the chest and goes out. It never goes to the center. You are afraid of the center, because if you go to the center you will become total. If you want to be fragmentary, this is the mechanism to be fragmentary.

You love: if you breathe from the center, you will flow in it totally. You are afraid. You are afraid to be so vulnerable, so open to someone, to anyone. You may call him your lover, you may call her your beloved, but you are afraid. The other is there. If you are totally vulnerable, open, you do not know what is going to happen. Then YOU ARE — completely, in another sense. You are afraid to be so completely given to someone. You cannot breathe; you cannot take a deep breath. You cannot relax your breathing so that it goes to the center — because the moment breathing goes to the center, the more your act becomes total.

As you are afraid of being total, you breathe shallow. You just breathe at the minimum, not at the maximum. That is why life seems so lifeless. If you are breathing at the minimum, life will become lifeless. You are living at the minimum, not at the maximum. You can live at the maximum: then life is an overflowing. But then there will be difficulty. You cannot be a husband, you cannot be a wife, if life is overflowing. Everything will become difficult.

If life is overflowing, love will be overflowing. Then you cannot stick to one. Then you will be flowing all over; all dimensions will be filled by you. And then the mind feels danger, so it is better not to be alive. The more you are dead, the more you are secure. The more you are dead, the more everything is in control. You can control: then you remain the master. You feel that you are the master because you can control. You can control your anger, you can control your love, you can control everything. But this controlling is possible only at the minimum level of your energy.

Everyone must have felt at some time or other that there are moments when he suddenly changes from the minimum level to the maximum. You go out to a hill station. Suddenly you are out of the city and the prison of it. You feel free. The sky is vast, and the forest is green, and the height touches the clouds. Suddenly you take a deep breath. You may not have observed it.

Now if you go to a hill station, observe. It is not really the hill station that makes the change. It is your breathing. You take a deep breath. You say, "Ah! Ah!" You touch the center, you become total for a moment, and everything is bliss. That bliss is not coming from the hill station. That bliss is coming from your center. You have touched it suddenly.

You were afraid in the city. Everywhere the other was present and you were controlling. You could not scream; you could not laugh. What a misfortune! You could not sing on the street and dance. You were afraid. A policeman was somewhere around the corner, or the priest or the judge or the politician or the moralist. Someone was just around the corner, so you could not just dance in the street.

Bertrand Russell has said somewhere, "I love civilization, but we have achieved civilization at a very great cost." You cannot dance in the streets, but you go to a hill station and suddenly you can dance. You are alone with the sky, and the sky is not an imprisonment. It is just opening, opening and opening — vast, infinite. Suddenly you take a breath deeply: it touches the center and the bliss. But it is not going to be so for a long time. Within an hour or two, the hill station will disappear. You may be there, but the hill station will disappear.

Your worries will come back. You will begin to think to make a call to the city, to write a letter to your wife, or you will begin to think that since after three days you are going back you should make the arrangements. You have just reached and you are making arrangements to leave.

You are back. That breath was not from you really. It suddenly happened. Because of the change of situation the gear changed. You were in a new situation. You could not breathe in the old way, so for a moment a new breath came in. It touched the center, and you felt the bliss.

Shiva says you are every moment touching the center, or if you are not touching you can touch it. Take deep, slow breaths. Touch the center; do not breathe from the chest. That is a trick. Civilization, education, morality, they have created shallow breathing. It will be good to go deep into the center, because otherwise you cannot take deep breaths.

Unless humanity becomes non-suppressive toward sex, man cannot breathe really. If the breath goes deep down to the abdomen, it gives energy to the sex center. It touches the sex center; it massages the sex center from within. The sex center becomes more active, more alive. Civilization is afraid of sex. We do not allow our children to touch their sex centers — their sex organs. We say, "Stop! Don't touch!"

Look at a child when he first touches his sex center, and then say "Stop!" and then observe his breathing. When you say "Stop! Don't touch your sex center!" the breath will become shallow immediately — because it is not only his hand which is touching the sex center: deep down the breath is touching it. And if the breath goes on touching it, it is difficult to stop the hand. If the hand stops, then basically it is necessary, required, that the breath should not touch, should not go deep. It must remain shallow.

We are afraid of sex. The lower part of the body is not only lower physically: it has become lower as a value. It is condemned as "lower". So do not go deep: just remain shallow. It is unfortunate that we can only breathe downwards. If some preachers were allowed, they would change the whole mechanism. They would only allow you to breathe upward into the head. Then you would absolutely not feel sex.

If we are to create a sexless humanity, then we will have to change the breathing system. The breath must go into the head, to the *"sahasrar"* (the seventh center in the head), then come back to the mouth. This should be the passage: from the mouth to the *sahasrar*. It must not go deep down because down is danger. The deeper you go, the nearer you reach to the deeper layers of biology. You reach to the center, and that center is just near the sex center — just near. It has to be because sex is life.

Look at it in this way: breath is life from above downwards; sex is life just from the other corner — from down upwards. Sex energy is flowing and breath energy is flowing. The breath passage is in the upper body and the sex passage is in the lower body. When they meet they create life; when they meet they create biology, bio-energy. So if you are afraid of sex, create a distance between the two. Do not allow them to meet. So, really, civilized man is a castrated man: that is why we do not know about breath, and this sutra will be difficult to understand.

Shiva says, "Whenever in-breath and out-breath fuse, at this instant touch the energy-less, energy-filled center." He uses very contradictory terms: "energy-less, energy-filled." It is energy-less because your bodies, your minds, cannot give any energy to it. Your body energy is not there, your mind energy is not there, so it is energy-less as far as you know your identity. But it is energy-filled because it has the Cosmic source of energy and not because of your body energy.

Your body energy is just fuel energy. It is nothing but petrol (gasoline). You eat something, you drink something: it creates energy. It is just giving fuel to the body. Stop eating and drinking and your body will fall dead. Not just now: it will take three months at least, because you have reservoirs of petrol. You have accumulated much energy; it can run at least for three months without going to any petrol station. It can run; it has a reservoir. For an emergency, any emergency, you may need it.

This is "fuel" energy. The center is not getting any fuel energy. That is why Shiva says it is energy-less. It is not dependent on your eating and drinking. It is connected with the

Cosmic source; it is Cosmic energy. That is why he says "energy-less, energy-filled center". The moment you can feel the center from where breath goes out or comes in, the very point where breath fuses, where the breaths fuse — that center, if you become aware of it, then, ENLIGHTENMENT.

The fourth technique : *"Or when breath is all out (up) and stopped of itself, or all in (down) and stopped — in such universal pause, one's small self vanishes. This is difficult only for the impure."* But then it is difficult for everyone, because, he says, "This is difficult only for the impure." But who is the pure one ? It is difficult for you; you cannot practise it. But you can feel it sometimes suddenly: You are driving a car and suddenly you feel there is going to be an accident. Breathing will stop. If it is out, it will remain out. If it is in, it will remain in. You cannot breathe in such an emergency; you cannot afford it. Everything stops, departs.

"Or when breath is all out (up) and stopped of itself, or all in (down) and stopped — in such universal pause, one's small self vanishes" : Your small self is only a daily utility. In emergencies you cannot remember it. Who you are, the name, the bank balance, the prestige, everything, just evaporates. Your car is just heading toward another car: a moment and there will be death. In this moment there will be a pause. Even for the impure there will be a pause. Suddenly breathing stops. If you can be aware in that moment, you can reach the goal.

Zen monks have tried this method very much in Japan. That is why their methods seem very weird, absurd, strange. They have done many inconceivable things. A teacher will throw someone out of the house. Suddenly the teacher will begin slapping the disciple without any rhyme or reason, without any cause.

You were sitting with your teacher and everything was okay. You were just chit-chatting, and he will begin to beat you in order to create the pause. If there is any cause the pause cannot be created. If you had abused the teacher and he starts beating you, there is a causality. Your mind understands : "I abused him, and he is beating me."

Really, your mind was expecting it already, so there is no gap. But, remember, a Zen teacher will not beat you if you abuse him. He will laugh, because then laughter can create the pause. You were abusing him and you were saying nonsense things to him, and you expected anger. But he starts laughing or dancing. That is sudden; that will create the pause. You cannot understand it. If you cannot understand, the mind stops. And when the mind stops, breathing stops. Either way: if breathing stops, mind stops; if mind stops, breathing stops.

You were appreciating the teacher, and you were feeling good, and you were thinking, "Now the teacher must be pleased." And suddenly he takes his staff and begins to beat you — and mercilessly, because Zen masters are merciless. He begins to beat you; you cannot understand what is happening. The mind stops; there is a pause. If you know the technique, you can attain to your Self.

There are many stories that someone attained Buddhahood because the teacher suddenly started beating him. You cannot understand it. What nonsense! How can one attain Buddhahood by being beaten by someone or by being thrown out of the window by someone? Even if someone kills you, you cannot attain Buddhahood. But if you understand this technique, then it becomes easy to understand.

In the West particularly, for the last thirty or forty years, Zen has become very much prevalent — a fashion. But unless they know this technique, they cannot understand Zen. They can imitate it, but imitation is of no use. Rather, it is dangerous. These are not things to be imitated.

The whole Zen technique is based on the fourth technique of Shiva. But this is unfortunate: now we will have to import Zen from Japan because we have lost the whole tradition; we do not know it. Shiva was the expert par excellence of this method. When he came to marry Devi with his *barat* — with his procession, the whole city must have felt the pause — the whole city!

Devi's father was not willing to marry his girl to this "hippie". Shiva was the original hippie. Devi's father was totally against him, and no father would permit this marriage — no father ! So we cannot say anything against Devi's father. No father would permit marriage to Shiva. And then Devi insisted, so he had to agree — non-willingly, unhappily, but he agreed.

Then came the marriage procession. It is said people began to run, seeing Shiva and his procession. The whole *barat* must have taken LSD, marijuana. They were "on". And, really, LSD and marijuana are just the beginning. Shiva knew and his friends and disciples knew the ultimate psychedelic — *soma rasa*. Aldous Huxley has named the ultimate psychedelic *"soma"* only because of Shiva. They were on, just dancing, screaming, laughing. The whole city fled. It must have felt the pause.

Any sudden unexpected, unbelievable thing can create the pause for the impure. But for the pure there is no need of such things. For the pure, the pause is always there. The pause is always there ! Many times, for pure minds, breathing stops — many times ! If your mind is pure (pure means you are not desiring, hankering, seeking anything), silently pure, innocently pure, you could be sitting, and suddenly your breath will stop.

Remember this : mind movement needs breath movement. Mind moving fast needs fast movement in breath. That is why, when you are in anger, breath will move fast. In the sex act, the breath will move very fast. That is why, in Ayurveda (a system of herbal medicine in India), it is said that your life will be shortened: if too much sex is allowed, your life will be shortened according to Ayurveda, because Ayurveda measures your life in breaths. If your breathing is too fast, your life will be shortened.

Modern medicine says that sex helps blood circulation, sex helps relaxation. And those who suppress their sex may get into trouble — particularly heart trouble. And they are right and Ayurveda is also right, but they seem contradictory. But Ayurveda was invented five thousand years before. Every man was doing much labour: life was labour, so there was no need to relax. There was no need to create artificial devices for blood circulation.

74

But now, for those who are not doing much physical labour, only sex is their labour. That is why modern medicine is also right for modern man. He is not doing any physical exertion, so sex gives the exertion: the heart beats more, the blood circulates faster, the breathing becomes deep and goes to the center. So after the sex act, you feel relaxed and you can fall into sleep easily. Freud says that sex is the best tranquillizer, and it is — at least for modern man.

In sex breathing will become fast; in anger breathing will become fast. In sex the mind is filled with desire, lust, impurity. When the mind is pure: no desire in the mind, no seeking, no motivation; you are not going anywhere, but just remaining here and now as an innocent pool — not even a ripple; then breathing stops automatically. There is no need for it.

On this path, the small self vanishes and you attain to the higher Self, the Supreme Self.

I think this will do for today.

4
Overcoming The Deceptions
Of The Mind

October 4, 1972, Bombay, India

QUESTIONS:

1. *How can awareness of the gap in breathing bring Enlightenment?*
2. *How to work and practise breath awareness simultaneously?*
3. *Is it impossible to understand these techniques intellectually?*

Question : *"How is it possible that by simply becoming aware at a particular point in the breathing process one can attain Enlightenment? How it is possible to become free from the unconscious by just being aware of such a small and momentary gap in the breathing?"*

This question is significant, and this question is likely to have occurred to many minds. So many things have to be understood. First, it is thought that spirituality is a difficult attainment. It is "neither": that is, it is neither difficult nor an attainment. Whatsoever you are, you are already spiritual; nothing new is to be added to your being. And nothing is to be discarded from your being: you are as perfect as possible. It is not that you are going to be perfect sometime in the future; it is not that you have to do something arduous to be yourself. It is not a journey to some other point somewhere else; you are not going somewhere else. You are already there. That which is to be attained is already attained. This idea must go deep. Only then will you be able to understand why such simple techniques can help.

If spirituality is some attainment, then, of course, it is going to be difficult — not only difficult, but really impossible. If you are not already spiritual, you cannot be. You never can be because how can one who is not spiritual be spiritual? If you are not Divine already, then there is no possibility; there is no way. And no matter what effort you will make, effort made by one who is not already Divine cannot create Divinity. If you are not Divine, your effort cannot create Divinity. Then it is impossible.

But the whole point is totally opposite: you are already that which you want to attain. The end of longing is already there, present in you. Here and now, this very moment, you are that which is known as Divine. The Ultimate is here; it is already the case. That is why simple techniques can help. It is not an attainment, but a discovery. It is hidden, and it is hidden in very, very small things.

The "persona" is just like clothes: your body is here, hidden in clothes. In the same way your spirituality is here, hidden in certain clothes. These clothes are your personality. You can be naked just here and now, and in the same way you can be naked in your spirituality also. But you do not know what the clothes are. You do not know how you are hidden in them; you do not know how to be naked. You have been with clothes so long — for lives and lives and lives you have been with clothes — and you have been so identified with the clothes that now you do not think that these are clothes. You think these clothes are you: that is the only barrier.

For example, you have some treasure, but you have forgotten or you have not yet recognized that this is a treasure, and you go on begging in the streets: you are a beggar. If someone says, "Go and look inside your house: you need not be a beggar; you can be an emperor this very moment," the beggar is bound to say, "What nonsense you are talking. How can I be an emperor this very moment? I have been begging for years and still I am a beggar, and even if I go on begging for lives together, I am not going to be an emperor. So how absurd and illogical your statement is that 'you can be an emperor this very moment'."

It is impossible. The beggar cannot believe it. Why? Because the begging mind is a long habit. But if the treasure is just hidden in the house, then from simple digging, removing the earth a little bit, the treasure will be there. And immediately he will not be a beggar again: he will become an emperor.

It is the same with spirituality. It is a hidden treasure. Nothing is to be achieved somewhere in the future. You have not yet recognized it, but it is there already in you. You are the treasure, but you go on begging.

So simple techniques can help. Digging earth, removing a little bit, is not a big effort, but you can become an emperor immediately. You have to dig a little bit to remove the earth. And when I say remove the earth, it is not only symbolically that I am saying it. Literally your body is part of the earth, and you have become identified with the body. Remove this earth a little bit, create a hole in it, and you will come to know the treasure.

That is why this question will occur to many. Really, to everyone this question will occur: "So small a technique like this — being aware of your breathing, being aware of the incoming breath and the outgoing breath, and then realizing the interval between the two — is this enough?" Such a simple thing! Is this enough for Enlightenment? Is this the only difference between you and Buddha, that you have not realized the gap between two breaths and Buddha has realized it — only this much? It seems illogical. The distance is vast between a Buddha and you. The distance seems infinite. The distance between a beggar and an emperor is infinite, but the beggar can immediately become an emperor if the treasure is already hidden.

Buddha was a beggar like you. He was not a Buddha always. At a particular point the beggar died, and he became the master. This is not a gradual process really; it is not that Buddha goes on accumulating, and then one day he is not the beggar and he becomes the emperor. No, a beggar can never become an emperor if it is going to be an accumulation: he will remain a beggar. He may become a rich beggar, but he will remain a beggar. And a rich beggar is a bigger beggar than a poor beggar.

Suddenly, one day Buddha realizes the inner treasure. Then he is no more a beggar: he becomes a master. The distance between Gautam Siddharth and Gautam Buddha is infinite. It is the same distance that is between you and a Buddha. But the treasure is hidden within you as much as it was hidden in Buddha.

A small — a VERY small — technique can be helpful. Take another example : one man is born with blind eyes, diseased eyes. For a blind man, the world is a different thing. A small operation may change the whole thing, because only the eyes have to be made all right. The moment the eyes are ready, the seer is hidden behind. He will begin to look from the eyes. The seer is already there: only windows are lacking. You are in a house with no windows. You can break a hole in the wall, and suddenly you will look out.

We are already that which we will be, which we should be, which we are to be. The future is already hidden in the present; the whole possibility is here in the seed. Only a window has to be broken. Only a small surgical operation is needed. If you can understand this, that spirituality is already there, already the case, then there is no problem concerning how such a small effort can help.

Really, no big effort is needed. Only small efforts are needed, and the smaller the better. And if you work effortlessly it is still better. That is why it happens, many times it happens, that the more you try to do, the harder it is to attain. Your very effort, your tension, your "occupiedness", your longing, your expectation, becomes the barrier. But with a very small effort, "an effortless effort" as they call it in Zen — doing as if not doing — it happens easily. The more you are mad after it, the less is the possibility, because where a needle is needed you are using a sword. The sword will not be helpful. It may be bigger, but where a needle is needed a sword will not do.

Go to a butcher: he has very big instruments. And go to a brain surgeon: you will not find such big instruments with the brain surgeon. And if you do find them, then escape immediately ! A brain surgeon is not a butcher. He needs very small instruments — the smaller the better.

Spiritual techniques are more subtle: they are not gross. They cannot be because the surgery is even more subtle. In the brain the surgeon is still doing something with gross matters, but when you are working on spiritual planes the surgery becomes more and more aesthetic. No gross matter is there. It becomes subtle: that is one thing.

Secondly, the question asks, "If something is smaller, how can a bigger step be possible through it?" This concept is irrational — unscientific. Now science knows that the smaller the particle, the more atomic, the more explosive — the bigger really. The smaller it is, the bigger the effect. Could you have conceived before 1945, could any imaginative poet or dreamer have conceived, that two atomic explosions would wipe out completely two big cities in Japan — Hiroshima and Nagasaki? Two hundred thousand people were simply wiped out of existence within seconds. And what was the explosive force used? An atom! The very smallest particle exploded two big cities. You cannot see the atom. Not only with eyes can you not see: you cannot see by any means. The atom cannot be seen with any instrument. We can only see the effects.

So do not think that the Himalayas are bigger because they have such a big body. The Himalayas are just impotent before an atomic explosion. One small atom can wipe out the whole Himalayas. Bigness in gross material is not necessarily power. On the contrary, the smaller the unit, the more penetrating. The smaller the unit, the more intensely it is filled with power.

These small techniques are atomic. Those who are doing bigger things do not know atomic science. You will think that a person who is working with atoms is a small person working with a small thing, and a person who is working with the Himalayas will look very big. Hitler was working with great masses; Mao is working with great masses. And Einstein and Planck, they were working in their laboratories with small units of matter — energy particles. But, ultimately, before Einstein's research, politicians were just impotent. They were working on a bigger canvas, but they did not know the secret of the small unit.

Moralists always work on big planes, but these are gross. The

83

thing looks very big. They devote their whole lives to moralizing, practising this and that, to *sanyam* (control): they go on controlling; the whole edifice looks very big.

Tantra is not concerned with this. Tantra is concerned with the atomic secrets in the human being, in the human mind, in human consciousness. And tantra has achieved atomic secrets. These methods are atomic methods. If you can attain them, their result is explosive — Cosmic.

Another point is to be noted. If you can say, "How is it that with such a small, simple exercise one can become Enlightened?" you are saying this without doing the exercise. If you do it, then you will not say that this is a small, simple exercise. It looks this way because within two or three sentences the whole exercise has been given.

Do you know the atomic formula? Two or three words, and the whole formula is given. And with those two or three words, those who can understand, those who can use those words, can destroy the whole earth. But the formula is very small.

These too are formulas, so if you just look at the formula it will look to be a very, very small, simple thing. It is not! Try to do it. When you do it, then you will know that it is not so easy. It looks simple, but it is one of the deepest things. We will analyze the process; then you will understand.

When you take your breath in, you never feel the breath. You have never felt the breath! You will immediately deny this. You will say, "This is not right. We may not be conscious continuously, but we feel the breath. No, you do not feel the breath: you feel the passage.

Look at the sea. Waves are there; you see the waves. But those waves are created by air, wind. You do not see the wind. You see the effect on the water. When you take breath in it touches your nostril. You feel the nostril, but you never know the breath. It goes down: you feel the passage. It comes back: again you feel the passage. You never feel the breath. You just feel the touch and the passage.

This is not what is meant when Shiva says, "Be aware." First, you will become aware of the passage, and when you become completely aware of the passage only then you will begin, by and by, to be aware of the breath itself. And when you become aware of the breath, then you will be capable of being aware of the gap, the interval. It is not so easy as it looks. It is not so easy!

For tantra, for the whole Indian seeking, there are layers of awareness. If I embrace you, first you will become aware of my touch upon your body, not of my love: my love is not so gross. And ordinarily we never become aware of love. We are aware only of the body in movement. We know loving movements, we know non-loving movements — but we have never known love itself. If I kiss you, you become aware of the touch, not of my love: that love is a very subtle thing. And unless you become aware of my love, the kiss is just dead; it means nothing. If you can become aware of my love, then only can you become aware of me, because that again is a deeper layer.

The breath goes in: you feel the touch, not the breath. But you are not even aware of that touch. If something is wrong, only then do you feel it. If you have some difficulty in breathing, then you feel it; otherwise you are not aware. The first step will be to be aware of the passage where breath is felt to be touching; then your sensitivity will grow. It will take years to become so sensitive that not the touch, but the movement of breath is known. Then, says tantra, you will have known "prana" — the vitality. And only then is there the gap where breath stops — where breath is not moving, or the center where the breath is touching, or the fusion point, or the turning where the breath — the ingoing breath — becomes outgoing. This will become arduous: then it will not be so simple.

If you do something, if you go into this center, only then will you know how difficult it is. Buddha took six years to come to this center beyond the breath. To come to this turning, he had a long, arduous journey of six years; then it happened. Mahavir was working on it for twelve years; then it happened. But the formula is simple, and theoretically this can happen this very moment — theoretically, remember. There is no barrier theoretically, so why should it not happen this very moment ? YOU are the barrier. Except for you this can happen this very moment. The treasure is there; the method is known to you. You can "dig", but you will not dig.

Even this question is a trick not to dig, because your mind says, "Such a simple thing ? Don't be a fool." How — how can you become a Buddha through "such a simple thing ? It is not going to be." And then you are not going to do anything, because "how can this happen ?" Mind is tricky. If I say this is very difficult, the mind says this is so difficult it is beyond you. If I say this is very simple, the mind says, "This is so simple that only fools can believe." And mind goes on rationalizing things, always escaping from doing.

Mind creates barriers. It will become a barrier if you think this is so simple. Or if this is too difficult, then what are you going to do ? You cannot do a simple thing, you cannot do a difficult thing. What are you going to do ? Tell me ! If you want to do a difficult thing, I will make it difficult. If you are going to do a simple thing, I will make it simple. It is both. It depends on how it is interpreted. But one thing is needed — that you are going to do. If you are not going to do, then the mind will always give you explanations.

Theoretically, it is possible here and how; there is no actual barrier. But there are barriers. They may not be actual. They may simply be psychological; they may just be your illusions : but they are there. If I say to you, "Do not be afraid — go ! The thing that you are thinking to be a snake is not a snake: it is just a rope," still the fear will be there. To you it appears to be a snake.

So whatsoever I say is not going to help. You are trembling; you want to escape and run away. I say it is just a rope, but your mind will say, "This man may be in conspiracy with the snake. There must be something wrong. This man is forcing me toward the snake. He may be interested in my death, or something else." If I try to convince you too much that this is a rope, that will only show that I am somehow interested in forcing you toward the snake. If I say to you that theoretically it is possible to see the rope as a rope this very moment, your mind will create many, many problems.

In reality there is no dilemma; in reality there is no problem. There never has been; there never will be. In mind there are problems, and you look at reality through the mind. Thus, the reality becomes problematic. Your mind works like a prison. It divides and creates problems. And not only that: it creates solutions which become deeper problems, because in fact, there are no problems to be solved. Reality is absolutely unproblematic; there is no problem. But you cannot see without problems. Wherever you see, you create problems: your "look" is problematic. I told you this breath technique; now the mind says, "This is so simple." Why? Why does the mind say this is so simple?

When for the first time the steam engine was invented, no one believed it. It looked so simple — unbelievable. Just the same steam that you know in your kitchen, in your kettle — the SAME steam — running an engine, running hundreds and hundreds of passengers and such a load? The same steam that you are so well acquainted with? This is not believable.

Do you know what happened in England? When the first train started, no one was ready to sit in it — no one! Many people were persuaded, bribed. They were given money to sit in the train. At the last point, they escaped. They said, "Firstly, steam cannot do such miracles. Such a simple thing as steam cannot do such miracles. And if the engine starts, that means that the Devil is at work somewhere. The Devil is running the thing: it is not the steam. And what is the guarantee that once the thing starts you will be capable of stopping it?"

No guarantee can be given because this was the first train. Never was it stopped before: it was only probable. There was no experience, so science could not say, "Yes it will stop." "Theoretically" it will stop, but the people were not interested in theories. They were interested in if there was any actual experience of stopping a train: "If it never stops then what will happen to us who will be sitting in it ?"

So twelve criminals from the jail were brought as passengers. Anyhow they were going to die, anyhow they were sentenced to death, so there was no problem if the train was not going to stop. Then the mad driver who thought that it was going to stop, the scientist who had invented it and these twelve passengers who were anyhow going to be killed, they alone would all be killed.

"Such a simple thing as steam," they said at that time. But now no one says this, because now it is working and you know it. Everything is simple; reality is simple. It seems complex only because of ignorance; otherwise everything is simple. Once you know it, it becomes simple, but the knowing is bound to be difficult — not because of reality, remember, but because of your mind. This technique is simple, but it is not going to be simple for you. Your mind will create difficulty. So try with it.

Another friend says, *"If I try this method of being aware of my breathing, if I pay attention to my breathing, then I cannot do anything else. The whole attention goes to it. And if I am to do anything else, then I cannot be aware of my breathing."*

This will happen, so in the beginning choose a particular period in the morning, or in the evening, or at anytime. For one hour just do the exercise; do not do aything else. Do not do anything else ! Just do the exercise. Once you become attuned to it, then it will not be a problem. You can walk on the street and you can be aware.

In awareness and in attention there is a difference. When you pay attention to anything, it is exclusive; you have to withdraw your attention from everywhere else. So it is "a tension" really. That is why it is called "attention". You pay attention to one thing at the cost of everything else. If you pay attention to your breathing, you cannot pay attention to your walking or to your driving. Do not try it while you are driving because then you cannot pay attention to both.

"Attention" means one thing exclusively. Awareness is a very different thing; it is not exclusive. It is not paying attention: it is "being attentive"; it is just being conscious. You are conscious when you are inclusively conscious. Your breathing is in your consciousness. You are walking and someone is passing, and you are also conscious of him. Someone is making noise on the road, some train passes by, some aeroplane flies: everything is inclusive. Awareness is inclusive, attention exclusive. But in the beginning it will be attention.

So first try in selected periods. For one hour just be attentive to your breathing. By and by you will be able to change your attention into awareness. Then do simple things — for example, walking: walk attentively with full awareness of walking and also of breathing. Do not create any opposition between the two actions of walking and breathing. Be a watcher of both. It is not difficult.

Look! For example, I can pay attention to one face here. If I pay attention to one face, all the faces will not be here for me. If I pay my attention to one face, then all the rest are bracketed out. If I pay attention only to the nose on that face, then the whole face, the remaining face, is bracketed out. I can go on narrowing down my attention to a single point.

The reverse is also possible. I pay attention to the whole face; then eyes and nose and everything are there. Then I have made my focus wider. I look at you not as an individual, but as a group. Then the whole group is in my attention. If I take you as different from the noise that is going on the street, then I am bracketing out the street. But I can look at you and the street as one whole. Then I can be aware of both you and the street. I can be aware of the whole Cosmos. It depends on your focus — on its becoming greater and greater. But first start from attention and remember that you have to grow into awareness. So choose a small period. The morning is good because you are fresh. Energies are vital; everything is rising; you are more alive in the morning.

Physiologists say that not only are you more alive, but your height is a little more in the morning than in the evening — your height ! If you are six feet, then in the morning you are six feet and one half inch. And in the evening you remain six feet: half an inch is lost because your spine settles down when it is tired. So in the morning, you are fresh, young, alive with energy.

Do this: do not make meditation the least thing on your schedule. Make it THE FIRST. Then, when you feel that now it is not an effort, when you can sit for an hour together completely immersed in breathing — aware, attentive; when you only know this: that you have achieved attention of breathing without any effort; when you are relaxed and enjoying it without any forcing; then you have attained it.

Then add something else — for example, walking. Remember both; then go on adding things. After a certain period you will be capable of being aware of your breath continuously, even in sleep. And unless you are aware even in sleep, you will not be able to know the depth. But this comes: by and by this comes.

One has to be patient and one has to start rightly. Know this, because the cunning mind will always try to give you a wrong start. Then you can leave it after two or three days and say, "This is hopeless." The mind will give you a wrong start. So always remember to begin rightly, because rightly begun means half done. But we start wrongly.

You know very well that attention is a difficult thing. This is because you are totally asleep. So if you start being attentive to breathing while you are doing something else, you cannot do it. And you are not going to leave the task. You will leave the effort of being attentive to breathing.

So do not create unnecessary problems for yourself. In 24 hours you can find a small corner. Forty minutes will do, so do the technique there. But the mind will give many excuses. The mind will say, "Where is the time ? There is already too much work to be done. Where is the time ?" Or, the mind will say, "It is not possible now, so postpone it. Sometime in the future when things are better, then you will do it."

Beware of what your mind says to you. Do not be too trusting of the mind. And we are never doubtful. We can doubt every-one but we never doubt our own minds.

Even those who talk too much of scepticism, of doubt, of reason, even they never doubt their own minds. And your mind has brought you to the state you are in. If you are in a hell, your mind has brought you to this hell, and you never doubt this guide. You can doubt any Teacher, any Master, but you never doubt your mind. With unflinching faith, you move with your mind as the Guru. And your mind has brought you to the mess, to the misery that you are. If you are going to doubt any-thing, doubt first your own mind. And whenever your mind says something, think twice.

Is it true that you do not have any time? Really? You do not have any time to meditate — to give one hour to meditation? Think twice. Ask again and again to the mind, "Is this the case, that I do not have any time?"

I don't see it. I have not seen a man who does not have more than enough time. I go on seeing people who are playing cards, and they say, "We are killing time." They are going to the movies and they say, "What to do?" They are killing time, gossiping, reading the same newspaper again and again, talking the same things they have been talking about for their whole lives, and they say, "We don't have any time." For unnecessary things they have enough time. Why?

With an unnecessary thing mind is not in any danger. The moment you think of meditation, mind becomes alert. Now you are moving in a dangerous dimension, because meditation means death of the mind. If you move in meditation, sooner or later your mind will have to dissolve — retire completely. The mind becomes alert and it begins to say many things to you: "Where is the time? And even if there is time, then more important things are to be done. First postpone it until later. You can meditate at any time. Money is more important. Gather money first, then meditate at your leisure. How can you meditate without money? So pay attention to money; then meditate later on."

Meditation can be postponed easily you feel, because it is not concerned with your immediate survival. Bread cannot be post-poned: you will die. Money cannot be postponed: it is needed for your basic necessities. Meditation can be postponed. It is not concerned with your survival: you can survive without it. Really, you can survive without it easily.

The moment yo go deep in meditation, you will not survive on this earth at least. You will disappear. From the circle of this life, from this wheel, you will disappear. Meditation is like death, so the mind becomes afraid. Meditation is like love, so the mind becomes afraid. "Postpone," it says. And you can go on postponing ad infinitum. Your mind is always saying things like this. And do not think I am talking about others. I am talking particularly about YOU.

I have come across many intelligent people who go on talking very non-intelligent things about meditation. One man came from Delhi. He is a big government official. He came only for the purpose to learn meditation here. He had come from Delhi, and he stayed seven days here. I told him to go to the morning meditation class on Chowpatty beach (in Bombay), but he said, "But that is difficult. I cannot get up so early." And he will never think over what his mind has told him. Is this so difficult ? Now you will know: the exercise can be simple, but your mind is not so simple. The mind says, "How can I get up in the morn-ing at six o'clock ?"

I was in a big city, and the Collector of that city came to meet me at eleven o'clock at night. I was just going to my bed, and he came and said, "No ! It is urgent. I am very disturbed. It is a question of life and death," he told me. "So please give me at least half an hour. Teach me meditation; otherwise I might com-mit suicide. I am very much disturbed. And I am so frustrated that something must happen in my inner world. My outer world is lost completely."

I told him, "Come in the morning at five o'clock." He said, "That is not possible." It is a question of life and death, but he cannot get up at five o'clock. He said, "That is not possible. I never get up so early." "Okay," I told him, "Then come at ten." He said, "That will also be difficult because by 10:30 I am to be present at my office."

He cannot take one day's leave, and it is a question of life and death. So I told him, "Is it a question of your life and death, or my life and death? Whose?" And he was not an unintelligent man. He was intelligent enough. These tricks were very intelligent.

So do not think that your mind is not playing the same tricks. It is very intelligent. And because you think it is your mind, you never doubt. It is not yours; it is just a social product. It is not yours! It has been given to you; it has been forced upon you. You have been taught and conditioned in a certain way. From the very childhood your mind has been created by others — parents, society, teachers. The past is creating your mind, influencing your mind. The dead past is forcing itself upon the living continuously. The teachers are just the agents — the agents of the dead, against the living. They go on forcing things upon your mind. But the mind is so intimate with you, the gap is so small, that you become identified with it.

You say, "I am a Hindu." Think again; reconsider it. YOU are not a Hindu. You have been given a Hindu mind. You were born just a simple, innocent being — not a Hindu, not a Mohammedan. But you were given a Mohammedan mind, a Hindu mind. You were forced, engaged, imprisoned in a particular condition, and then life goes on adding to this mind, and this mind becomes heavy — heavy on you. You cannot do anything; the mind starts forcing its own way upon you. Your experiences are being added to the mind. Constantly, your past is conditioning your every present moment. If I say something to you, you are not going to think about it in a fresh way, in an open way. Your old mind, your past, will come in between, will begin to talk and chatter for or against.

Remember, your mind is not yours, your body is not yours: it comes from your parents. Your mind is also not yours: it also comes from your parents. Who are you?

Either one is identified with the body or with the mind. You think you are young, you think you are old, you think you are a Hindu, you think you are a Jain, that you are a Parsi. You are not! You were born as a pure consciousness. These are all imprisonments. These techniques which look so simple to you will not be so simple, because this mind will create constantly many, many complexities and problems.

Just a few days before, a man came to me, and he said, "I am trying your method of meditation, but tell me, in what scripture is it given? If you can convince me that it is given in my religious scripture, then it will be easier for me to do."

But why will it be easier for him to do if it is written in a scripture? Because then the mind will not create a problem. The mind will say, "Okay! This belongs to us, so do it." If it is not written in any scripture, then the mind will say, "What are you doing?" The mind goes against it.

I said to the man, "You have been doing this method for three months. How are you feeling?" He said, "Wonderful. I am feeling very wonderful. But tell me, give some authority from the scriptures." His own feeling is not an authority at all. He says, "I am feeling wonderful. I have become more silent, more peaceful, more loving. I am feeling wonderful." But his own experience is not the authority. The mind asks for an authority in the past.

I told him, "It is not written anywhere in your scriptures. Rather, many things which are against this technique are written." His face became sad. And then he said, "Then it will be difficult for me to do it and to continue it."

Why is his own experience not of any value? The past — the conditioning, the mind — is constantly molding you and destroying your present. So remember, and be aware. Be sceptical and doubting about your mind. Do not trust it. And if you can attain to this maturity of not trusting your mind, only then will these techniques be really simple, helpful, functioning. They will work miracles; they can work miracles.

These techniques, these methods, cannot be understood intellectually at all. I am trying the impossible, but then why am I trying ? If they cannot be understood intellectually, then why am I talking to you ? They cannot be understood intellectually, but there is no other way to make you aware of certain techniques which can change your life totally. You can understand only intellect, and this is a problem. You cannot understand anything else: you can understand only the intellect. And these techniques cannot be understood intellectually. So how to communicate ?

Either you should become capable of understanding without intellect being brought in, or some method should be found so that these techniques can be made intellectually understandable. The second is not possible, but the first is possible.

You will have to start intellectually, but do not cling to it. When I say "Do", try doing. If something begins to happen within you, then you will be capable of throwing your intellect aside and reaching toward me directly without the intellect, without any meditation, without the meditator. But start doing something. We can go on talking for years and years. Your mind can be stuffed with many things, but that is not going to help. Rather, it may harm you because you will begin to know many things. And if you know many things you will become confused. It is not good to know many things. It is good to know a little and to practise it. A single technique can be helpful: something done is always helpful. What is the difficulty in doing it ?

Deep down somewhere there is fear. If you do it, the fear is that it may be that something stops happening: that is the fear. It may look paradoxical, but I have been meeting so many — so many persons — who think they want to change. They say they need meditation; they ask for a deep transformation. But deep down they are also afraid. They are dual — double; they have two minds. They go on asking about what to do, never doing it. Why then do they go on asking ? Just to deceive themselves that they are really interested in transforming themselves. That is why they are asking.

This gives a facade, an appearance, that they are really, sincerely interested in changing themselves. That is why they are asking, going to this Guru and that, finding, trying, but they never do anything. Deep down they are afraid.

Eric Fromme has written a book, "Fear of Freedom." The title seems contradictory. Everyone thinks that they like freedom; everyone thinks that they are endeavouring for freedom — in this world and in "that world" also. "We want *Moksha* (Liberation): we want to be freed from all limitations, from all slaveries. We want to be totally free," they say. But Eric Fromme says that man is afraid of freedom. We want, we go on saying that we want, we go on convincing ourselves that we want, but deep down we are afraid of freedom. We do not want! Why? Why this duality?

Freedom creates fear, and meditation is the deepest freedom possible. You are not freed only from outward limitations: you are freed from inner slavery — the very mind, the base of slavery. You are freed from the whole past. The moment you have no mind, the past has disappeared. You have transcended the history. Now there is no society, no religion, no scripture, no tradition, because they all have their abode in the mind. Now there is no past, no future, because past and future are part of the mind, the memory and the imagination.

Then you are here and now in the present. Now there is not going to be any future. There will be now and now and now — eternal now. Then you are freed completely; you transcend all tradition, all history, body, mind, everything. One becomes free of the fearful. Such freedom? Then where will YOU be? In such freedom, can you exist? In such freedom, in such vastness, can you have your small "I" — your ego? Can you say "I am"?

You can say "I am in bondage" because you can know your boundary. When there is no bondage there is no boundary. You become just like a state — nothing more: absolute nothingness, emptiness. That creates fear, so one goes on talking about meditation — about how to do it, and one goes on without doing it.

All the questions arise out of this fear. Feel this fear. If you know it, it will disappear. If you do not know it, it will continue.

Are you ready to die in the spiritual sense? Are you ready to be NOT?

Whenever anyone came to Buddha, he would say: "This is the basic truth — that you are not. And because you are not, you cannot die, you cannot be born; and because you are not, you cannot be in suffering, in bondage. Are you ready to accept this?" Buddha will ask, "Are you ready to accept this? If you are not ready to accept this, then do not try meditation now. First try to find out whether you really are or you are not. Meditate on this first. Is there any self? Is there any substance within or are you just a combination?"

If you are going to find out, you will find that your body is a combination. Something has come from your mother, something has come from your father, and all else has come from food. This is your body. In this body you are NOT; there is no self. Contemplate on the mind: something has come from here, something from there. Mind has nothing that is original. It is just accumulation.

Find out if there is any self in the mind. If you move deep, you will find that your identity is just like an onion. You peel off one layer, and another layer comes up; you peel off another layer, and still another layer comes up. You go on peeling layers off, and ultimately you come to a nothingness. With all the layers thrown off, there is nothing inside. Body and mind are like onions. When you have peeled off both body and mind, then you come to encounter a nothingness, an abyss, a bottomless Void. Buddha called it "Shunya".

To encounter this Shunya, to encounter this Void, creates fear. That fear is there. That is why we never do meditation. We talk about it, but we never do anything about it. That fear is there. You know deep down that there is a Void, but you cannot escape this fear. Whatsoever you do, the fear will remain — unless you encounter it: that is the only way. Once you encounter your nothingness, once you know that within you are just like a space, Shunya, then there will be no fear. Then there cannot be any fear, because this Shunya, this Void, cannot be destroyed. This Void is not going to die. That which was going to die is no more; it was nothing but the layers of an onion.

That is why, many times, in deep meditation, when one comes nearer to this nothingness, one becomes afraid and starts trembling. One feels that one is going to die. One wants to escape from this nothingness back to the world. And many go back; then they never turn within again. And as I see it, everyone of you have tried in some life or other some meditative technique. You have been near to the nothingness, and then fear gripped you and you escaped. And deep in your past memories, that memory is there: that becomes the hindrance. Whenever you again think of trying meditation, that past memory deep down in your unconscious mind again disturbs you and says, "Go on thinking; do not do it. You have done it once."

It is difficult to find a man (and I have looked into many) who has not tried meditation once or twice in some life. The memory is there, but you are not conscious of it, you are not aware of where the memory is. It is there. Whenever you begin to do something, that becomes a barrier, and this and that begins to stop you in many ways. So if you are really interested in meditation, find out about your own fear of it. Be sincere about it: Are you afraid? If you are afraid, then first something has to be done about your fear, not about meditation.

Buddha used to try many devices. Sometimes someone would say to him, "I am afraid of trying meditation." And this is a must: the Teacher must be told that you are afraid. You cannot deceive the Teacher, and there is no need. It is deceiving yourself. So whenever someone would say, "I am afraid of meditation," Buddha would say, "You are fulfilling the first requirement." If you say yourself that you are afraid of meditation, then something becomes possible. Then something can be done because you have uncovered a deep thing. So what is the fear? Meditate on it. Go and dig out where it comes from, what the source is.

All fear is basically death oriented — ALL fear! Whatsoever its form, mode — whatsoever its shape, name, all fear is death oriented. If you move deep, you will find that you are afraid of death.

If someone would come to Buddha and say, "I am afraid of death; I have found out," then Buddha would say, "Then go to the burning *ghat* — go to the cemetery, and meditate on a funeral pyre. People are dying daily: they will be burned. Just remain there at the *marghat* (cemetery) and meditate on the burning pyre. When their family members have gone, you remain there. Just look into the fire, at the burning body. When everything is becoming smoke, you just look at it deeply. Do not think: just meditate on it for three months, six months, nine months.

"When it becomes a certainty to you that death cannot be escaped, when it becomes absolutely certain that death is the way of life, that death is implied in life, that death is going to be, that there is no way out and you are already in it, only then come to me."

After meditating on death, after seeing every day — night and day — dead bodies being burned, dissolved into ashes, just a smoke remains and then disappears, after meditating for months together, a certainty will arise — the certainty that death is certain. It is the only certainty really. The only thing certain in life is death. Everything else is uncertain: it may be or it may not be, but you cannot say that it may be or it may not be for death. It is; it is going to be. It has already occurred. The moment you entered life, you entered death. Now nothing can be done about it.

When death is certain there is no fear. Fear is always with things which can be changed. If death is to be, fear disappears. If you can change, if you can do something about death, then fear will remain. If nothing can be done, if you are already in it, then it is absolutely certain that fear disappears. And when fear of death disappears, Buddha would allow you to meditate. He would say, "Now you can meditate."

So you also go deep into your mind. And listening to these techniques will be helpful only when your inner barriers are broken, when inner fears disappear and you are certain that death is the reality. So if you die in meditation, there is no fear: death is certain. Even if death occurs in meditation, there is no fear. Only then can you move — and then you can move at rocket speed because the barriers are not there.

It is not distance that takes time, but the barriers. You can move this very moment if there is no barrier. You are already there but for the barrier. It is a hurdle race, and you go on putting more and more hurdles. You feel good when you cross a hurdle. You feel good that now you have crossed the hurdle. And the idiocy of it, the foolishness of it, is that the hurdle was placed there by you in the first place. It was never there. You go on placing hurdles, then jumping over them, then feeling good, then you go on putting more hurdles, then jumping. You move in a circle and never, never reach to the center.

Mind creates hurdles because mind is afraid. It will give you many explanations as to why you are not doing meditation. Do not believe it. Go deep; find out the basic cause. Why does a person go on talking about food, and yet he never eats? What is the problem! The man seems mad!

Another man goes on talking about love and never loves, another man goes on talking about something and never doing anything about it. This talking becomes obsessive; it becomes a compulsion. One goes on; one sees talking as a doing. By talking you feel that you are doing something, so you feel at ease. You are doing "something" — at least talking, at least reading, at least listening. This is not doing. This is deceptive. Do not fall into the deception.

I will be talking here about these 112 methods not to feed your mind, not to make you more knowledgeable, not to make you more informed. I am not trying to make you a pundit. I am talking here in order to give you a certain technique which can change your life. So whichever method appeals to you, do not start talking about it: do it! Be silent about it and do it. Your mind will raise many questions. Just inquire deeply first before asking me. Inquire deeply first whether those questions are really significant or if your mind is just deceiving you.

Do, then ask. Then your questions become practical. And I know which question has been asked through doing and which question has been asked just through curiosity, just through intellect. So by and by I will not answer your intellectual questions at all. Do something. Then your questions become significant.

These questions which say, "This exercise is a very simple one" are not asked after doing. This is NOT so simple. In the end I must repeat again, YOU ARE ALREADY THE TRUTH. ONLY A CERTAIN AWAKENING IS NEEDED. You are not to go anywhere else. You are to go into yourself, and the going is possible this very moment. If you can put aside your mind, you enter here and now.

These techniques are for putting your mind aside. These techniques are not really for meditation: they are for putting the mind aside. Once the mind is not there, YOU ARE!

I think this is enough for today, or even more than enough.

5
Five Techniques Of Attentiveness

October 5, 1972, Bombay, India

SUTRAS:

5. *Attention between eyebrows, let mind be before thought. Let form fill with breath essence to the top of the head and there shower as light.*

6. *When in worldly activity, keep attentive between two breaths, and so practising, in a few days be born anew.*

7. *With intangible breath in center of forehead, as this reaches heart at the moment of sleep, have direction over dreams and over death itself.*

8. *With utmost devotion, center on the two junctions of breath and know the knower.*

9. *Lie down as dead. Enraged in wrath, stay so. Or stare without moving an eyelash. Or suck something and become the sucking.*

When one of the great Greek philosophers, Pythagoras, reached Egypt to enter a school — a secret esoteric school of mysticism, he was refused. And Pythagoras was one of the best minds ever produced. He could not understand. He applied again and again, but he was told that unless he goes through a particular training of fasting and breathing he cannot be allowed to enter the school.

Pythagoras is reported to have said, "I have come for knowledge, not for any sort of discipline." But the school authorities said, "We cannot give you knowledge unless you are different. And, really, we are not interested in knowledge at all. We are interested in actual experience. And no knowledge is knowledge unless it is lived and experienced. So you will have to go on a forty-day fast, continuously breathing in a certain manner, with a certain awareness on certain points."

There was no other way, so Pythagoras had to pass through this training. After forty days of fasting and breathing, aware, attentive, he was allowed to enter the school. It is said that Pythagoras said, "You are not allowing Pythagoras. I am a different man. I am reborn. And you were right and I was wrong because then my whole standpoint was intellectual. Through this purification my center of being has changed. From the intellect it has come down to the heart. Now I can feel things. Before this training I could only understand through the intellect, through the head. Now I can feel. Now Truth is not a concept to me, but a life. It is not going to be a philosophy, but, rather, an experience — existential."

What was that training he went through ? This fifth technique was the technique that was given to Pythagoras. It was given in Egypt, but the technique is Indian.

The fifth technique: *"Attention between eyebrows, let mind be before thought. Let form fill with breath essence to the top of the head and there shower as light."*

This was the technique given to Pythagoras. Pythagoras went with this technique to Greece. And, really, he became the fountainhead, the source, of all mysticism in the West. He is the father of all mysticism in the West.

This technique is one of the very deep methods. Try to understand this: "Attention between the eyebrows..." Modern physiology, scientific research, says that between the two eyebrows is the gland which is the most mysterious part in the body. This gland, called the pineal gland, is the third eye of the Tibetans — *"Shivanetra"*: the eye of the Shiva, of the tantra. Between the two eyes there is a third eye existing, but it is non-functioning. It is there; it can function any moment. But it is not functioning naturally. You have to do something about it to open it. It is not blind. It is simply closed. This technique is to open the third eye.

"Attention between the eyebrows..." Close your eyes, then focus both of your eyes just in the middle of the two eyebrows. Focus just in the middle, with closed eyes, as if you are looking with your two eyes. Give total attention to it.

This is one of the simplest methods of being attentive. You cannot be attentive to any other part of the body so easily. This gland absorbs attention like anything. If you give attention to it, your both eyes become hypnotized with the third eye. They become fixed; they cannot move. If you are trying to be attentive to any other part of the body, it is difficult. This third eye catches attention, forces attention. It is magnetic for attention. So all the methods all over the world have used it. It is the simplest to train attention because not only are you trying to be attentive:

the gland itself helps you; it is magnetic. Your attention is brought to it forcibly. It is absorbed.

It is said in the old tantra scriptures that for the third eye attention is food. It is hungry; it has been hungry for lives and lives. If you pay attention to it, it becomes alive. It becomes alive! The food is given to it. And once you know that attention is food, once you feel that your attention is magnetically drawn, attracted, pulled by the gland itself, attention is not a difficult thing then. One has only to know the right point. So just close your eyes, let your two eyes move just in the middle, and feel the point. When you are near the point, suddenly your eyes will become fixed. When it will be difficult to move them, then know you have caught the right point.

"Attention between the eyebrows, let mind be before thought. . . " If this attention is there, for the first time you will come to experience a strange phenomenon. For the first time you will feel thoughts running before you; you will become the witness. It is just like a film screen: thoughts are running and you are a witness. Once your attention is focused at the third-eye center, you become immediately the witness of thoughts.

Ordinarily you are not the witness: you are identified with thoughts. If anger is there, you become anger. If a thought moves, you are not the witness: you become one with the thought — identified, and you move with it. You become the thought; you take the form of the thought. When sex is there you become sex, when anger is there you become anger, when greed is there you become greed. Any thought moving becomes identified with you. You do not have any gap between you and the thought.

But focused at the third eye, suddenly you become a witness. Through the third eye, you become the witness. Through the third eye, you can see thoughts running like clouds in the sky or people moving on the street.

You are sitting at your window looking at the sky or at people in the street: you are not identified. You are aloof, a watcher on the hill — different. Now if anger is there, you can look at

THE BOOK OF THE SECRETS

it as an object. Now you do not feel that YOU are angry. You
feel that you are surrounded by anger: a cloud of anger has
come around you. But you are not the anger — and if you are not
the anger, anger becomes impotent. It cannot affect you; you remain untouched. The anger will come and go, and you will
remain centered in yourself.

This fifth technique is a technique of finding the witness.
"Attention between the eyebrows, let the mind be before
thought": Now look at your thoughts; now encounter your
thoughts. "Let form fill with breath essence to the top of the
head and there shower as light": When attention is focused at
the third-eye center, between the two eyebrows, two things
happen. One, suddenly you become a witness. This can happen
in two ways. You become a witness, and you will be centered at
the third eye.

Try to be a witness. Whatsoever is happening, try to be a
witness. You are ill, the body is aching and painful, you have
misery and suffering, whatsoever: be a witness to it. Whatsoever
is happening, do not identify yourself with it. Be a witness — an
observer. Then if witnessing becomes possible, you will be
focused in the third eye.

Secondly, the vice versa is the case also. If you are focused
in the third eye, you will become a witness. These two things are
part of one. So the first thing: by being centered in the third
eye there will be the arising of the witnessing Self. Now you can
encounter your thoughts. This will be the first thing. And the
second thing will be that now you can feel the subtle, delicate
vibration of breathing. Now you can feel the form of breathing,
the very essence of breathing.

First try to understand what is meant by "the form" by "the
essence of breathing". While you are breathing, you are not
only breathing air. Science says you are breathing only air — just
oxygen, hydrogen, and other gases in their combined form of air.
They say you are breathing "air" ! But tantra says that air is just
the vehicle, not the real thing. You are breathing "prana" —

vitality. Air is just the medium; prana is the content. You are breathing prana — not only air.

Modern science is still not able to find out whether there is something like prana. But some researchers have felt something mysterious. Breathing is not simply air. It has been felt by many modern researchers also. In particular, one name is to be mentioned — Wilhelm Reich, a German psychologist who called it "orgone energy". It is the same thing as prana. He says that while you are breathing, air is just the container, and there is a mysterious content which can be called "orgone" or "prana" or "elan vital". But that is very subtle. Really, it is not material. Air is the material thing: the container is material. But something subtle, non-material, is moving through it.

The effects of it can be felt. When you are with a very vital person, you will feel a certain vitality arising in you. If you are with a very sick person, you will feel sucked, as if something has been taken out of you. When you go to the hospital, why do you feel so tired? You are being sucked from everywhere. The whole hospital atmosphere is ill, and everyone there needs more elan vital, more prana. So if you are there, suddenly your prana begins to flow out of you. Why do you feel suffocated sometimes when you are in a crowd? Because your prana is being sucked. While you are alone under the sky in the morning, under the trees, suddenly you feel a vitality in you — the prana. Each one needs a particular space. If that space is not given, your prana is sucked.

Wilhelm Reich did many experiments, but he was thought to be a mad man. Science has its own superstitions, and science is a very orthodox thing. Science cannot feel yet that there is anything more than air, but India has been experimenting with it for centuries.

You may have heard or you have even seen someone going into Samadhi (Cosmic Consciousness) — underground Samadhi — for days together, with no air penetrating. One man went into such underground Samadhi in Egypt, in 1880, for forty years. Those who had buried him all died, because he was to come out of his Samadhi in 1920, forty years afterwards. In 1920, no one believed that they would find him alive, but he was found alive. He lived afterwards for ten years more. He had become completely pale, but he was alive. And there was no possibility of air reaching to him.

He was asked by medical doctors and others, "What is the secret of it?" He said, "We do not know. We only know this, that prana can enter and flow anywhere." Air cannot penetrate, but prana can penetrate. Once you know that you can suck prana directly, without the container, then you can go into Samadhi for centuries even.

By being focused in the third eye, suddenly you can observe the very essence of breath — not breath, but the very essence of breath, prana. And if you can observe the essence of breath, prana, you are on the point from where the jump, the breakthrough, happens.

The sutra says, "Let form fill with breath essence to the top of the head..." And when you come to feel the essence of breathing, prana, just imagine that your head is filled with it. Just imagine. No need of any effort. I will explain to you how imagination works. When you are focused at the third eye center, imagine, and the thing happens — then and there.

Now your imagination is just important. You go on imagining, and nothing happens. But sometimes, unknowingly, in ordinary life also, things happen. You are imagining about your friend, and suddenly there is a knock on the door. You say it is a coincidence that the friend has come. Sometimes your imagination works just like coincidence. But whenever this happens, now try and remember, and analyze the whole thing. Whenever it happens that you feel your imagination has become actual, go inside and observe. Somewhere your attention must have been near the third eye. Whenever this coincidence happens, it is not a coincidence. It looks that way because you do not know the secret science. Your mind must have moved unknowingly near the third-eye center. If your attention is in the third eye, just imagination is enough to create any phenomenon.

This sutra says that when you are focused between the eyebrows and you can feel the very essence of breathing, "let form fill." Now imagine that this essence is filling your whole head — particularly the top of the head, the "*Sahasrar*" (the highest psychic center). And the moment you imagine, it will be filled. "There (at the top of the head) shower as light": This prana essence is showering from the top of your head as light. And it WILL begin to shower, and under the shower of light you will be refreshed, reborn, completely new. That is what inner rebirth means.

So two things: first, focused at the third eye, your imagination becomes potent, powerful. That is why so much insistence has been given on purity: before doing these practices, be pure. Purity is not a moral concept for tantra. Purity is significant — because if you are focused at the third eye and your mind is impure, your imagination can become dangerous: dangerous to you, dangerous to others. If you are thinking to murder someone, if this idea is in the mind, just imagining may kill the man. That is why so much insistance on being pure first.

Pythagoras was told to go through fasting, through particular breathing — this breathing, because here one is travelling in a very dangerous land: because wherever there is power there is danger. And if the mind is impure, whenever you will get power your impure thoughts will take hold of it immediately.

You have imagined many times to kill, but the imagination cannot work, fortunately. If it works, if it is actualized immediately, then it will become dangerous — not only to others, but to yourself also, because so many times you have thought to commit suicide. If the mind is focused at the third eye, just thinking of suicide will become suicide. You will not have any time to change. Immediately it will happen.

You might have observed someone being hypnotized. When someone is hypnotized, the hypnotist can say anything and immediately the hypnotized person follows. Howsoever absurd the order, howsoever irrational or even impossible, the hypnotized person follows it. What is happening? This fifth technique is at the base of all hypnotism. Whenever someone is being hypnotized he is told to focus his eyes at a particular point — on some light, some dot on the wall, or anything, or on the eyes of the hypnotist.

When you focus your eyes at any particular point, within three minutes your inner attention begins to flow toward the third eye. And the moment your inner attention begins to flow toward the third eye, your face begins to change. And the hypnotist knows when your face begins to change. Suddenly your face loses all vitality. It becomes dead, as if deeply asleep. Immediately the hypnotist knows when your face has lost the lustre, the aliveness. It means that now attention is being sucked by the third-eye center. Your face has become dead; the whole energy is running toward the third-eye center.

Now the hypnotist immediately knows that anything said will happen. He says, "Now you are falling into a deep sleep": you will fall immediately. He says, "Now you are becoming unconscious": you will become unconscious immediately. Now anything can be done. If he says, "Now you have become Napoleon or Hitler," you will become. You will begin to behave like a Napoleon, you will begin to talk like Napoleon. Your gestures will change. Your unconscious will take the order and will create the actuality. If you are suffering from a disease, now it can be ordered that the disease has disappeared, and it will disappear. Or, any new disease can be created.

Just by putting an ordinary stone from the street on your hand, the hypnotist can say, "This is fire on your hand." You will feel intense heat; your hand will get burned — not only in the mind, but actually. Actually your skin will get burned. You will have a burning sensation. What is happening? There is no fire. There is just an ordinary stone — cold. How? How does this burning happen? You are focused at the third-eye center, your imagination is being given suggestions by the hypnotist, and they are being actualized. If the hypnotist says, "Now you are dead," you will die immediately. Your heart will stop. It WILL stop.

This happens because of the third eye. In the third eye, imagination and actualization are not two things. Imagination is the fact. Imagine, and it is so. There is nó gap between dream and reality. There is NO gap between dream and reality! Dream, and it will become real. That is why Shankara has said that this whole world is nothing but the dream of the Divine — the DREAM of the Divine! This is because the Divine is centered in the third eye — always, eternally. So whatsoever the Divine dreams, it becomes real. If you are also centered in the third eye, whatsoever you dream will become real.

Sariputta came to Buddha. He meditated deeply, then many things, many visions, started coming, as it happens with anyone who goes into deep meditation. He began to see heavens, he began to see hells, he began to see angels, gods, demons. And they were actual, so real, that he came running to Buddha to tell him that such and such a vision had come to him. But Buddha said, "It is nothing — just dreams. Just dreams!" But Sariputta said, "They are so real. How can I say that they are dreams? When I see a flower in my vision it is more real than any flower in the world. The fragrance is there; I can touch it. When I see you," he said to Buddha, "it is not as real. That flower is more real than your being here just before me, so how can I differentiate what is real and what is dream?" Buddha said, "Now that you are centered in the third eye, dream and reality are one. Whatsoever you are dreaming will be real, and *vice versa* also."

For one who is centered in the third eye, dreams will become real and the whole reality will become just a dream, because when your dream can become real, you know there is no basic difference between dream and reality. So when Shankara says that this whole world is just *maya*, a dream of the Divine, it is not a theoretical proposition, it is not a philosophical statement. It is, rather, the inner experience of one who is focused in the third eye.

When you are focused in the third eye, just imagine that the essence of prana is showering from the top of the head, just as if you are sitting under a tree and flowers are showering, or you are just under the sky and suddenly a cloud begins to shower, or you are just sitting in the morning and the sun rises and rays begin to shower. Imagine, and immediately there is a shower — a shower of light falling down from the top of your head. This shower recreates you, gives you a new birth. You are reborn.

The sixth technique : *"When in worldly activity, keep attentive between the two breaths, and so practising, in a few days, be born anew."*

"When in worldly activity, keep attentive between the two breaths..." Forget breaths. Keep attentive in between. One breath has come: before it returns, before it is exhaled out, there is the gap, the interval. One breath has gone out: before it is taken in again, the gap. "In worldly activity keep attentive between the two breaths, and so practising, in a few days be born anew": But this has to be done continuously. This sixth technique has to be done continuously. That is why this is mentioned: "When in worldly activity..." Whatsoever you are doing, keep your attention in the gap between the two breaths. But it must be practised while in activity.

We have discussed one technique that is just similar. Now there is only this difference, that this has to be practised while in worldly activity. Do not practise it in isolation. This practice is to be done while you are doing something else. You are eating: go on eating, and be attentive of the gap. You are walking: go on walking and be attentive of the gap. You are going to sleep: lie down; let sleep come. But you go on being attentive of the gap.

Why in activity ? Because activity distracts the mind. Activity calls your attention again and again. Do not be distracted. Be fixed at the gap. And do not stop activity: let the activity continue. You will have two layers of existence — doing and being. We have two layers of existence: the world of doing and the world of being. The circumference and the center. Go on working on the periphery, on the circumference; do not stop it. But

go on working attentively on the center also. What will happen?
Your activity will become an acting, as if you are playing a part.

You are playing a part — for example, in a drama. You have
become Ram or you have become Christ. You go on acting as
Christ or as Ram, and still you remain yourself. In the center,
you know who you are; on the periphery you go on acting Ram,
Christ or anyone. You know you are not Ram: you are acting.
You know who you are. Your attention is centered in you; your
activity continues on the circumference.

If this method is practised, your whole life will become a long
drama. You will be an actor playing roles, but constantly centered in the gap. If you forget the gap, then you are not playing
roles: you have become the role. Then it is not a drama. You
have mistaken it as life. That is what we have done. Everyone
thinks he is living life. It is not life: it is just a role — a part
which has been given to you by the society, by the circumstances,
by the culture, by the tradition, the country, the situation. You
have been given a role. You are playing it; you have become
identified with it. To break that identification, this technique.

Krishna has many names. Krishna is one of the greatest actors.
He is constantly centered in himself and playing — playing
many plays, many games, but absolutely non-serious. Seriousness
comes from identification. If you really become Ram in the
drama, then there are bound to be problems. Those problems
will come out of your seriousness. When Sita is stolen, you may
get a heart attack and the whole play would have to be stopped.
If you really become Ram a heart attack is certain, even heart
failure.

But you are just an actor. Sita is stolen, but nothing is stolen.
You will go back to your home and you will sleep peacefully. Not
even in dream will you feel that Sita is stolen. When really Sita
was stolen, Ram himself was weeping, crying and asking the
trees, "Where has my Sita gone? Who has taken her?" But
this is the point to understand: if Ram is really weeping and
asking the trees, he has become identified. He is no more Ram;
he is no more a Divine person.

This is the point to remember: that for Ram, his real life also was just a part. You have seen other actors playing Ram, but Ram himself was just playing a part — on a greater stage, of course.

India has a very beautiful story about it. I think that the story is unique. Nowhere else in any part of the world does such a thing exist. It is said that Valmiki wrote the "Ramayana" before Ram was born, and then Ram had to follow. So, really, the first act of Ram was also just a drama. The story was written before Ram was born and then Ram had to follow, so what can he do ? When a man like Valmiki writes the story, Ram has to follow. So everything was fixed in a way. Sita was to be stolen and the war had to be fought.

If you can understand this, then you can understand the theory of destiny, *bhagya* — fate. It has a very deep meaning. And the meaning is that if you take it that everything is fixed for you, your life becomes a drama. If you are playing Ram's act in the drama, you cannot change it. Everything is fixed, even your dialogue. If you say something to Sita, it is just repeating something that is fixed. You cannot change it if life is taken as fixed.

For example, you are going to die on a particular day: it is fixed. And when you will be dying you will be weeping, but it is fixed. And such and such persons will be around you: it is fixed. If everything is fixed, everything becomes a drama. If everything is fixed, it means you are just to enact it. You are not asked to live it: you are just asked to enact it.

This technique, the sixth technique, is just to make yourself a psychodrama — just a play. You are focused in the gap between two breaths, and life moves on, on the periphery. If your attention is at the center, then your attention is not really on the periphery: that is just "sub-attention"; it just happens somewhere near your attention. You can feel it, you can know it, but it is not significant. It is as if it is not happening to you. I will repeat this: if you practise this sixth technique, your whole life will be as if it is not happening to you — as if it is happening to someone else.

The seventh technique : *"With intangible breath in center of forehead, as this reaches heart at the moment of sleep, have direction over dreams and over death itself."* More and more you are entering deeper layers. "With intangible breath in center of forehead": If you have known the third eye, then you know the intangible breath, the invisible prana in the center of forehead, and then you know the showering — that the energy, the light, showers. ". . .As this reaches heart": when the shower will reach your heart, "at the moment of sleep, have direction over dreams and over death itself."

Take this technique in three parts. One, you must be able to feel the prana in breath, the intangible part of it, the invisible part of it, the immaterial part of it. It comes if you are attentive between the two eyebrows. Then it comes easily. If you are attentive in the gap, then too it comes, but a little less easily. If you are aware of the center at your navel where breath comes and touches and goes out, it also comes, but with less ease. The easiest point where to know the invisible part of breath is to be centered at the third eye. But wherever you are centered, it comes. You begin to feel the prana flowing in.

If you can feel the prana flowing in you, you can know when you are going to die. Six months before your day of death you begin to know, if you can feel the invisible part of breath. Why do so many saints declare their day of death ? It is easy, because if you can see the content of the breath, the prana flowing into you, the moment the process reverses you can feel it. Before you die, six months before you die, the process reverses: prana begins to flow out of you. Then the breath is not taking it in. Rather, on the contrary, the breath is taking it out — the same breath.

You cannot feel it because you do not know the invisible part — you know only the visible; you know only the vehicle: the vehicle will be the same. Now the breath is carrying prana in, leaving it there. Then the vehicle goes back vacant. Then again it is filled with the prana and it comes in. So the ingoing breath and the outgoing breath are not the same, remember.

The ingoing breath and the outgoing breath are the same as vehicles, but the incoming breath is filled with prana and the outgoing breath is empty. You have sucked the prana, and the breath has become empty.

The reverse happens when you are nearing death. The incoming breath comes "prana-less", empty. Because your body cannot suck prana from the Cosmos, you are going to die; there is no need. The whole process has reversed. And when the breath goes out, it takes your prana out. One who has been able to see the invisible can know his day of death immediately. Before six months the process reverses.

This sutra is very, very significant : "With intangible breath in center of forehead, as this reaches heart at the moment of sleep, have direction over dreams and over death itself." While you are falling into sleep, this technique has to be practised — then only, not at any other time. While you are falling asleep, only then. That is the right moment to practise this technique. You are falling asleep. By and by, by and by, sleep is overtaking you. Within moments, your consciousness will dissolve; you will not be aware. Before that moment comes, become aware — aware of the breath and the invisible part prana, and feel it coming to the heart.

Go on feeling that it is coming to the heart, it is coming to the heart. The prana enters from your heart into the body. Go on feeling, go on feeling that the prana is coming into the heart, and let sleep come while you are continuously feeling it. You go on feeling, and let sleep come and drown you.

If this happens — that you are feeling invisible breath coming into the heart and sleep overtakes you — you will be aware in dreams. You will know that you are dreaming. Ordinarily we do not know that we are dreaming. While you dream you think that this is reality. That too happens because of the third eye. Have you seen anyone asleep ? His eyes move upwards and become focused in the third eye. If you have not seen, then see.

Your child is sleeping: just open his eyes and see where his eyes are. His pupils have gone up and they are focused in the third eye. I say look at children. Do not look at grown-ups: they are not believable because their sleep is not deep. They will be just thinking that they are asleep. Look at children: their eyes move up. They become focused in the third eye. Because of this focusing in the third eye, you take your dreams as real; you cannot feel they are dreams. They are real. You will know when you get up in the morning. Then you will know that "I was dreaming". But this is the later, retrospective realization. You cannot realize in the dream that you are dreaming. If you realize it, then there are two layers: dream is there, but you are awake, you are aware. For one who becomes aware in dreams, this sutra is wonderful. It says, "Have direction over dreams and over death itself."

If you can become aware of dreams, you can do two things. You can create dreams — one. Ordinarily you cannot create dreams. How impotent man is! You cannot even create dreams. You CANNOT create dreams! If you want to dream a particular thing, you cannot dream it; it is not in your hands. How powerless man is! Even dreams·cannot be created. You are just a victim of dreams, not the creator. A dream happens to you; you cannot do anything. Neither can you stop it nor can you create it.

But if you move into sleep remembering the heart being filled with prana, continuously being touched by prana with every breath, you will become a master of your dreams — and this is a rare mastery. Then you can dream whatsoever dreams you like. Just note while you are falling asleep that "I want to dream this dream", and that dream will come to you. Just say, "While falling asleep I do not want to dream that dream," and that dream cannot enter your mind.

But what is the use of becoming the master of your dreaming? Isn't it useless? No, it is not useless. Once you become master of your dreams you will never dream. It is absurd. When you are master of your dreams, dreaming stops; there is no need for it. And when dreaming stops, your sleep has a different quality altogether, and the quality is the same as of death.

Death is deep sleep. If your sleep can become as deep as death, that means there will be no dreaming. Dreaming creates superficiality in sleep. You move on the surface because of the dreams. Because of hanging onto the dreams, you move on the surface. When there is no dreaming, you just drop into the sea; its depth is reached.

Death is the same. That is why India has always been saying that sleep is a short duration of death and death is a long sleep. Qualitatively they are the same. Sleep is a day-to-day death. Death is a life-to-life phenomenon, a life-to-life sleep. Every day you are tired: you fall into sleep and you regain your vitality, your aliveness, in the morning. You are reborn. After a life of 70 or 80 years, you are tired completely. Now such short durations of death won't do. You need a great death. After that great death or great sleep, you are reborn with a totally new body.

Once you can know dreamless sleep and can be aware in it, then there will be no fear of death. No one has ever died, no one can die : that is the only impossibility. Just a day before I was telling you that death is the only certainty, and now I say to you that death is impossible. No one has ever died and no one can die: that is the only impossibility. Just a day before because the universe is life. You are again and again reborn, but the sleep is so deep that you forget your old identity. Your mind is washed clean of the memories.

Think of it in this way. Today you are going to sleep: it is just as if there were some mechanism (and soon we will have this) like that which can erase on a tape recorder, which can wipe a tape clean so that whatsoever is recorded is no more there. The same is possible with memory because memory is really just a deep recording. Sooner or later we will find a mechanism which can be put on the head, and it will clean your mind completely. In the morning you will no more be the same person because you won't be able to remember who went to sleep. Then your sleep will look like death. There will be a discontinuity. You won't be able to remember who went to sleep.

This is happening naturally. When you die and when you are reborn, you cannot remember who died. You start again.

With this technique, first you will become the master of your dreams — that is, dreaming will cease. Or, if you want to dream you will be able to dream, but dreaming will become voluntary. It will not be non-voluntary; it will not be forced upon you; you will not be a victim. Then your quality of sleep will become just like that of death. Then you will know that death is sleep.

That is why this sutra says, "Have direction over dreams and over death itself": Now you will know that death is just a long sleep — and helpful and beautiful because it gives you new life; it gives you everything anew. Death ceases to be. With cessation of dream, death ceases to be.

There is another meaning to gaining power over death, direction over death: if you can come to feel that death is just a sleep, you will be able to direct it. If you can direct your dreams, you can direct your death also. You can choose where you are to be born again, to whom, when, in what form: you will become master of your birth also.

Buddha died. I am not referring to his last life, but to his last-but-one life ago — before he became Buddha. Before dying he said, "I will be born to such and such parents. Such will be my mother, such will be my father, but my mother will die immediately. When I will be born, my mother will die immediately. When I will be born, my mother will have 'these' dreams." Not only do you gain power from your dreams : you gain power from others dreams also. So Buddha (as an example) said that " 'These' dreams will be there. When I will be in the womb, my mother will have 'these' dreams. So whenever any woman has these dreams in this sequence, know well I am going to be born to her."

And it happened. Buddha's mother dreamed the same sequence. The sequence was known all over India, because it was no ordinary statement. It was known to everyone, particularly those who were interested in religion and the deeper things of life and the esoteric ways of life. It was known, so the dreams were interpreted. Freud was not the first interpreter and, of course, not the deepest. Only in the West was he the first.

So Buddha's father immediately called dream interpreters, the Freuds and Jungs of those days, and he asked, "What does this sequence mean ? I am afraid. These dreams are rare, and they go on repeating in the same sequence. There are one, two, three, four, five, six dreams continuously repeating. There are the same dreams as if one is seeing the same film again and again. What is happening ?"

So they told, "You are going to be a father of a great soul — one who is going to be a Buddha. But, then, your wife is going to be in danger, because whenever this Buddha is born it is difficult for the mother to survive." The father asked, "Why ?" The interpreter said, "We cannot say why, but this soul who is going to be born has made a statement that when he will be born again the mother will die immediately."

Later on Buddha was asked, "Why did your mother die immediately ?" He said, "Giving birth to a Buddha is such a big event that everything else becomes futile afterwards. So the mother cannot exist. She will have to be born again to start anew. It is such a climax giving birth to a Buddha, it is such a peak, that the mother cannot exist beyond it."

So the mother died. And Buddha had said in his previous life that he will be born while his mother will be standing under a palm tree. And it happened. The mother was standing under a palm tree — standing while Buddha was born. And he had said, "I will be born while my mother is standing under a palm tree, and I will take seven steps. Immediately, I will walk. These are the signs I give to you," he said, "so that you will know that a Buddha is born." And he directed everything.

And this is not only so about Buddha. It is so about Jesus, it is so about Mahavir, it is so about many others. Every Jain Teethanker has predicted in his previous life how he is going to be born. And they have given particular dream sequences that such and such will be the symbols, and they have told how it will happen.

You can direct. Once you can direct your dreams you can direct everything, because dream is the very stuff of this world. This life is made out of the stuff of dreams. Once you can direct your dreams, you can direct everything. This sutra says, ". . . Over death itself." Then one can give a certain birth, a certain life to oneself. We are just victims. We do not know why we are born, why we die. Who directs us — and why? There seems to be no reason. It all seems just a chaos, just accidental. It is because we are not masters. Once we are masters it is not like this.

The eighth technique: *"With utmost devotion, center on the two junctions of breath and know the knower."*

There is a slight difference in techniques, slight modifications. But though they are slight in the techniques, for you they may be great. A single word makes a great difference. "With utmost devotion, center on the two junctions of breath": the incoming breath has one junction where it turns, the outgoing breath has another junction where it turns. With these two turnings (and we have discussed these turnings), a slight difference is made — that is, slight in the technique, but for the seeker it may be great. Only one condition is added ("With utmost devotion"), and the whole technique becomes different.

In the first form of it there was no question of devotion — just a scientific technique. You do it, and it works. But there are persons who cannot do such dry, scientific techniques. Those who are heart oriented, those who belong to the world of devotion, for them a slight difference has been made: "With utmost devotion, center on the two junctions of breath and know the knower."

If you are not of the bent of the scientific attitude, if you are not a scientific mind, then try this "With utmost devotion": with faith, love, trust, "center on the two junctions of breath and know the knower." How to do this — how? You can have devotion about someone: about Krishna, about Christ, you can have devotion. But how can you have devotion about yourself, about this junction of breathing? The phenomenon seems absolutely non-devotional. But that depends.

123

Tantra says that the body is the temple. Your body is the temple of the Divine, the abode of the Divine, so do not treat your body as an object: it is sacred; it is holy. And while you are taking a breath in, it is not only you who are taking the breath: it is the Divine within you. You are eating, you are moving or walking. Look at it in this way: it is not you, but the Divine moving in you. Then the whole thing becomes absolutely devotional.

It is said about many saints that they love their bodies. They treated their bodies as if their bodies belonged to their beloveds. You can treat your body in this way or you can treat it just like a mechanism. That again is an attitude. You can treat it with guilt, sin; you can treat it as something dirty; you can treat it as something miraculous — as a miracle; you can treat it as the abode of the Divine. It depends on you. If you can treat your body as a temple, then this technique will be helpful — "With utmost devotion..."

Try it. While you are eating, try it. Do not think that YOU are eating. Think that it is the Divine who is eating in you. And look at the change. You are eating the same thing; you are the same. But immediately everything becomes different. You are giving the food to the Divine. You are taking a bath — a very ordinary, trivial thing. But change the attitude: feel that you are giving a bath to the Divine in you. Then this technique will be easy: "With utmost devotion, center on the two junctions of breath and know the knower."

The ninth technique: *"Lie down as dead. Enraged in wrath, stay so. Or stare without moving an eyelash. Or suck something and become the sucking."*

"Lie down as dead..." Try it: suddenly you have gone dead. Leave the body! Do not move it, because you are dead. Just imagine that you are dead. You cannot move the body, you cannot move the eyes, you cannot cry, you cannot scream, you cannot do anything: you are just dead. And then feel how it feels. But do not deceive. You can deceive: you can slightly move the body. Do not move. If some mosquito is there, then treat the body as if it is dead. It is one of the most used techniques — one of the MOST used techniques!

Raman Maharshi attained his Enlightenment through this technique, but it was not a technique for him in his life. In his life it suddenly happened spontaneously. But he must have persisted in some past life, because nothing happens spontaneously. Everything has a causal link, a causality. Suddenly, one night, Raman felt (he was just young — fourteen or fifteen at the time) that he was going to die. And it was so certain in his mind that death had taken over. He couldn't move his body. He felt as if he was paralyzed. Then he felt a sudden choking, and he knew that now the heart was going to drop. He could not even cry and say to another that "I am going to die".

Sometimes it happens in some nightmare: you cannot cry; you cannot move. Even when you become awake for a few moments you cannot do anything. That happened. He had absolute power over his consciousness, but no power over his body. He knew he was there — that he was present, conscious, alert, but he felt he was going to die. And the certainty became so certain that there was no other possibility, so he just gave up. He closed his eyes and remained there just to die; he waited there just to die.

By and by the body became stiff. The body died, but then it became a problem. He knew that the body had died, but he was there and he knew it. He knew that he was alive and that the body had died. Then he came back. In the morning the body became okay but the same man never returned — because he had known death. He had known a different realm, a different dimension of consciousness.

He escaped from the house. That death experience changed him completely. He became one of the very few Enlightened persons of this age.

This is the technique; this happened spontaneously to Raman. But it is not going to happen spontaneously to you. But try it. In some life it may become spontaneous. It may happen while you are trying it. And if it is not going to happen, the effort is

125

never wasted. It is in you; it remains in you as a seed. Sometime, when the time is ripe and the rains will fall, it will sprout.

Every spontaneity is just like this. The seed was sown sometime, but the time was not ripe; there were no rains. In another life the time becomes ripe. You are more mature, more experienced, more frustrated with the world. Then, suddenly, in a certain situation, there are rains and the seed explodes.

"Lie down as dead. Enraged in wrath, stay so": of course, while you are dying it will not be a happy moment. It is not going to be so blissful while you are feeling that you are dead. Fear will take you, anger may come in the mind, or frustration, sadness, sorrow, anguish, anything. It will differ from individual to individual.

The sutra says, "Enraged in wrath, stay so." If you feel enraged, stay so. If you feel sad, stay so. If you feel anxiety, fear, stay so. You are dead and you cannot do anything, so stay so. Whatsoever is in the mind, the body is dead and you cannot do anything, so stay.

That saying is beautiful. If you can stay for a few minutes, suddenly you will feel that everything has changed. But we start moving. If there is some emotion in the mind, the body begins to move. That is why we call it "emotion": it creates "motion" in the body. If you are angry, suddenly your body begins to move. If you are sad, your body begins to move. That is why it is called "emotion": because it creates motion in the body. Feel dead and do not allow emotions to move your body. Let them be there, but you "stay so" — fixed, dead. Whatsoever is there, no movement. Stay! No movement.

"Or stare without moving an eyelash": This "or stare without moving an eyelash" was the method of Meher Baba. For years together he was staring just at the roof of his room. For years together he was just lying dead on the floor, staring at the roof without moving an eyelash, without moving his eyes. He would lie down for hours together, just staring, not doing anything. Staring with the eyes is good, because you become fixed again in the third eye. And once you are fixed in the third eye, even if you want to move the eyelashes, you cannot. They become fixed.

Meher Baba attained through this staring, and you say "how with these small exercises. . ." But for three years he was staring at the roof not doing anything. Three years is a long time. Do it for three minutes, and you will feel as if you have been lying there for three years. Three minutes will become very, very long. It will look as if time is not passing and as if the clock has stopped.

Meher Baba stared and stared and stared. By and by thoughts ceased, movement ceased, and he became just a consciousness. He became just a staring. Then he remained silent for his whole life. He became so silent inside by this staring that it became impossible for him to formulate words again.

Meher Baba was in America. There was one man who could read others' thoughts, who could do mind reading. And he was really one of the rarest mind readers. He would close his eyes, sit before you, and within a few minutes he would become attuned with you and he would begin to write what you are thinking. Thousands and thousands of times he was examined, and he was always right, always correct. So someone brought him to Meher Baba. He sat there, and this was the only failure of his life — the only failure. But then again we cannot say it was a failure. He stared and stared and tried, and he began to perspire. But he couldn't catch a single word.

Pen in his hand, he remained there and said, "What type of man is this? I cannot read because there is nothing to read. This man is absolutely vacant. I even forget that someone is sitting there. After closing my eyes, I have to open them again and look to see whether that man is there or whether he has escaped. So it is difficult to concentrate, because the moment I close my eyes I feel I am being deceived — as if that man has escaped and there is no one before me. I have to open my eyelids again, and I find that this man is there. And he is not thinking at all." That staring, that constant staring, had stopped his mind completely.

"Or stare without moving an eyelash. Or suck something and become the sucking": These are slight modifications. Anything will do. You are dead: it is enough.

"Enraged in wrath and then stay so": even this part can become one technique. You are in anger: lie down; remain in the anger. Do not move from it; do not do anything. Just remain still.

Krishnamurti goes on talking about this. His whole technique depends on this single thing: "Enraged in wrath, stay so." If you are angry, then be angry, and remain angry. Do not move. If you can stay so, anger will go and you will come out a different man. If you are in anxiety, do not do anything. Remain there, stay there. The anxiety will go; you will come out a different man. And once you have looked at anxiety without being moved by it, you will be the master.

"Or stare without moving an eyelash. Or suck something and become the sucking": this last one is physical and easy to do, because sucking is the first thing a child has to do. Sucking is the first act of life. When the child is born, he begins to cry. You may not have tried to penetrate into why there is this crying. He is not really crying. It appears to us that he is crying. He is just sucking air. And if the child cannot cry, within a few minutes he will be dead because crying is the first effort to suck the air. The child was not breathing while he was in the womb. He was alive without breathing. He was doing the same which yogis are doing underground. He was just getting prana without breathing — pure prana from the mother.

That is why the love between the child and the mother is an altogether different thing from other loves, because the purest prana — energy — joins both. Now this can never happen again. There was a subtle pranic relationship. The mother was giving her prana to the child, and child was not breathing at all. When he is born, he is thrown out of the mother into an unknown world. Now the prana — the energy — will not reach him so easily. He has to breathe himself.

The first cry is an effort to suck, and then he will suck the milk from the mother's breast. These are the first basic acts which you have done. Whatsoever YOU have done comes later. These are the first life acts. They can be practised also: This sutra says, "Or suck something and become the sucking." Suck something: just suck the air, but forget the air and become the sucking. What does this mean? You are sucking something: you are the sucker, not the sucking. You are standing behind and sucking.

This sutra says do not stand behind. Move in the act and become the sucking. Try anything that will do. You are running: become the running; do not be the runner. Become the running and forget the runner. Feel that there is no runner inside, just the process of running. You are the process, a river-like process running. Nobody is there inside. It is quiet inside and there is only a process.

Sucking is good, but you will feel that it is very difficult because we have forgotten it completely — but not really completely, however, because we go on substituting for it. The mother's breast is substituted by a cigarette: you go on sucking it. It is nothing but the nipple, the mother's breast and the nipple. And when the warm smoke flows in, it is just like warm milk.

So those who were not really allowed to suck the mother's breast as much as they wanted will smoke later on. This is a substitute, but the substitute will do. While you are smoking a cigarette become the sucking. Forget the cigarette, forget the smoker. Become the smoking.

There is the object you are sucking, there is the subject who is sucking, and the process in between of sucking. Become the sucking, become the process. Try it. You will have to try it with many things; then you will find out what is right for you.

You are drinking water. The cold water is going in: become the drinking. Do not drink the water. Forget the water; forget yourself and your thirst. Just become the drinking — the very process: become the coolness, the touch, the entry, and the sucking that has to be given to the process.

Why not? What will happen? If you become the sucking,

what will happen ? If you can become the sucking, immediately you will become innocent — like a first-day, newly born child — because that is the first process. You will be regressed in a way, but the hankering is there. The very being of man hankers after sucking. He tries many things, but nothing helps because the point is missed. Unless you become the sucking, nothing will help. So try it.

I gave this method to one man. He had tried many things; he had tried many, many methods. Then he came to me, so I asked him, "If I give you only one thing to choose in the whole world, what are you going to choose ?" And I told him immediately to close his eyes and tell me, and not think about it. He became afraid, hesitant, so I told him, "Do not be afraid; do not be hesitant. Be frank and tell me." He said, "This is absurd, but a breast appears before me." And then he began to feel guilty. So I said, "Do not feel guilty. Nothing is wrong in a breast; it is one of the most beautiful things. So why be guilty ?"

But he said, "This has always been an obsession with me." And he said to me, "Please tell me first; then you can proceed with your method and the technique: first tell me why I am so much interested in the breasts of a woman ? Whenever I look at a woman, the first thing I see is the breast. The whole body is secondary."

And it is not so only with him. It is so with everyone — with almost everyone. And it is natural, because the breast of the mother was the first acquaintance with the universe. It is basic. The first contact with the universe was the mother's breast. That is why breasts are so appealing. They look beautiful; they attract; they have a magnetic force. That magnetic force comes from your unconscious. That was the first thing with which you came in contact, and the contact was lovely. It felt beautiful. It gives you food, instant vitality, love, everything. The contact was soft, receptive, inviting. It has remained so in the mind of man.

So I told that man, "Now I will give you the method." And this was the method I gave him: "Suck something and become the sucking." I told him, "Just close your eyes. Imagine your mother's breasts or anybody's breasts that you like. Imagine, and start sucking as if there is a real breast. Start sucking."

He started sucking. Within three days he was sucking so fast, so madly, he became so much enchanted by it, that he told me, "It has become a problem. I want to suck the whole day. And it is so beautiful and such deep silence is created by it."

Within three months the sucking became a very, very silent gesture. The lips stopped. You couldn't even have judged that he was doing something. But inner sucking had started. He was sucking the whole day. It became a mantra, a *japa* (mantra repetition).

After three months he came to me and said, "Something strange is happening to me. Something sweet is falling from my head onto my tongue continuously — and it is so sweet, and so energy filling, that I do not need any food. There is no hunger left. Eating has become just a formality. I take something in order not to create any problems in the family. But something is continuously coming to me. It is so sweet — life-giving."

I told him to continue. Three months more, and one day he came just mad, dancing to me, and he said, "Sucking has disappeared, but I am a different man. I am no more the same man who had come to you. Some door has opened within me. Something has broken and there is no desire left. Now I do not want anything — not even God, not even *Moksha* (Liberation). I do not want anything. Now everything is okay as it is. I accept it and I am blissful."

Try this: Just suck something and become the sucking. It may be helpful to many because it is so basic.

This much for today.

6
Devices To Transcend Dreaming

October 6, 1972, Bombay, India

QUESTIONS:

1. How to be conscious while dreaming?
2. Why make efforts if we are merely actors on a set stage?

One friend has asked, *"Will you please explain to us what are some of the other factors which can make one conscious while dreaming?"*

This is a significant question for all those who are interested in meditation, because meditation is really a transcending of the process of dreaming. You are constantly dreaming — not only in the night, not only while you are asleep: you are dreaming the whole day. This is the first point to be understood. While you are awake you are still dreaming.

Just close your eyes at any time of the day. Relax the body and you will feel that the dreaming is there. It never disappears. It is only suppressed by our daily activities. It is like the stars in the day. In the night you see the stars. In the day you cannot see them, but they are there always. They are simply suppressed by the sunlight.

If you go into a deep well, then you can see the stars in the sky even in the day. A certain darkness is needed to see the stars. So go into a deep well and look from the bottom, and you will be able to see the stars in the day also. The stars are there. It is not that in the night they are there and in the day they are not. They are always there. In the night you can see them easily. In the day you cannot see them because the sunlight becomes a barrier.

The same is true with dreaming. It is not that you dream while you are asleep. In sleep you can feel dreams easily because the daily activity of the day is no more. Thus, that inner activity can be seen and felt. When you get up in the morning, the dreaming continues inside while you start acting on the outside.

This process of activity, of daily activity, simply suppresses the dreaming. The dreaming is there. Close your eyes, relax in an armchair, and suddenly you can feel: the stars are there; they have not gone anywhere. The dreams are there always. There is a continuous activity.

The second point: If the dreaming continues, you cannot be said to be really awake. In the night you are more asleep, in the day you are less asleep. The difference is relative, because if the dreaming is there you cannot be said to be really awake. Dreaming creates a film over the consciousness. This film becomes like smoke: you are surrounded by it. You cannot be really awake while you are dreaming — whether in the day or in the night. So the second thing: you can only be said to be awake when there is no dreaming at all.

We call Buddha the Awakened One. What is this awakening? This awakening is really the cessation of inner dreaming. There is no dream inside. You move there, but there is no dream. It is as if there were no star in the sky. It has become pure space. When there is no dreaming, you become pure space.

This purity, this innocence, this non-dreaming consciousness, is what is known as Enlightenment — the awakening. For centuries spirituality all over the world, East or West, has said that man is asleep. Jesus says this, Buddha says this, the Upanishads talk about this: man is asleep. So while you are asleep in the night, you are just relatively more asleep; in the day you are less asleep. But spirituality says that man is asleep. This has to be understood.

What is meant by this? Gurdjieff, in this century, emphasized much this fact that man is asleep. "Rather," he said, "man is a sort of sleep. Everyone is deeply asleep."

What is the reason for saying that? You cannot know, you cannot remember, who you are. Do you know who are you?

If you meet a person in the street and you ask him who he is and he cannot reply, what will you think? You will think that he is either mad, intoxicated or just asleep. If he cannot answer who he is, what are you going to think about him? On the spiritual path everyone is like that. You cannot answer who you are.

This is the first meaning when Gurdjieff or Jesus or anyone says that man is asleep: you are not conscious about yourself. You do not know yourself; you have never met yourself. You know many things in the objective world, but you do not know the subject. Your state of mind is as if you had gone to see a film. On the screen the film is running, and you have become so absorbed in it that the only thing you know is the film, the story, whatsoever is appearing on the screen. Then if someone asks you who you are, you cannot say anything.

Dreaming is just the film — JUST the film! It is the mind reflecting the world. In the mirror of the mind the world is reflected: that is what dreaming is. And you are so deeply involved in it, so much identified with it, that you have completely forgotten who you are. This is what "asleep" means: the dreamer is lost in the dreaming. You see everything except yourself; you feel everything except yourself; you know everything except yourself. This self-ignorance is the sleep. Unless dreaming ceases completely, you cannot awaken unto yourself.

You might have felt it sometimes while looking at a film for three hours, and suddenly the film stops and you come back to yourself. You remember that three hours have passed. You remember that it was just a film. You feel your tears. You have been weeping because the film was a tragedy to you, or you were laughing, or you were doing something else, and now you laugh about yourself. What nonsense you were doing! It was just a film, just a story. There was nothing on the screen — just a play of light and shadow, just an electrical play. Now you laugh: you have come back to yourself. But where were you for these three hours?

You were not at your center. You had moved completely to

the periphery. There where the film was moving you had gone. You were not at your center; you were not with yourself. You were somewhere else.

This happens in dreaming; this is what our life is. The film event is only for three hours, but this dreaming is running for lives and lives and lives. Even if suddenly the dreaming stops, you will not be able to recognize who you are. Suddenly you will feel very faint, even afraid. You will try to move again into the film because that is known. You are acquainted with it, you are well adjusted to it.

For when it happens, there is a path, particularly in Zen, which is known as a sudden path — a path of sudden Enlightenment. There are techniques in these 112 methods, there are many techniques, which can give you sudden awakening. But it can be too much, and you may not be capable of bearing it. You may just explode. You may die even, because you have lived with dreaming so long that you have no memory of who you are if there is no dreaming.

If this whole world should suddenly disappear and you alone are left, it would be such a great shock that you would die. The same would happen if suddenly all dreaming disappeared from the consciousness. Your world will disappear because your world was your dreaming.

We are not really in the world. Rather, "the world" consists not of outside things to us, but of our dreams. So everyone lives in his own dreamworld.

Remember, it is not one world that we go on talking about. Geographically it is, but psychologically there are as many worlds as there are minds. Each mind is a world of its own. And if your dreaming disappears, your world disappears. Without dreams it is difficult for you to live. That is why sudden methods are not used generally. Only gradual methods are used.

It is good to note this: gradual methods are used not because there is any need of gradual processes. You can suddenly jump into Realization this very moment. There is no barrier; there has never been any barrier. You are already that Realization, you can jump this very moment. But that may prove dangerous, fatal. You may not be capable of bearing it. It is going to be too much for you.

You are attuned only to false dreams. Reality you cannot face; you cannot encounter it. You are a hothouse plant. You can live in your dreams. They help you in many ways. They are not just dreams: for you they are the reality.

Gradual methods are used not because Realization needs time. Realization needs NO TIME! Realization needs no time at all. Realization is not something to be attained in the future, but with gradual methods you will attain it in the future. So what are the gradual methods doing? They are not really helping you to "Realize Realization": they are helping you to bear it. They are making you capable, strong, so that when the happening happens you can bear it.

There are seven methods through which immediately you can force your way into Enlightenment. But you will not be capable of bearing it. You may go blind: too much of light. Or you may suddenly die: too much of bliss.

This dreaming, this deep sleep we are in, how can it be transcended? This question is meaningful in transcending it: "Will you please explain to us what are some of the other factors which can make one conscious while dreaming?" I will talk about two methods more. One we discussed yesterday. Today, two more that are even easier.

One is to start acting, behaving, as if the whole world is just a dream. Whatsoever you are doing, remember this is a dream. While eating, remember this is a dream. While walking, remember this is a dream. Let your mind continuously remember while you are awake that everything is a dream. This is the reason for calling the world *maya*, illusion, dream. This is not a philosophical argument.

Unfortunately, when Shankara was translated into English, German and French, into Western languages, he was understood to be just a philosopher. That has created much misunderstanding. In the West there are philosophers — for example:

Berkeley — who say that the world is just a dream, a projection of the mind. But this is a philosophical theory. Berkeley proposes it as an hypothesis.

When Shankara says that the world is a dream, it is not philosophical — not a theory. Shankara proposes it as a help, as a support for a particular meditation. And this is the meditation: if you want to remember while dreaming that this is a dream, you will have to start while you are awake. As the case is, while you are dreaming you cannot remember that this is a dream. You think that this is a reality.

Why do you think that this is a reality? Because the whole day you are thinking everything is a reality. That has become the attitude — a fixed attitude. While awake, you were taking a bath: it was real. While awake, you were eating: it was real. While awake, you were talking with a friend: it was real. For the whole day, the whole life, whatsoever you are thinking your attitude is that this is real. This becomes fixed. This becomes a fixed attitude in the mind.

So while you are dreaming in the night, the same attitude goes on working: that this is real. So let us first analyze. There must be some similarity between dreaming and reality; otherwise this attitude would be somewhat difficult.

I am seeing you. Then I close my eyes and I go into a dream, and I see you in my dream. In both seeings there is no difference. While I am actually seeing you, what am I doing? Your picture is reflected in my eyes. I am not seeing YOU. Your picture is mirrored in my eyes, and then that picture is transformed through mysterious processes — and science is still not in a position to say how. That picture is transformed chemically and carried somewhere inside the head, but science is still not able to say where — where exactly this thing happens. It is not happening in the eyes: eyes are just windows. I am not seeing you by the eyes. I am seeing you THROUGH the eyes.

In the eyes you are reflected. You may be just a picture; you may be a reality; you may be a dream. Remember, dreams are three-dimensional. I can recognize a picture because a picture is two-dimensional. Dreams are three-dimensional, so they look exactly like you. And the eyes cannot say whether whatsoever is seen is real or unreal. There is no way to judge: the eyes are not the judge.

Then the picture is transformed into chemical waves. Those chemical waves are electric waves: they go somewhere in the head. It is still unknown where the point is where the eyes come in contact with the surface of seeing. Just waves reach to me and then they are decoded. Then I again decode them, and in this way I know what is happening.

I am always inside, and you are always outside, and there is no meeting. So whether you are real or just a dream is a problem. Even this very moment, there is no way to judge whether I am dreaming or you are really here.

Listening to me, how can you say that really you are listening to me — that you are not dreaming ? There is no way. That is why the attitude which you maintain the whole day is carried over into the night. And while you are dreaming you take it as real.

Try the opposite; that is what Shankara means. He says that the whole world is an illusion, he says the whole world is a dreaming — remember this. But we are stupid people. If Shankara says, "This is a dream," then we say, "What is the need to do anything ?" If this is just a dream, then there is no need to eat. Why go on eating and thinking that this is a dream ? Don't eat ! But then remember — when you feel hunger, it is a dream. Or eat, and when you feel that you have eaten too much, remember, this is a dream.

Shankara is not telling you to change the dream, remember, because the effort to change the dream is again falsely based on the belief that it is real; otherwise there is no need to change anything. Shankara is just saying that whatever is the case is a dream.

Remember this: do not do anything to change it. Just remember it constantly. Try to remember for three weeks continuously that whatsoever you are doing it is just a dream. In the beginning it is very difficult. You will fall again and again into the old pattern of the mind: you will start thinking that this is a reality. You will have to constantly awaken yourself to remind yourself that "this is a dream". If for three weeks continuously you can maintain this attitude, then in the fourth or fifth week, any night while dreaming, you will suddenly remember that "this is a dream".

This is one way to penetrate dreams with consciousness, with awareness. If you can remember in the night while dreaming that this is a dream, then in the day you will not need any effort to remember that this is also a dream. You will know it then.

In the beginning, while you are practising this, it will be just a make-believe. You start just in faith that "this is a dream". But when you can remember in dreaming that "this is a dream", it will become a reality. Then in the day, when you get up, you will not feel that you are getting up from sleep: you will feel you are simply getting up from one dreaming to another. Then it will become a reality. And if the whole twenty-four hours becomes dreaming, and you can feel and remember it, you will be standing at your center. Then your consciousness will have become double-arrowed.

You are feeling dreams, and if you are feeling them as dreams you will start to feel the dreamer — the subject. If you take dreams as real, you cannot feel the subject. If the film has become real, you forget yourself. When the film stops and you know that it was unreal, your reality erupts — breaks out. You can feel yourself: this is one way.

Another: this has been one of the oldest Indian methods. That is why we have insisted on the world being unreal. We do not mean it philosophically; we do not say that this house is unreal so that you can pass through the walls. We do not mean that! When we say that "this house is unreal", it is a device. This is not an argument against the house.

So Berkeley proposed that the whole world is just a dream. One day, in the morning, he was walking with Dr. Johnson.

Dr. Johnson was a hard realist, so Berkeley said, "Have you heard about my theory? I am working on it: I feel that the whole world is unreal, and it cannot be proved that it is real. And the burden of proving it is on those who say that it is real. I say it is unreal — just like dreams."

Johnson was not a philosopher, but he had a very astute logical mind. They were on the street, just passing, walking in the morning — on a lonely street. Johnson then takes one stone in his hand and hits Berkeley's leg. Blood oozes out, and Berkeley screams. Johnson says, "Why are you screaming if the stone is just a dream? Whatsoever you say, you believe in the reality of the stone. What you are saying is one thing, and your behaviour is something different and contrary. If your house is just a dream, then to where are you returning? Where are you returning after the morning walk? If your wife is just a dream, you will not meet her again."

Realists have always argued this way, but they cannot argue this way with Shankara because his is not a philosophical theory. It is not saying anything about the reality; it is not proposing anything about the universe. Rather, it is a device to change your mind — to change the basic fixed attitude so that you can look at the world in a different — an altogether different — way.

This is a problem — continously a problem for Indian thought — because for Indian thought everything is just a device for meditation. We are not concerned about its being true or untrue. We are concerned about its utility in transforming man.

This is emphatically different from the Western mind. When they propose a theory, they are concerned with whether this is true or unture, with whether this can be proved logically or not. When we propose anything, we are not concerned about its truth: we are concerned about its utility; we are concerned about its capacity, its capability, to transform the human mind. It may be true, it may not be true. Really, it is neither. It is simply a device.

I have seen flowers outside. In the morning the sun rises and everything is just beautiful, and you have never been outside, and you have never seen flowers, and you have never seen the morning sun. You have never seen the open sky; you do not know what beauty is. You have lived in a closed prison. I want to lead you out. I want you to come out under the open sky to meet these flowers. How am I to do it ?

You do not know flowers. If I talk about flowers, you think, "He has gone mad. There are no flowers." If I talk about the morning sun, you think, "He is a visionary. He sees visions and dreams. He is a poet." If I talk about the open sky, you will laugh. You will start laughing because where is the open sky ? There are "only walls and walls and walls".

So what am I to do ? I must devise something which you can understand and which helps you to go out, so I say that the house is on fire and I start running. It becomes infectious: you run after me and go out. Then you will know that what I said was neither true nor false. It was just a device. Then you will know flowers and then you can forgive me.

Buddha was doing that, Mahavir was doing that, Shiva was doing that, Shankara was doing that. We can forgive them later on. We have always forgiven them because once we go out we know what they were doing. And then we understand that it was useless to argue with them because it was not a question of arguing.

The fire was nowhere, but we could not understand only that language. Flowers were, but we could not understand the language of the flowers. Those symbols were meaningless for us. So this is one way. Then there is a second method at the other pole. This method makes one pole; the other method makes another pole of the same thing. One is to start feeling, remembering, that everything is a dream. The other is not to think anything about the world, but just to go on remembering that YOU ARE.

Gurdjieff used this second method. This second method comes from Sufi tradition, from Islam. They worked on it very deeply. Remember "I am" — whatsoever you are doing. You are drinking water, you are eating your food: remember, "I am." Go on eating and go on remembering, "I am, I am." Do not forget it! It is difficult because you already think that you know you are. So what is the need to go on remembering this? You never remember it, but it is a very, very potential technique.

When walking remember, "I am." Let the walking be there; go on walking. But be constantly fixed in this self-remembering of "I am, I am, I am". Do not forget this. You are listening to me: just do it here. You are listening to me: do not be so much merged, involved, identified. Whatsoever I am saying, remember, go on remembering. Listening is there, words are there, someone is talking, you are — "I am, "I am, I am": let this "I am" be a constant factor of awareness.

It is very difficult. You cannot remember continuously even for a single minute. Try it. Put your watch before your eyes, and look at the hands moving. One second, two seconds, three seconds — go on looking at it. Do two things: look at the movement of the hand which is showing seconds, and continuously remember, "I am, I am." With every second go on remembering, "I am." Within five or six seconds you will feel that you have forgotten. Suddenly you will remember that "Many seconds have passed and I have not remembered 'I am'".

Even to remember for one complete minute is a miracle. And if you can remember for one minute, the technique is for you. Then do it. Through it you will be capable of going beyond dreams and of knowing that dreams are dreams.

How does it work? If the whole day you can remember "I am", then this will penetrate your sleep also. And when you will be dreaming, continuously you will remember, "I am." If you can remember "I am" in the dream, suddenly the dream becomes just a dream. Then the dream cannot deceive you. Then the dream cannot be felt as reality. This is the mechanism: the dream is felt as reality because you are missing the self-remembering: you are missing, "I am." If there is no remembering of oneself, then dream becomes reality. If there is the remembering of oneself, then reality, the so-called reality, becomes just a dream.

This is the difference between dreaming and reality. For a meditative mind, or for the science of meditation, this is the only difference. If you are, then the whole reality is just a dream. If you are not, then the dreaming becomes reality.

Nagarjuna says, "Now I am, for the world is not. While I was not, the world was. Only one can exist." That doesn't mean that the world has disappeared. Nagarjuna is not talking about this world. He is talking about the world of dreaming. Either you can be or the dreams can be. Both cannot be.

So the first step will be to continue remembering "I am" constantly; simply, "I am." Do not say "Ram", do not say "Shyam". Do not use any name, because you are not that. Simply use, "I am."

Try it in any activity and then feel it. The more real you become inside, the more unreal becomes the surrounding world. The reality becomes "I", and the world becomes unreal. The world is real or the "I" is real. Both cannot be real. You are feeling that you are just a dream now. Then the world is real. Change the emphasis. Become real, and the world will become unreal.

Gurdjieff worked on this method continuously. His chief disciple P. D. Ouspensky relates that when Gurdjieff was working on him with this method, and he was practising for three months continuously this remembering of "I am, I am, I am", after three months everything stopped. Thoughts, dreaming, everything, stopped. Only one note remained inside like eternal music: "I am, I am, I am, I am." But then this was not an effort. This was a spontaneous activity going on: "I am." Then Gurdjieff called Ouspensky out of the house. For three months he had been kept in the house and wasn't allowed to move out.

Then Gurdjieff said, "Come with me." They were residing in a Russian town — Tiflis. Gurdjieff called him out and they went into the street. Ouspensky writes in his diary, "For the first time I could understand what Jesus meant when he said that man is asleep. The whole city looked to me as if asleep. People were moving in their sleep; shopkeepers were selling in their sleep;

customers were buying in their sleep. The whole city was asleep. I looked at Gurdjieff: only he was awake. The whole city was asleep. They were angry, they were fighting, they were loving, buying, selling, doing, everything."

Ouspensky says, "Now I could see their faces, their eyes: they were asleep. They were not there. The inner center was missing; it was not there." Ouspensky said to Gurdjieff, "I do not want to go there any more. What has happened to the city? Everyone seems asleep, drugged."

Gurdjieff said, "Nothing has happened to the city. Something has happened to you. You have been undrugged. The city is the same. It is the same place you moved in three months ago. But you couldn't see that other people are asleep because you were also asleep. Now you can see because a certain quality of awareness has come to you. With three months of practising "I am" continuously, you have become aware in a very small measure. You have become aware! A part of your consciousness has gone beyond dreaming. That is why you can see that everyone is asleep, dead, moving, drugged, as if hypnotized."

Ouspensky says, "I couldn't bear that phenomenon — everyone asleep! Whatsoever they are doing, they are not responsible for it. They are not! How can they be responsible?" He came back and he asked Gurdjieff, "What is this? Am I deceived somehow? Have you done something to me that the whole city seems asleep? I cannot believe my own eyes."

But this will happen to anyone. If you can remember yourself, then you will know that no one is remembering himself, and in this way each goes on moving. The whole world is asleep. But start while you are awake. Any moment that you remember start, "I am."

I do not mean that you have to repeat the words "I am"; rather, have the feeling. Taking a bath, feel, "I am." Let there be the touch of the cold shower, and let yourself be there behind, feeling it and remembering, "I am." Remember, I am not saying that verbally you have to repeat, "I am." You can repeat it, but that repetition will not give you awareness. Repetition may even create more sleep. There are many people who are repeating many things. They go on repeating "Ram-Ram-Ram", and if they are just repeating without awareness, then this "Ram-Ram-Ram" becomes a drug. They can sleep well through it.

That is why Mahesh Yogi has so much appeal in the West: because he is giving mantras to repeat. And in the West sleep has become one of the most serious problems. Sleep is totally disturbed. Natural sleep has disappeared. Only through tranquilizers and drugs can you sleep. Otherwise sleep has become impossible. This is the reason for Mahesh Yogi's appeal: it is because if you constantly repeat something, that repetition gives you deep sleep; that is all.

So the so-called transcendental meditation is nothing but a psychological tranquilizer. It is nothing — just a tranquilizer. It helps, but it is good for sleep — not for meditation. You can sleep well. A more calm sleep will be there. It is good, but it is not meditation at all. If you repeat a word constantly, it creates a certain boredom — and boredom is good for sleep.

So anything monotonous, repetitive, can help sleep. The child in the mother's womb sleeps for nine months continuously, and the reason for this you may not be knowing. The reason is only the "tick-tock, tick-tock" of the heart of the mother. Continuously there is the beat — the heartbeat. It is one of the most monotonous things in the world. With the same beat continuously repeating, the child is drugged. He goes on sleeping.

That is why, whenever the child is crying, screaming, creating any problem, the mother puts his head near her heart. Then suddenly he feels good and goes down into sleep. Again it is due to heartbeat. He becomes again a part of the womb. That is why, even if you are not a child and your wife, your beloved, puts your head on her heart, you will feel sleepy from the monotonous beat.

Psychologists suggest that if you cannot sleep, then concentrate on the clock. Just concentrate on the clock's "tick-tock, tick-tock": it repeats the heartbeat, and you can fall asleep. Anything repetitive will help.

So this "I am", the remembering of "I am", is not a verbal mantra. It is not going to be repeated verbally. Feel it! Be sensitive to your being. When you touch someone's hand do not only touch his hand: feel your touch also. Feel yourself also — that you are here in this touch, present totally. While eating, do not only eat: feel yourself eating as well. This feeling, this sensitivity, must penetrate deeper and deeper into your mind.

One day, suddenly, you are awake at your center, functioning for the first time. And then the whole world becomes a dream. And then you can know that your dreaming is a dreaming. And when you know that your dreaming is a dreaming, dreaming stops. It can continue only if it is felt as real. It is stopped if it is felt as unreal.

And once dreaming stops in you, you are a different man. The old man is dead; the sleepy man is dead. That human being which you were you are no more. For the first time, you become aware. For the first time, in the whole world that is asleep, you are awake. You become a Buddha, an Awakened One.

With this awakening, there is no misery. After this awakening, there is no death. Through this awakening, there is no more fear. You become, for the first time, free of everything. To be free of sleep, to be free of dreaming, is to be free of everything. You attain freedom. Hate, anger, greed disappear. You become just love. Not loving: you become just love!

One question more, and it is relatively the same: *"If we are all actors in a play that is already written, how can meditation transform us without the play itself containing a chapter for our transformation at a specific time? And if such a chapter is there already waiting to unfold at its due time, why meditate? Why make any effort at all?"*

This is the same: it contains the same fallacy. I am not saying that everything is determined. I am not proposing this as a theory to explain the universe. It is a device.

India has always been working with this device of fate. It is not meant by this that everything is predetermined. This is not meant at all! The only reason to propose this is that if you take it that everything is determined, everything becomes a dream. If you take things in this way, if you believe this way — that everything is predetermined, that, for example, you are going to die on a particular day — EVERYTHING becomes a dream. It is not determined It is not fixed! No one is that much interested in you, and the universe is completely unaware of you and when you are going to die. It is so useless a thing. Your death is irrelevant to the universe.

Do not think yourself so important that the whole universe is determining your day of death — the time, the minute, the moment — no! You are NOT the center. It makes no difference to the universe whether you are or you are not. But this fallacy goes on working in the mind. It is created in childhood and it becomes unconscious.

A child is born. He cannot give anything to the world, but he has to take many things. He cannot repay, he cannot give back anything. He is so impotent — just helpless. He will need food, he will need love, he will need shelter, he will need warmth. Everything is to be supplied.

A child is born absolutely helpless — particularly man's child. No animal is so helpless. That is why no animal could create a family. There is no need! But man's child is so helpless, so absolutely helpless, he cannot exist without there being a mother to protect, a father, a family, a society. He cannot exist alone. He will die immediately.

He is so much dependent. He will need love, he will need food, he will need everything, and he will demand everything. And the mother will supply, the father will supply, the family will supply. The child begins to think that he is the center of the whole world. Everything is to be supplied to him; he has but to demand. Just to demand is enough: no other effort is needed.

So the child begins to think himself as the center, and everything just goes on around him, for him. The whole Existence seems to be created for him. The whole Existence was waiting for him to come and demand. And everything will be fulfilled.

This is a necessity, that his demands should be fulfilled; otherwise he will die.

But this necessity becomes very dangerous. He grows up with this attitude that "I am the center". By and by he will demand more. A child's demands are very simple; they can be supplied. But as he will grow his demands will become more and more complex. Sometimes it will not be possible to supply them, to fulfill them. Sometimes it may be absolutely impossible. He may demand the moon or anything.

The more he will grow, the more the demands will become complex, impossible. Then frustration sets in, and the child begins to think that now he is being deceived. He has taken it for granted that he was the center of the world. Now problems will be there, and by and by he will be dethroned. He will be dethroned. When he becomes an adult, he wlil be completely dethroned. Then he will know that he is not the center. But deep down the unconscious mind goes on thinking in terms that he is the center.

People come and ask me whether their fate is determined. They are asking whether they are so important, so significant for this universe, that their fate must be determined beforehand. "What is my purpose ?" they ask. "Why was I created ?" This childhood nonsense that you are the center creates these questions like, "For what purpose am I created ?"

You are not created for any purpose. And it is good that you are not created for any purpose; otherwise you would be a machine. A machine is created for some purpose. Man is not created for some purpose, for something — no ! Man is just the outflowing, overflowing creation. Everything simply is. Flowers are there and stars are there and you are there. Everything is just an overflowing, a joy, a celebration of Existence without any purpose.

But this theory of fate, of predetermination, is what creates problems, because we take it as a theory. We think that everything is determined, but nothing is determined. However, this technique uses this as a device. When we say everything is determined, this is not said to you as a theory. The purpose is this: that if you take life as a drama, predetermined, then it becomes a dream. For example, if I knew that this day, this night, I was going to talk to you, and it is predetermined what words I should speak on this day, and if it is so fixed that nothing can be changed — that I cannot utter a single new word, then suddenly I am not related at all with this whole process because then I am not the source of action.

If everything is determined and if every word is to be spoken by the universe itself or by the Divine or by whatsoever name you choose, then I am no more the source of it. Then I can become an observer — a simple observer.

If you take life as predetermined, then you can observe it. Then you are not involved. If you are failure, it was predetermined; if you are a success, it was predetermined. If both are predetermined, both become of equal value — synonymous. Then one is Ravan, one is Ram, and everything is predetermined. Ravan need not feel guilty, Ram need not feel superior. Everything is predetermined, so you are just actors. You are just on a stage playing a role.

To give you the feeling that you are playing a role, to give you the feeling that this is only a predetermined pattern that you are fulfilling, to give you this feeling so that you can transcend it, this is the device. It is very difficult because we are so much accustomed to thinking of fate as a theory — not only as a theory, but as a law. We cannot understand this attitude of taking these laws and theories as devices.

I will explain this to you. One example will be helpful. I was in a city. One man came: he was a Mohammedan. But I didn't know, I was not aware. And he was dressed so that he looked like a Hindu. He not only looked like a Hindu, but as he talked with me he was of the Hindu type. He was not a Mohammedan type.

He asked me one question. He said, "Mohammedans, Christians, say that there is only one life. Hindus, Buddhists and Jains say there are many lives — a long sequence of lives, that unless one is Liberated, one goes on and on being reborn again and again. So what do you say? If Jesus was an Enlightened man, he must have known. Or, Mohammed, or Moses, they must have known too if they were Enlightened men that there are many lives and not just one. And if you say that they are right, then what about Mahavir, Krishna, Buddha and Shankara? One thing is certain, that they cannot all be Enlightened.

"If Christianity is right, then Buddha is wrong, then Krishna is wrong, then Mahavir is wrong. And if Mahavir, Krishna and Buddha are right, then Mohammed, Jesus and Moses are wrong. So tell me. I am very much puzzled; I am in a mess — confused. And both cannot be right. How can both be right? Either there are many lives or there is one. How can both be right?" He was a very intelligent man, and he had studied many things, so he said, "You cannot just escape and say that both are right. Both cannot be right. It is logically so. Both cannot be right."

But I said, "This need not be. Your approach is absolutely wrong. Both are devices. Neither is right, neither is wrong. Both are devices." It became impossible for him to understand what I meant by device.

Mohammed, Jesus and Moses, they were talking to one type of mind, and Buddha, Mahavir, Krishna, they were talking to a very different mind. There are really two source religions — the Hindu and the Jewish. So all the religions born out of India, all the religions born out of Hinduism, believe in rebirth, in many births, and all the religions born out of Jewish thinking — Mohammedanism, Christianity — they believe in one life. These are two devices.

Try to understand it. Because our minds are fixed, we take things as theories, not as devices. So many times people come to me and say, "One day you said this is right, and another day you said that is right, and both cannot be right." Of course, both cannot be right, but no one is saying that both are right. I am not concerned at all with which is right and which is wrong. I am only concerned with which device works.

In India they use this device of many lives. Why? There are

many points. All the religions born in the West, particularly out of Jewish thinking, they were religions of poor people. Their prophets were uneducated. Jesus was not educated, Mohammed was not educated, Moses was not. They were all uneducated, unsophisticated, simple, and they were talking with masses who were not sophisticated at all, which were poor. They were not rich.

For a poor man, one life is more than enough — more than enough! He is starving, dying. If you say to him that there are so many lives, that you will go on being reborn and reborn, that you will move in a wheel of a thousand and one lives, the poor man will just feel frustrated about the whole thing. "What are you saying?" a poor man will ask. "One life is too much, so do not talk of a thousand and one lives, of a million lives. Do not speak this. Give us heaven immediately after this life." God becomes a reality only if He can be achieved after this life — immediately.

Buddha, Mahavir, Krishna, they were talking to a very rich society. Today it has become difficult to understand because the whole wheel has turned. Now the West is rich and the East is poor. Then the West was poor and the East was rich. All the Hindu *Avatars*, all the *Teerthankers* (World Teachers) of the Jains, all the *Buddhas* (Awakened Ones), they were all princes. They belonged to royal families. They were cultured, educated, sophisticated, refined in every way. You cannot refine Buddha more. He was absolutely refined, cultured, educated. Nothing can be added. Even if Buddha comes today, nothing can be added.

So they were talking to a society which was rich. Remember, for a rich society, there are different problems. For a rich society, pleasure is meaningless, heaven is meaningless. For a poor society, heaven is very meaningful. If the society is living in heaven, heaven becomes meaningless. So you cannot propose this. You cannot create an urge to do something for heaven: they are already in it — and bored.

So Buddha, Mahavir, Krishna, they do not talk about heaven.

They talk of freedom. They do not talk of a pleasant world beyond. They talk of a transcendental world where there is neither pain nor pleasure. Jesus' heaven would not have appealed to them. They were already in it.

And, secondly, for a rich man the real problem is boredom. For a poor man, promise him pleasure in the future. For a poor man, suffering is the problem. For a rich man, suffering is not the problem. For a rich man, boredom is the problem. He is bored of all pleasures.

Mahavir, Buddha and Krishna, they all used this boredom, and they said, "If you do not do anything you are going to be born again and again. This wheel will move. Remember, the same life will be repeated. The same sex, the same richness, the same food, the same palaces again and again: a thousand and one times, you will be moving in a wheel."

To a rich man who has known all pleasures, this is not a good prospect, this repetition. Repetition is the problem. That is the suffering for him. He wants something new, and Mahavir and Buddha say, "There is nothing new. This world is old. Nothing is new under the heavens. Everything is just old. And you have tasted all these things before and you will go on tasting them. You are in a wheel, moving. Go beyond it; take a jump out of the wheel."

For a rich man, if you create a device which intensifies his feeling of boredom, only then can he move toward meditation. For a poor man, if you talk about boredom you are talking meaningless things. A poor man is never bored — never! Only a rich man is bored. A poor man is never bored: he is always thinking of the future. Something is going to happen, and everything will be okay. The poor man needs a promise, but if the promise is very long it becomes meaningless. It must be immediate.

Jesus is reported to have said that "In my lifetime, in your lifetime, you will see the Kingdom of God." That statement has haunted the whole of Christianity for twenty centuries — because Jesus said, "In YOUR life, immediately, you are going to see the Kingdom of God." And the Kingdom of God has not come even yet, so what did he mean ? And he said, "The world is going to end soon, so do not waste time ! Time is short." Jesus said, "Time is very short. It is foolish to waste it. Immediately, the world is going to end and you will have to reply, so repent."

Jesus created a feeling of immediacy through the concept of one life. He knew, but Buddha and Mahavir also knew. Whatsoever they knew is not told. Whatsoever they devised is known. This was a device to create immediacy, urgency, so that you would begin to act.

India was an old country, rich. There was no question of urgency in future promises. There was only one way possible to create urgency, and that was to create more boredom. If a man feels he is going to be born again and again, again and again, infinitely, ad infinitum, he immediately comes and asks, "How — how to be freed from this wheel ? This is too much. Now I cannot continue it any more because whatsoever can be known I have known. If this is to be repeated, it is a nightmare. I do not want to repeat it. I want something new."

So Buddha and Mahavir say, "There is nothing new under ths sky. Everything is old and a repetition. And you have repeated for many, many lives, and you will go on repeating for many, many lives. Beware of the repetition. Beware of your boredom and take a jump."

The device is different, but the purpose is the same. Take a jump ! Move ! Transform yourself ! Whatsoever you are, transform yourself from it.

If we take religious statements as devices, then there is no contradiction. Then Jesus and Krishna, Mohammed and Mahavir, they mean the same thing. They create different routes for different people, different techniques for different minds, different appeals for different attitudes. But those are not principles to be fought and argued about. They are devices to be used, transcended and thrown.

This much for today.

7
Techniques To Put You At Ease

October 7, 1972, Bombay, India

SUTRAS:

10. While being caressed, sweet princess, enter the caress as everlasting life.

11. Stop the doors of the senses when feeling the creeping of an ant. Then.

12. When on a bed or a seat, let yourself become weightless, beyond mind.

Man has a center, but he lives off of it — off the center. That creates an inner tension, a constant turmoil, anguish. You are not where you should be; you are not at your right balance. You are off balance, and this being off balance, off center, is the base of all mental tensions. If it becomes too much, you go mad. A "madman" means one who has gone "out of himself" completely. The Enlightened man is just the reverse of the madman. He is centered in himself.

You are in between. You have not gone completely out of yourself, and you are not at your center either. You just move in the gap. Sometimes you move very, very far away, so you have moments when you are temporarily mad. In anger, in sex, in anything in which you have moved too far away from yourself, you are temporarily mad. Then there is no difference between you and the madman. The difference is only that he is permanently there and you are temporarily there. You will come back.

When you are in anger it is madness, but it is not permanent. Qualitatively, there is no difference: quantitatively, there is a difference. The quality is the same, so sometimes you touch madness and sometimes, when you are relaxed, totally at ease, you touch your center also. Those are the blissful moments. They happen. Then you are just like a Buddha or like a Krishna, but only temporarily, momentarily. You will not stay there. Really, the moment you realize that you are blissful, you have moved. It is so momentary that by the time you have recognized the bliss it is finished.

We go on moving between these two, but this movement is dangerous. This movement is dangerous because then you cannot create a self-image, a fixed self-image. You do not know who you are. If you constantly move from madness to being centered in yourself, if this movement is constant, you cannot have a solid image of yourself. You will have a liquid image. Then you do not know who you are. It is very difficult. That is why you even become afraid if you are expecting blissful moments, so you try to fix yourself somewhere in between.

This is what we mean by a normal human being: he never touches his madness in anger and he never touches that total freedom, that ecstasy, either. He never moves from a solid image. Normal man is really a dead man between these two points. That is why all those who are exceptional — great artists, painters, poets — they are not normal. They are very liquid. Sometimes they touch the center, sometimes they go mad. They move fast between these two. Of course, their anguish is great, their tension is much. They have to live between two worlds constantly changing themselves. That is why they feel that they have no identity. They feel, in the words of Colin Wilson, that they are "outsiders". In your world of normality they are outsiders.

It will be helpful to define these four types: first is the normal man who has a fixed solid identity, who knows who he is — a doctor, an engineer, a professor, a saint — who knows who he is and never moves from there. He constantly clings to the identity, to the image. Second are those who have liquid images — poets, artists, painters, singers. They do not know who they are. Sometimes they become just normal, sometimes they go mad, sometimes they touch the ecstasy that a Buddha touches. Third are those who are permanently mad. They have gone outside themselves; they never come back into their home. They do not even remember that they have a home. And fourth are those who have reached their home — Buddha, Christ, Krishna.

This fourth category — those who have reached their home — they are totally relaxed. In their consciousness there is no tension, no effort, no desire. In one word, there is no "becoming". They do not want to become anything. They are, they have been. No becoming! And they are at ease with their being. Whatsoever they are, they are at ease with it. They do not want to change it; do not want to go anywhere. They have no future. This very moment is eternity for them. No longing, no desire. That does not mean that a Buddha will not eat or a Buddha will not sleep. He will eat, he will sleep, but these are not desires. A Buddha will not project these desires. He will not eat tomorrow: he will eat today.

Remember this: you go on eating in the tomorrow; you go on eating in the future; you go on eating in the past, in the yesterday. It rarely happens that you eat today. While you are eating today, your mind will be moving somewhere else. While you will be trying to go to sleep, you will start eating tomorrow, or else the memory of the past will come.

A Buddha eats today. This very moment he lives. He does not project his life into the future; there is no future for him. Whenever future comes, it comes as the present. It is always today; it is always now. So Buddha eats, but he never eats in the mind — remember this. There is no cerebral eating. You go on eating in the mind. It is absurd because the mind is not meant for eating. All your centers are confused. Your entire body-mind arrangement is mixed up; it is mad.

A Buddha eats, but he never thinks of eating. And that applies for everything. So a Buddha is as ordinary as you while he is eating. Do not think that a Buddha is not going to eat, or that when the hot sun is there he is not going to perspire, or when cold winds come he will not feel cold. He will feel it, but he will feel always in the present — never in the future. There is no becoming. If there is no becoming, there is no tension. Understand this very clearly. If there is no becoming, how can there be any tension? Tension means you want to be something else which you are not.

You are A and you want to be B; you are poor and you want to be a rich man; you are ugly and you want to be beautiful; or, you are stupid and you want to be a wise man. Whatsoever the wanting, whatsoever the desire, the form is always this: A wants to become B. Whatsoever you are, you are not content with it. For contentment something else is needed: that is the constant structure of a mind that is desiring. When you will get it, again the mind will say that this is not enough, that something else is needed. The mind always moves on and on. Whatsoever you get becomes useless. The moment you get it, it is useless. This is desire. Buddha has called it *"trishna"*: this is becoming.

You move from one life to another, from one world to another, and this goes on. It can continue ad infinitum. There is no end to it. There is no end to desire, desiring. But if there is no becoming, if you accept totally whatsoever you are — ugly or beautiful, wise or stupid, rich or poor, whatsoever you are, if you accept it in its totality — becoming ceases. Then there is no tension. Then the tension cannot exist. Then there is no anguish. You are at ease: you are not worried. This non-becoming mind is a mind that is centered in the Self.

On quite the opposite pole is the madman. He has no Being: he is only a becoming. He has forgotten what he is. The A is forgotten completely and he is trying to be B. He no longer knows who he is: he only knows his desired goal. He doesn't live here and now: he lives somewhere else. That is why he looks crazy to us, mad, because you live in this world and he lives in the world of his dreams. He is not part of your world: he is living somewhere else. He has completely forgotten his reality here and now. And with himself he has forgotten the world around him which is real. He lives in an unreal world. For him, that is the only reality.

A Buddha lives this very moment in the Being, and the madman is just the opposite: he never lives in the here and now, in the Being, but always in the becoming — somewhere on the horizon. These are the two polar opposites.

So, remember, the madman is not against you: he is against

Buddha. And remember also, Buddha is not against you: he is against the madman. You are in between. You are both mixed. You have madnesses, you have moments of Enlightenment, but both are mixed.

Sometimes, a glimpse into the center suddenly happens — if you are relaxed. There are moments when you are relaxed. You are in love: for a few moments, for a single moment, your lover, your beloved, is with you. It has been a long desire, a long effort, and at last your beloved is with you. For a moment the mind goes "off". There has been a long effort to be with the beloved. The mind has been hankering and hankering and hankering, and the mind has always been thinking, thinking, about the beloved. Now the beloved is there and suddenly, the mind cannot think. The old process cannot be continued. You were asking for the beloved. Now the beloved is there, so the mind simply stops.

In that moment when the beloved is there, there is no desire. You are relaxed; suddenly you are thrown to yourself. Unless a lover can throw you to yourself, it is not love. Unless you become yourself in the presence of the beloved, it is not love. Unless mind completely ceases to function in the presence of the lover or the beloved, it is not love.

Sometimes it happens that mind ceases, and for a moment there is no desire. Love is desireless. Try to understand this: you may desire love, but love is desireless. When love happens, there is no desire. Mind is quiet, calm, relaxed. No more becoming, nowhere to go.

But this happens only for a few moments, if it happens at all. If you have really loved someone, then it will happen for a few moments. It is a shock. The mind cannot function because the whole function has become useless, absurd. The one for whom you were longing is there, and the mind cannot think what to do now.

For a few moments the whole mechanism stops. You are relaxed in yourself. You have touched your Being, your center, and you feel to be at the source of well-being. A bliss fills you;

163

a fragrance surrounds you. Suddenly you are not the same man you were.

That is why love transforms so much. If you are in love, you cannot hide it. That is impossible ! If you are in love, it will show. Your eyes, your face, the way you walk, the way you sit, everything will show it, because you are not the same man. The desiring mind is not there. You are like a Buddha just for a few moments. This cannot be continued for long because it is just a shock. Immediately the mind will try to find some ways and excuses to think again. For example, the mind may start thinking you have attained your goal, you have attained your love, so now what: what are you going to do. Then the prophesizing starts, argument starts. You begin thinking, "Today I have reached my beloved, but will it be the same tomorrow also ?" The mind has started working. And the moment mind is working you have moved again into becoming.

Sometimes, even without love, just through fatigue, tiredness, one stops desiring. Then too one is thrown to oneself. When you are not away from yourself, you are bound to be at your Self, no matter what may be the cause of it. When one is tired totally, fatigued, when one does not even feel like thinking or desiring, when one is frustrated completely without any hope, then suddenly one feels at home. Now he cannot go anywhere. All the doors are closed; hope has disappeared — and with it desire, with it becoming.

It will not be for long because your mind has a mechanism. It can go off for a few moments, but suddenly it will come alive again because you cannot exist hopelessly: you will have to find some hope. You cannot exist without desire. Because you do not know how to exist without desire, you will have to create some desire.

In any situation where it happens that suddenly the mind ceases functioning, you are at your center. You are on a holiday, in a forest or at a hill station, or on a beach: suddenly your routine mind will not work. The office is not there, the wife is not there, the husband is not there. Suddenly there is a very new situation, and the mind will need some time to function in it, to be adjusted to it. The mind feels unadjusted. The situation is so new that you relax, and you are at your center.

In these moments you become a Buddha, but these will only be moments. Then they will haunt you, and then you would like to reproduce them again and again and repeat them. But, remember, they happened spontaneously so you cannot repeat them. And the more you try to repeat them, the more it will be impossible for them to come to you.

That is happening to everyone. You loved someone, and in the first meeting your mind ceased for a few moments. Then you got married. Why did you get married? To repeat those beautiful moments again and again. But when they happened you were not married, and they cannot happen in marriage because the whole situation is different. When two people meet for the first time, the whole situation is new. Their minds cannot function in it. They are so overwhelmed by it — so filled by the new experience, by the new life, the new flowering! Then the mind starts functioning and they think. "This is such a beautiful moment! I want to go on repeating it every day, so I should get married."

Mind will destroy everything. Marriage means mind. Love is spontaneous; marriage is calculating. Getting married is a mathematical thing. Then you wait for those moments, but they will never come again. That is why every married man and woman is frustrated — because they are waiting for certain things that did happen in the past. Why are they not happening again? They cannot happen because you are missing the whole situation. Now you are not new; now there is no spontaneity. Now love is a routine. Now everything is expected and demanded. Now love has become a duty, not a fun. It was fun in the beginning; now it is a duty. And duty cannot give you the same bliss that fun can give. It is impossible! Your mind has created the whole thing. Now you go on expecting, and the more you expect the less is the possibility of its happening.

This happens everywhere — not only in marriage. You go to a

Guru and the experience is new. His presence, his words, his way of life, are new. Suddenly your mind stops functioning. Then you think, "This is the man for me, so I must go every day." Then you get married to him. By and by frustration sets in because you have made it a duty, a routine. Now those same experiences will not be coming. Then you think this man has deceived you or that you were fooled somehow. Then you think, "The first experience was hallucinatory. I must have been hypnotized or something. It was not real."

It was real. Your routine mind makes it unreal. And then the mind tries to expect, but the first time it happened you were not expecting. You had come without any expectations. You were just open to receive whatsoever was happening.

Now you come every day with expectations, with a closed mind. It cannot happen. It always happens in an open mind; it always happens in a new situation. That doesn't mean that you have to change your situation daily. It only means do not allow your mind to create a pattern. Then your wife will be new every day, your husband will be new every day. But do not allow the mind to create a pattern of expectations; do not allow the mind to move in the future. Then your Guru will be every day new, your friend will be every day new. And everything is new in the world except the mind. Mind is the only thing which is old. It is always old.

The sun is rising anew every day. It is not the old sun. The moon is new; the day, the night, the flowers, the trees, everything is new, except your mind. Your mind is always old — remember, always — because mind needs the past, the accumulated experience, the projected experience. Mind needs the past and life needs the present. Life is always blissful, mind never is. Whenever you allow your mind to come in, misery sets in.

These spontaneous moments will not be repeated again, so what to do? How to be in a relaxed state continuously? These three sutras are for this. These are three techniques concerning the feeling of ease, techniques to relax the nerves.

How to remain in the Being? How not to move in the becoming? It is difficult, arduous, but these techniques can help. These techniques will throw you upon yourself.

The first technique: *"While being caressed, Sweet Princess, enter the caressing as everlasting life."*

"While being loved, Sweet Princess, enter the loving as everlasting life": Shiva starts with love. The first technique is concerned with love, because love is the nearest thing in your experience in which you are relaxed. If you cannot love, it is impossible for you to relax. If you can relax, your life will become a loving life.

A tense man cannot love. Why? A tense man always lives with purposes. He can earn money, but he cannot love because love is purposeless. Love is not a commodity. You cannot accumulate it; you cannot make a bank balance of it; you cannot strengthen your ego out of it. Really, love is the most absurd act, with no meaning beyond it, no purpose beyond it. It exists in itself, not for anything else.

You earn money FOR something: it is a means. You build a house for someone to live in it: it is a means. Love is not a means. Why do you love? For what do you love? Love is the end in itself. That is why a mind that is calculative — logical, a mind that thinks in terms of purpose, cannot love. And the mind that always thinks in terms of purpose will be tense, because purpose can only be fulfilled in the future — never here and now.

You are building a house: you cannot live in it just NOW. You will have to build it first. You can live in the future, not now. You earn money: the bank balance will be created in the future, not now. Means you will have to use now, and ends will come in the future.

Love is always here; there is no future to it. That is why love is so near to meditation. That is why death is also so near to meditation — because death is also always here and now: it can never happen in the future. Can you die in the future? You can die only in the present. No one has ever died in the future. How can you die in the future? Or, how can you die in the past? The past has gone. It is no more, so you cannot die in it. The future has not yet come, so how can you die in it?

Death always occurs in the present. Death, love, meditation — they all occur in the present. So if you are afraid of death, you cannot love. If you are afraid of love, you cannot meditate. If you are afraid of meditation, your life will be useless — useless not in the sense of any purpose: useless in the sense that you will never be able to feel any bliss in it. It will be futile.

It may seem strange to connect these three: love, meditation, death. It is not! They are similar experiences. So if you can enter in one, you can enter in the remaining two.

Shiva starts with love. He says: "While being carassed (loved), Sweet Princess, enter the caressing (the loving) as everlasting life."

What does it mean? Many things! One: while you are loved, the past has ceased, the future is not. You move in the dimension of the present. You move in THE NOW. Have you ever loved someone? If you have ever loved, then you know that the mind is no longer there. That is why the so-called wise men say that lovers are blind, mindless, mad. They say rightly in essence. Lovers ARE blind because they have no eyes for the future to calculate what they are doing. They are blind: they cannot see the past. What has happened to lovers? They just move here and now without any consideration of past or future, without any consideration of consequences. That is why they are called blind. They are! They are blind for those who are calculating, and they are seers for those who are not calculating. Those who are not calculating will see love as the real eye, the real vision.

So the first thing: in the moment of love, past and future are no more. Then, one delicate point is to be understood: when there is no past and no future, can you call this moment the present? It is the present only between the two — between the past and the future. It is relative. If there is no past and no future, what does it mean to call it the present? It is meaningless. That is why Shiva doesn't use the word "present". He says, "everlasting life." He means "eternity" — enter "eternity".

We divide time into three parts — past, present, future. That division is false — absolutely false. Time is really past and future. The present is not part of time. The present is part of eternity. That which has passed is time; that which is to come is time. That which is, is not time because it never passes. It is always there. The now is always here. It is ALWAYS here! This now is eternal.

If you move from the past, you never move in the present. From the past you always move into future. There comes no moment which is present. From the past you always move into the future. From the present you can never move into the future. From the present you go deeper and deeper, into more present and more present. This is everlasting life.

We may say it in this way: From past to future is time. Time means you move on a plane, on a straight line. Or, we may call it as horizontal. The moment you are in the present the dimension changes: you move vertically — up or down, toward the height or toward the depth. But then you never move horizontally. A Buddha, a Shiva, they live in eternity, not in time.

Jesus was asked, "What will happen in your Kingdom of God?" The man who asked him was not asking about time. He was asking about what is going to happen to his desires — about how they will be fulfilled. He was asking whether there will be life everlasting or whether there will be death, whether there be any misery or whether there will be inferior and superior men. He was asking things of this world when he asked, "What is going to happen in your Kingdom of God?" And Jesus replied (the reply is like that of a Zen monk), "There shall be time no longer."

The man who was replied in this way may not have understood at all. "There shall be time no longer": only this one thing Jesus said. "There shall be time no longer," because time is horizontal and the Kingdom of God is vertical: it is eternal.

It is always here! You have only to move away from time to enter into it.

So love is the first door. Through it, you can move away from time. That is why everyone wants to be loved; everyone wants to love. And no one knows why so much significance is given to love, why there is such a deep longing for love. And unless you know it rightly, you can neither love nor be loved because love is one of the deepest phenomena upon this earth.

We go on thinking that everyone is capable of love as he is. This is not the case: it is not so. That is why you are frustrated. Love is a different dimension. And if you try to love someone in time, you will be defeated in your effort. In time, love is not possible.

I remember one anecdote. Meera was in love with Krishna. She was a housewife — the wife of a prince. The prince became jealous of Krishna. Krishna was no more; Krishna was not present; Krishna was not a physical body. There was a gap of 5,000 years between Krishna's physical existence and Meera's physical existence. So, really, how can Meera be in love with Krishna? The time gap was so great.

One day the prince asked Meera — her husband asked her, "You go on talking about your love, you go on dancing and singing around Krishna. But where is he? With whom are you so much in love? With whom are you talking continuously?" Meera was talking with Krishna, singing, laughing, fighting. She looked mad. She was, in our eyes. The prince said, "Have you gone mad? Where is your Krishna? Whom are you loving? With whom are you conversing? And I am here, and you have completely forgotten me."

Meera said, "Krishna is here; you are not here: because Krishna is eternal; you are not. He will always be here; he was always here; he is here. You will not be here; you were not here. You were not here one day; you will not be here another day. So how I can believe that between these two non-existences you are here? How is an existence possible between two non-existences?"

The prince is in time, but Krishna is in eternity. So you can be near the prince, but the distance cannot be destroyed. You will be distant. You may be very, very distant in time from Krishna, but you can be near. It is a different dimension, however.

I look in front of me and there is a wall; I move my eyes and there is a sky. When you look in time, there is always a wall. When you look beyond time, there is the open sky — infinite. Love opens the infinity, the everlastingness of Existence. So, really, if you have ever loved, love can be made a technique of meditation. This is the technique: "While being loved, Sweet Princess, enter loving as everlasting life."

Do not be a lover standing aloof — out. Become loving and move into eternity. When you are loving someone, are you there as the lover ? If you are there, then you are in time and love is just false — just pseudo. If you are still there and you can say, "I am," then you can be physically near, but spiritually you are poles apart.

While in love, YOU must not be — only love, only loving. Become loving. While caressing your lover or beloved become the caress. While kissing, do not be the kisser or the kissed. Be the kiss. Forget the ego completely: dissolve it into the act. Move into the act so deeply that the actor is no more. And if you cannot move in love, it is difficult to move in eating or walking — very difficult because love is the easiest approach for dissolving the ego. That is why those who are egoists cannot love. They may talk about it; they may sing about it; they may write about it: but they cannot love. The ego cannot love !

Shiva says become "loving". When you are in the embrace, become the embrace, become the kiss. Forget yourself so totally that you can say, "I am no more. Only love exists." Then the heart is not beating, but love is beating. Then the blood is not circulating: love is circulating. And eyes are not seeing: love is seeing. Then hands are not moving to touch: love is moving to touch.

Become love and enter everlasting life. Love suddenly changes your dimension. You are thrown out of time and you are facing eternity. Love can become a deep meditation — the deepest possible. And lovers have known sometimes what saints have not known. And lovers have touched that center which many yogis have missed. But it will be just a glimpse unless you transform your love into meditation. Tantra means this: the transformation of love into meditation. And now you can understand why tantra talks so much about love and sex. Why ? Because love is the easiest natural door from where you can transcend this world — this horizontal dimension.

Look at Shiva with his consort Devi. Look at them ! They don't seem to be two: they are one. The oneness is so deep that it has even gone into symbols. We all have seen the Shivalinga. It is a phallic symbol — Shiva's sex organ. But it is not alone. It is based in Devi's vagina.

The Hindus of the old days were very daring. Now when you see a Shivalinga, you never remember that it is a phallic symbol. We have forgotten; we have tried to forget it completely.

Jung remembers in his autobiography, in his memoirs, a very beautiful and funny incident. He came to India and went to see Konark, and in the temple of Konark, there are many, many Shivalingas, many phallic symbols. The pundit who was taking him around explained everything to him except the Shivalinga. And they were so many, it was difficult to escape this. Jung was well aware, but just to tease the pundit he went on asking, "But what are these ?" So the pundit at last said into his ear, in Jung's ear, "Do not ask me here. I will tell you afterwards. This is a private thing."

Jung must have laughed inside. These are the Hindus of today. Then outside the temple the pundit came near and said, "It was not good of you to ask before others. I will tell you now. It is a secret." And then again in Jung's ear, he said, "They are our private parts."

When Jung went back, he met one great scholar — a scholar of oriental thought, myth, philosophy — Heinrich Zimmer. He related this anecdote to Zimmer. Zimmer was one of the most gifted minds who ever tried to penetrate Indian thought. And he was a lover of India and of its ways of thinking — of the oriental, non-logical, mystic approach toward life. When he heard this from Jung, he laughed and said, "This is good for a change. I have always heard about great Indians — Buddha, Krishna, Mahavir. What you relate tells not about any great Indians, but about Indians."

Love for Shiva is the great gate. And for him sex is not something to be condemned. For him sex is the seed and love is the flowering of it, and if you condemn the seed you condemn the flower. Sex can become love. If it never becomes love, then it is crippled. Condemn the crippledness, not the sex. Love must flower. Sex must become love. If it is not becoming, it is not the fault of sex. It is your fault.

Sex must not remain sex; that is the tantra teaching. It must be transformed into love. And love also must not remain love. It must be transformed into light, into meditative experience, into the last, ultimate, mystic peak. How to transform love ? Be the act and forget the actor. While loving, be love — simply love. Then it is not your love or my love or anybody else's. It is simply LOVE. When you are not there, when you are in the hands of the Ultimate source or current, when you are in love, it is not you who is in love. When the love has engulfed you, you have disappeared; you have just become a flowing energy.

D. H. Lawrence, one of the most creative minds of this age, was knowingly or unknowingly a tantra adept. He was condemned in the West completely. His books were banned. There were many cases in the courts only because he had said, "Sex energy is the only energy. And if you condemn it and suppress it you are against the universe, and then you will never be capable of knowing the higher flowering of this energy. And when suppressed it becomes ugly, and this is the vicious circle."

Priests, moralists, so-called religious people, Popes, *Shankara-charyas* (Hindu religious heads) and others, they go on condemning sex. They say that this is an ugly thing. And when you suppress it, it becomes ugly. So they say, "Look ! What we

173

said is true. It is proved by you. Look! Whatsoever you are doing is ugly and you know it is ugly."

But it is not sex which is ugly. It is these priests who have made it ugly. And once they have made it ugly, they are proved right. And when they are proved right, you go on making it more and more ugly — uglier.

Sex is innocent energy — life flowing in you, Existence alive in you. Do not cripple it! Allow it to move toward the heights. That is, sex must become love. What is the difference? When your mind is sexual, you are exploiting the other. The other is just an instrument to be used and thrown. When sex becomes love, the other is not an instrument, the other is not to be exploited, the other is not really the other. When you love, it is not self-centered. Rather, the other becomes significant — unique.

It is not that you are exploiting him — no! On the contrary, you both are joined in a deep experience. You are partners of a deep experience, not the exploiter and the exploited. You are helping each other to move into a different world of love. Sex is exploitation. Love is moving together into a different world.

If this moving is not momentary and if this moving becomes meditative — that is, if you can forget yourself completely, and the lover and the beloved disappear, and there is only love flowing, then says Shiva, "Everlasting life is yours."

The second technique: *"Stop the doors of the senses when feeling the creeping of an ant. Then."*

This looks very simple, but it is not so simple. I will read it again: "Stop the doors of the senses when feeling the creeping of an ant. Then." This is only an example; anything will do. Stop the doors of the senses when feeling the creeping of an ant, and then — THEN — the thing will happen. What is Shiva saying?

You have a thorn in your foot: it is painful; you are suffering. Or, one ant is there creeping on your leg. You feel the creeping and suddenly you want it to be thrown away. Take any experience! You have a wound: it is painful! You have a headache, or any pain in the body: anything will do as an object. It is only an example — the creeping of an ant. Shiva says, "Stop the doors of the senses when feeling the creeping of an ant." Whatsoever you are feeling, stop all the doors of the senses.

What is to be done ? Close your eyes, and think that you are just blind and you cannot see. Close your ears and think that you cannot hear. With all of the five senses, you just close them. How can you close them ? It is easy. Stop breathing for a single moment: all your senses will be closed. When the breath has stopped and all the senses are closed, where is this creeping ? Where is the ant ? Suddenly you are removed — far away.

One of my friends, an old friend, very aged, fell down from the staircase. And doctors said that now he will not be able to move from his bed for three months. He would have to rest for three months. And he was a very restless man; it was difficult for him. I went to see him, so he said, "Pray for me and bless me so that I may die, because these three months are more than death. I cannot remain stone-like." And others said, "Don't move."

I told him, "This is a good opportunity. Just close your eyes and think that you are only a stone. You cannot move. How can you move ? You are a stone — just a stone, a statue. Close your eyes. Feel that you are now a stone — a statue." He asked me what will happen. I told him, "Just try. I am sitting here, and nothing can be done. Nothing can be done ! You will have to be here for three months anyhow, so try. He would have never tried, but the situation was so impossible that he said, "Okay ! I will try because something may happen. I don't believe it," he said. "I don't believe that something can happen just by thinking that I am stone-like, dead like a statue, but I will try." So he tried.

I was also not thinking that something was going to happen, because the man was such. But sometimes, when you are in an impossible situation, hopeless, things begin to happen. He closed his eyes. I waited because I was thinking within two or three minutes he would open them and he would say, "Nothing happened." But he would not open his eyes, and thirty minutes passed. I could feel and see that he had become a statue. All the tension on his forehead disappeared. His face was changed.

I had to leave, but he would not open his eyes. And he was so silent, as if dead. His breathing calmed down, and because I had to leave, I had to tell him, "I want to go now, so please open your eyes and tell me what has happened." He opened his eyes a different man. And he said, "This is a miracle. What have you done to me?" I told him, "I have not done anything at all." He said, "You must have done something because this is a miracle. When I began to think that I am just like a stone, like a statue, suddenly the feeling came to me that even if I wanted to move my hands it was impossible to do so. I wanted so many times to open my eyes, but they were like stone so I couldn't open them."

He said, "I even became worried about what you will be thinking, as it was so long, but what could I do? I couldn't move myself for these thirty minutes. And when every movement ceased, suddenly the world disappeared and I was alone, deep down in me myself. Then the pain disappeared."

There was severe pain; he could not sleep in the night without a tranquilizer. But the pain disappeared. I asked him how he felt when the pain was disappearing. He said, "First I began to feel that it was somewhere distant. The pain was there, but very far away as if happening to someone else. And then by and by, by and by, as if someone is going away and away and you cannot see him, it disappeared. The pain disappeared! For at least ten minutes, the pain was no more. How can a stone body have pain?"

This sutra says, "Stop the doors of the senses": become stone-like, closed to the world. When you are closed to the world, really, you are closed to your own body also, because your body is not part of you; it is part of the world. When you are closed completely to the world, you are closed to your own body also. Then, Shiva says, then the thing will happen.

So try it with the body. Anything will do. You will not need some ant creeping on you. Otherwise you will think that "When

176

the ant will creep, I will meditate." And such helpful ants are difficult to find, so anything can do. You are lying on your bed; you feel the cold sheets: become dead. Suddenly the sheets will go away, away, away, and they will disappear. Your bed will disappear; your bedroom will disappear; the whole world will disappear. You are closed, dead, a stone, like a Leibnitzian monad with no window outside — no window! You cannot move!

And then, when you cannot move, you are thrown back to yourself, you are centered in yourself. Then, for the first time, you can look from your center. And once you can look from your center, you can never be the same man again.

The third technique: *"When on a bed or a seat, let yourself become weightless, beyond mind."*

You are sitting here: Just feel that you have become weightless. There is no weight. You will feel that somewhere or other there is weight, but go on feeling the weightlessness. It comes. A moment comes when you feel that you are weightless — that there is no weight. When there is no weight you are no more a body, because the weight is of the body — not of you. You are weightless.

That is why there were so many experiments done: Someone would be dying, and many scientists all over the world have tried many times to weigh the person. If there is a slight difference, if when a man is alive the weight is more and if when a man is dead the weight is less, then scientists can say that something has moved from the body — that a soul or the Self or something that was there is no more, because for science nothing can be weightless — nothing!

Weight is basic to all matter. Even sun rays have weight. It is very, very slight, minute, and they are difficult to weigh, but scientists have weighed them. If you can collect all the sun rays on a five-square-mile plot of ground, their weight will be similar to a hair. But sun rays do have weight; they have been weighed. Nothing can be weightless for science. And if something can be weightless, then it is immaterial. It cannot be matter. And science

177

believed for these twenty or twenty-five years that there is nothing except matter.

So when a man dies, if something leaves the weight must differ. But it never differs; the weight remains the same. Sometimes it even becomes more: that is the problem. The alive man weighs less and the dead man becomes more weighty. That created new problems because they were really trying to find out if some weight is lost. Then they can say something has left. But it seemed that, on the contrary, something has come in. What has happened? Weight is material, but you are not a weight. You are immaterial.

If you try this technique of weightlessness, you just have to conceive of yourself as weightless — and not only to conceive, but to feel that your body has become weightless. If you go on feeling, feeling, feeling, a moment comes when suddenly you realize that you are weightless. You are already, so you can realize it anytime. You have only to create a situation in which you can feel again that you are weightless.

You have to dehypnotize yourself. This is the hypnosis: the belief that "I am a body and that is why I feel weight". If you can dehypnotize yourself into realizing that you are not a body, you will not feel weight. And when you do not feel weight you are beyond mind, says Shiva: "When on a bed or on a seat let yourself become weightless, beyond mind." Then the thing can happen. The mind also has weight: each one's mind has a different weight.

At one time there were some proposals that the weightier the mind, the more intelligent. And generally it is true, but not absolutely, because sometimes very small minds were very great men, and sometimes some stupid idiots weighed very much. But generally it is true, because when you have a bigger mechanism of the mind you weigh more. The mind is also a weight, but your consciousness is weightless. To feel this consciousness, you have to feel weightlessness. So try it: walking, sitting, sleeping, you can try it.

Some observations: why does the dead body become more

weighty sometimes? Because the moment the consciousness leaves the body, the body becomes unprotected. Many things can enter it immediately. They were not entering because of you. Many vibrations can enter into a dead body: they cannot enter in you. You were there: the body was alive, resistant to many things. That is why once you are ill, it begins to be a long sequence — one illness, then another and then another: because once you are ill, you become unprotected, vulnerable, non-resistant. Then anything can enter. Your presence protects the body. So sometimes a dead body can gain weight: the moment you leave it, anything can enter into the body.

Secondly, when you are happy you always feel weightless; when you are sad you always feel more weight, as if something is pulling you down. The gravitation becomes much more. When you are sad, you are more weighty. When you are happy, you are light. You feel it. Why? Because when you are happy, whenever you feel a blissful moment, you forget the body completely. When you are sad, suffering, you cannot forget the body. You feel the weight of it. It pulls you down — down to the earth, as if you are rooted. Then you cannot move: you have roots in the earth. In happiness, you are weightless. In sorrow, sadness, you become weighty.

In deep meditation, when you forget your body completely, you can levitate. Even the body can go up with you. It happens many times. Scientists have been observing one woman in Bolivia. While meditating she goes up four feet, and now it has been a scientific observation. Many films have been taken, many photographs. Before thousands and thousands of observers suddenly the woman goes up and gravity becomes nil, nullified. As of yet there is no explanation for what is happening, but that same woman cannot go up while not in meditation. And if her meditation is disturbed, suddenly she falls down.

What happens? Deep in meditation you forget your body completely, and the identification is broken. The body is a very small thing; you are very big. You have infinite power. The body has nothing in comparison to you,

It is as if an emperor has become identified with his slave, so as the slave goes begging, the emperor goes begging. As the slave weeps, the emperor weeps. When the slave says, "I am no one," the emperor says, "I am no one." Once the emperor recognizes his own being, once he recognizes that he is the emperor and this man is just a slave, everything will change suddenly.

You are infinite power identified with a very finite body. Once you Realize your Self, then weightlessness becomes more and the weight of the body less. Then you can levitate: the body can go up.

There are many many stories which cannot yet be proven scientifically, but they will be proven — because if one woman can go up four feet, then there is no barrier. Another can go a thousand feet, another can go completely into the cosmos. Theoretically, there is no problem: four feet or four hundred or four thousand feet make no difference.

There are stories about Ram and about many others who have disappeared completely with the body. Their bodies were never found dead on this earth. Mohammed disappeared completely — not only with his body: it is said with his horse also. These stories look impossible, they look mythological — but they are not necessarily so.

Once you know the weightless force, you have become the master of gravity. You can use it: it depends on you. You can disappear completely with your body.

But to us weightlessness will be a problem. The technique of "siddhasan", the way Buddha sits, is the best way to be weightless. Sit on the earth — not on any chair or anything, but just on the floor. And it is good if the floor is not of cement or anything artificial. Just sit on the ground so that you are the nearest to nature. It is good if you can sit naked. Just sit naked on the ground, in the Buddha posture — siddhasan, because siddhasan is the best posture in which to be weightless. Why ? Because you feel more weight if your body is leaning this way or that way. Then your body has more area to be affected by gravity. If I am sitting on this chair, then a greater area of my body is affected by gravity.

While you are standing less area is affected, but you cannot stand for too long. Mahavir always meditated standing — always, because then one covers the least area of gravity. Just your feet are touching the ground. When you are standing on your feet, straight, the least amount of gravity works on you — and gravity is weight.

Sitting in a Buddha posture locked (your legs are locked, your hands are locked) also helps, because then your inner electricity becomes a circuit. Let your spine be straight.

Now you can understand why so much emphasis has been given to a straight spine, because with a straight spine less and less area is covered. Gravity affects you less. With closed eyes, balance yourself completely, center yourself. Lean to the right and feel the gravity; lean to the left and feel the gravity; lean forward and feel the gravity; lean backward and feel the gravity. Then find the center where the least pull of gravity is felt, the least weight is felt, and remain there. Then forget the body and feel that you are not weight: you are weightless. Then go on feeling this weightlessness. Suddenly you become weightless; suddenly you are not the body; suddenly you are in a different world of bodilessness.

Weightlessness is bodilessness. Then you transcend mind also. Mind is also part of the body, part of matter. Matter has weight; you do not have any weight. This is the base of this technique.

Try any, but stick to it for a few days so that you can feel whether it is working or not.

Enough for today.

8
Total Acceptance And Non-Division: The Meaning Of Tantric Purity

October, 8, 1972, Bombay, India

QUESTION:

1. *What does tantra mean by purity?*

One of the things being asked about is: *"What does tantra mean by purification of the mind, purity of the mind, as a basic condition to further progress?"*

Whatsoever is ordinarily meant by purity is not what is meant by tantra. Ordinarily, we divide everything into bad and good. The division may be for any reason: it may be hygienically, morally or any other way, but we divide life into two — good and bad. And, ordinarily, whenever we say purity we mean goodness. The "bad" qualities should not be allowed and the "good" qualities should be there. But for tantra this division of good and bad is meaningless. Tantra does not look at life through any dichotomy, any duality, any division. Then "What is meant by 'purity' in tantra?" is a very relevant question.

If you ask a saint, he will say that anger is bad, sex is bad, greed is bad. If you ask Gurdjieff, he will say that negativity is bad — that whatsoever emotion is negative is bad and to be positive is good. If you ask Jains, Buddhists, Hindus, Christians or Mohammedans, they may differ in their definition of good and bad — but they have definitions. They call certain things bad and certain things good. So to define purity is not difficult for them. Whatsoever they take as good is pure, whatsoever they take as bad is impure.

But for tantra it is a deep problem. Tantra makes no superficial division between good and bad. Then what is purity? Tantra says that to divide is impure and to live in non-division is purity. So for tantra purity means innocence — undifferentiated innocence.

A child is there: you call him pure. He gets angry, he has greed, so why do you call him pure ? What is pure in childhood ? Innocence ! There is no division in the mind of a child. The child is unaware of any division into what is good and what is bad. That unawareness is the innocence. Even if he gets angry, he has no mind to be angry. It is a pure and simple act. It happens, and when anger goes, it goes. Nothing is left behind. The child is again the same, as if the anger has never been there. The purity is not touched. The purity is the same. So a child is pure because there is no mind.

The more mind grows, the more the child will become impure. Then anger will be there as a considered thing, not spontaneously. Then sometimes the child will suppress the anger — if the situation does not permit it. And when anger becomes suppressed, then sometimes it will be transferred onto another situation also. When there is really no need to be angry, he will get angry, because the suppressed anger will need some outlet. Then everything will become impure because the mind has come in.

A child can be a thief in our eyes, but a child himself is never a thief because the very concept that things belong to individuals doesn't exist in his mind. If he takes your watch, your money, or anything, it is not a theft for him because the very notion that things belong to someone is non-existent. His theft is pure while even your non-theft is not pure. The mind is there.

Tantra says that when someone becomes again like a child, he is pure. Of course, he is not a child — only like a child. The difference is there and the similarity is there. The similarity is the innocence regained. Again someone is like a child. A child is standing naked: no one feels the nakedness because a child is still unaware of the body. His nakedness has a quality different from your nakedness. You are aware of the body.

The sage must regain this innocence. Mahavir stands again naked. That nakedness again has the same quality of innocence.

He has forgotten his body; he is no longer the body. But the difference is also there, and the difference is great. The child is simply ignorant: hence, the innocence. But the sage is wise: that is the reason for his innocence.

The child will one day become aware of his body and will feel the nakedness. He will try to hide, he will become guilty, and he will feel shame. He will come to be aware. So his innocence is an innocence of ignorance. Knowledge will destroy it.

That is the meaning of the Biblical story of Adam and Eve being expelled from Eden. They were naked like children. They were not aware of the body; they were not aware of anger, greed, lust, sex or anything. They were unaware. They were like children — innocent.

But God had forbidden them to eat the fruit of the Tree of Knowledge. The tree of Knowledge was forbidden, but they ate because anything forbidden becomes inviting. Anything forbidden becomes attractive ! They were living in a big garden with infinite trees, but the Tree of Knowledge became most important and significant because it was forbidden. Really, this "forbidden-ness" became the attraction, the invitation. They were as if magnetized, hypnotized by the tree. They couldn't escape it. They had to eat.

But this story is beautiful became the tree is named "Tree of Knowledge". The moment they ate the fruit of knowledge they became non-innocent. They became aware; they came to realize that they were naked. Immediately, Eve tried to hide her body. With the awareness of body they became aware of everything — anger, lust, greed, everything. They became adult, so they were expelled from the garden.

So in the Bible knowledge is sin. They were thrown out of the garden, they were punished, because of knowledge. Unless they become again like children — innocent, non-knowing — they cannot enter the garden. They can enter the Kingdom of God again only if they fulfill this condition of becoming innocent again.

The whole thing is just the story of humanity. Every child is expelled from the garden, not only Adam and Eve. Every child lives his childhood in innocence without knowing anything. He is pure, but the purity is of ignorance. It cannot continue. Unless it becomes a purity of wisdom, you cannot rely on it. It will have to go. Sooner or later you will have to eat the fruit of knowledge.

Each child will have to eat the fruit of knowledge. It was easy in the Garden of Eden: just the Tree was there. As a substitute for the Tree, we have schools, colleges and universities. Each child will have to pass, will have to become non-innocent, will have to lose his innocence. The very world needs knowledge, the very existence needs knowledge. You cannot exist in it without knowledge. And the moment knowledge comes, division enters. You begin to divide between what is good and what is bad.

So for tantra the division into good and bad is impurity. Before it you are pure, after it you are pure, in it you are impure. But knowledge is a necessary evil. You cannot escape it. One has to go through it: that is part of life. But one need not remain in it always. One can transcend it. Transcendence makes you again pure and innocent. If divisions lost their meaning, if the knowledge which differentiates between good and evil were no more, you would again look at the world from an innocent attitude.

Jesus says, "Unless you become like children, you cannot enter into my Kingdom of God." "Unless you become like children": this is the purity of tantra.

Lao Tse says, "One inch of division, and heaven and hell are set apart." No-division is the mind of the sage — no-division at all! A sage doesn't know what is good or what is bad. He is like children, but unlike them also because he has known this division. He has passed through this division and transcended it; he has gone beyond it. He has known darkness and light, but now he has gone beyond it. Now he sees darkness as part of light and light as part of darkness. Now there is no division. Light and darkness have both become one — degrees of one phenomenon. Now he sees everything as degrees of one. Howsoever polar opposite they are, they are not two. Life and death, love and hate, good and bad, everything, is part of one phenomenon, one energy. The difference is only of degrees, and they can never be divided. It cannot be demarked that from "this point" there is division. There is no division.

What is good ? What is bad ? From where can you define them and demark them as separate ? They are always one. They are only different degrees of the same. Once this is known and felt your mind becomes again pure. This is the purity meant by tantra. So I will define tantric purity as innocence, not as goodness.

But innocence can be ignorant. Then it is of no use. It has to be lost; you have to be thrown out of it: otherwise you cannot mature. Giving up knowledge and transcendence of knowledge are both part of maturing, part of being really adult. So go through them, but do not remain there. Move ! Go on moving ! A day comes when you are beyond them.

That is why tantric purity is difficult to understand and can be misunderstood: it is delicate ! So to recognize a tantric sage is virtually impossible. Ordinary saints and sages can be recognized because they follow you — your standards, your definitions, your morality. A tantric sage is even difficult to recognize because he transcends all divisions. So, really, in the whole history of human growth, we really know nothing about tantric sages. Nothing is mentioned or recorded about them because it is so difficult to recognize them.

Confucius went to Lao Tse. Lao Tse's mind is that of a tantrically awakened sage. He never knew about the word "tantra": the word is meaningless for him. He never knew anything about tantra, but whatsoever he has said is tantra. Confucius is representative of our mind. He is the arch-representative. He continually thinks in terms of good and bad, of what should be done and what should not be done. He is a legalist — the greatest legalist ever born. He went to see Lao Tse, and he asked Lao Tse, "What is good ? What ought one to do ? What is bad ? Define clearly."

Lao Tse said that definitions create a mess because defining means dividing: "This is this, and that is that." You divide and say A is A and B is B: you have divided. You say A cannot be B: then you have created a division, a dichotomy, and the Existence is one. A is always becoming B, A is always moving into B. Life is always becoming death, life is always moving into death, so how can you define? Childhood is moving into youth and youth is moving into old age; health is moving into disease and disease is moving into health. So where can you demark them as separate?

Life is one movement, and the moment you define you create a mess because definitions will be dead and life is an alive movement. So definitions are always false. Lao Tse says that defining creates non-truth, so do not define. Do not say what is good and what is bad.

So Confucius said, "What are you saying? Then how can people be led and guided? Then how can they be taught? How can they be made moral and good?"

Lao Tse said, "When someone tries to make someone else good, that is a sin in my eyes. Who are you to lead? Who are you to guide? And the more guides there are, the more confusion. Leave everyone to himself. Who are you?"

This type of attitude seems dangerous. It is! Society cannot be founded on such attitudes. Confucius goes on asking, and the whole point is that Lao Tse says, "Nature is enough. No morality is needed. Nature is spontaneous. Nature is enough. No imposed laws and disciplines are needed. Innocence is enough. No morality is needed. Nature is spontaneous, nature is enough. No imposed laws and disciplines are needed. Innocence is enough. Knowledge is not needed."

Confucius came back very much disturbed. He could not sleep for nights. And his disciples asked, "Tell us something about the meeting. What happened?" Confucius answered, "He is not a man. He is a danger, a dragon. He is not a man. Never go to that side where he is. Whenever you hear about Lao Tse, just escape from that place. He will disturb your mind completely."

And that is right, because the whole tantra is concerned with how to transcend the mind. It is bound to destroy the mind. Mind lives with definitions, laws and disciplines. Mind is an "order". But remember, tantra is not disorder, and that is a very subtle point to be understood.

Confucius could not understand Lao Tse. When Confucius left, Lao Tse was laughing and laughing and so his disciples asked, "Why are you laughing so much? What has happened?

Lao Tse is reported to have said, "The mind is such a barrier to understanding. Even the mind of a Confucius is a barrier. He could not understand me at all, and whatsoever he will say about me will be a misunderstanding. He thinks he is going to create order in the world. You CANNOT create order in the world. Order is inherent in it; it is always there. When you try to create order, you create disorder." Lao Tse said, "He will think that I am creating disorder, and, really, he is the one who is creating disorder. I am against all imposed orders because I believe in a spontaneous discipline which comes and grows automatically. You need not impose it."

Tantra looks at things in this way. For tantra, innocence is spontaneity, *Sahajata* — to be oneself without any imposition — to be simply oneself, growing like a tree: not the tree of your garden, but the tree of your forest, growing spontaneously; not guided, because every guidance is a misguidance (for tantra, every guidance is a misguidance); not guided, not guarded, not directed, not motivated, but simply growing.

The inner law is enough; no other law is needed. And if you need some other law, it only shows that you do not know the inner law. You have lost contact with it. So the real thing is not something imposed. The real thing is again regaining the balance, again moving to the center, again returning to the home so that you gain the real inner law.

But for morality, for religions — so-called religions, order is to be imposed, goodness is to be imposed from above, from without. Religions, moral teachings, priests, Popes, they all take you as inherently bad, remember this. They do not believe in the goodness of man; they do not believe in any inner goodness.

They believe that you are evil — that unless you are taught to be good, you cannot be good; unless goodness is forced from without, there is no possibility, of it coming from within.

So for priests, for religious people, for moralists, you are naturally bad. Goodness is going to be a discipline imposed from without. You are a chaos. Order has to be brought in by them. They will bring the order, and they have made the whole world a mess, a confusion, a madhouse, because they have been ordering for centuries and centuries, disciplining for centuries and centuries. They have taught so much that the taught ones have gone mad.

Tantra believes in your inner goodness: remember this difference. Tantra says that everyone is born good, that goodness is your nature. It is the case! You are already good! You need a natural growth. You do not need any imposition. That is why nothing is taken as bad. If anger is there, if sex is there, if greed is there, tantra says they are also good. The only thing lacking is that you are not centered in yourself; that is why you cannot use them. That is why you cannot use them!

Anger is not bad. Really, the problem is that you are not inside. That is why anger creates havoc. If you are present there inside, anger becomes a healthy energy, anger becomes health. Anger is transformed into energy. It becomes good. Whatsoever is there is good. Tantra believe in the inherent goodness of everything. Everything is holy. Nothing is unholy and nothing is evil. For tantra there is no Devil, only Divine Existence.

Religions cannot exist without the Devil. They need a God and they need a Devil also. So do not be misguided if you see only a God in their temples. Just behind that God, the Devil is hiding, because no religion can exist without the Devil.

Something has to be condemned, something has to be fought, something has to be destroyed. The total is not accepted, only part. This is very basic. You are not accepted totally by any religion, only partially. They say, "We accept your love, but not your hate. Destroy hate." And this is a very deep problem, because when you destroy hate completely love is also destroyed — because they are not two. They say "We accept your silence, but we do not accept your anger." Destroy anger, and your aliveness is destroyed. Then you will be silent, but not an alive man — only a dead one. That silence is not life. It is just death.

Religions always divide you into two — the evil and the divine. They accept the divine and are against the evil. The evil has to be destroyed. So if someone really follows them, he will come to conclude that the moment you destroy the Devil, the God is destroyed. But no one really follows them. No one can follow them because the very teaching is absurd. So what is everyone doing ? Everyone is just deceiving. That is why there is so much hypocrisy. That hypocrisy has been created by religion. You cannot do whatsoever they are teaching you to do, so you become a hypocrite. If you follow them you will die; if you do not follow them you feel guilty that you are irreligious. So what to do ?

The cunning mind makes a compromise. It goes on paying lip service to them, saying, "I am following you," but it goes on doing whatsoever it wants to do. You continue your anger, you continue your sex, you continue your greed, but you always go on saying that greed is bad, anger is bad, sex is bad — that it is a sin. This is hypocrisy. The whole world has become hypocritical. No man is honest. Unless these dividing religions disappear, no man can be honest. This will look contradictory because all the religions are teaching to be honest. But they are the foundation stones of all dishonesty. They make you dishonest: because they teach you to do impossible things which you cannot do, you become hypocrites.

Tantra accepts you in your totality, in your wholeness, because tantra says, either accept wholly or reject wholly: there is no in between. A man is a whole — an organic whole. You cannot divide it. You cannot say that "We will not accept 'this' ", because that which you reject is organically joined to that which you accept.

It is like this: my body is there. Someone comes and says, "We accept your blood circulation, but we do not accept the noise of your heart. This continuous beating of your heart we do not accept. We accept your blood circulation. It is okay: it is silent." But my blood circulation is through my heart, and the beating is basically related with blood circulation. It happens because of it. So what am I to do ? My heart and my blood circulation are an organic unity. They are not two things: they are one.

So either accept me totally or reject me totally, but do not try to divide me because then you will create a dishonesty — a deep dishonesty. If you go on condemning my heartbeat, then I will also start condemning my heartbeat. But the blood won't be able to circulate and I cannot be alive without it. So what to do ? Go on as you are, and go on all the time saying something else which you are not, which you cannot be.

It is not difficult to see how heart and blood circulation are related, but it is difficult to see how love and hate are related. They are one. When you love someone, what are you doing ? It is one movement, like breath going out. When you love some-one, what are you doing ? You are going out to meet him. It is a breath going out. When you hate someone, it is a breath coming back.

When you love, you are attracted to someone. When you hate, you are repelled. Attraction and repulsion are two waves of one movement. Attraction and repulsion are not two things; you cannot divide them. You cannot say: "You can breathe in but you cannot breathe out, or you can breathe out but you cannot breathe in. You are allowed only one thing. Either go on breath-ing out or go on breathing in. Do not do both."

How can you breathe in if you are not allowed to breathe out ? And if you are not allowed to hate, you cannot love.

Tantra says that we accept the whole man because man is an organic unity. Man is a deep unity; you cannot discard any-thing. And this is as it should be — because if man is not an organic unity, then in this universe nothing can be an organic unity. Man is the peak of organic wholeness. The stone lying on the street is a unity. The tree is a unity. The flower and the bird are unities. Everyhing is a unity, so why not man? And man is the peak — a great unity, a very complex organic whole. Really, you cannot deny anything.

Tantra says, "We accept you as you are. That does not mean there is no need to change; that doesn't mean that now you have to stop growing. Rather, on the contrary, it means that we accept the base of growth." Now you can grow, but this growth is not going to be a choice. This growth is going to be a choiceless growth.

Look! For example, when a Buddha becomes Enlightened, we can ask, "Where has his anger gone — where?" He was with anger, he was with sex, so where has his sex gone? Where is it that his anger has gone? Where is his greed? We cannot recognize any anger in him now. When he is Enlightened we cannot recognize any anger in him.

Can you recognize the mud in the lotus? The lotus comes from the mud. If you have never seen a lotus growing from the mud and a lotus flower is brought to you, can you conceive that this beautiful lotus flower has come up from the ordinary mud of a pond? This beautiful lotus coming from ugly mud! Can you recognize the mud anywhere in it? It is there, but transformed. Its fragrance is coming from that same ugly mud. The rosiness of the petals is coming from the same ugly mud. If you hide this lotus flower in mud again, within days it will disappear again into its mother. Then again you won't be able to recognize where that lotus has gone. Where? Where is the fragrance? Where are those beautiful petals?

You cannot recognize yourself in Buddha, but he is there. Of course, on a greater and higher plane — transformed. The sex is there, the anger is there, the hate is there. Everything which belongs to man is there. He is a man, but he has come to his ultimate growth. He has become a lotus flower; you cannot recognize the mud. But that doesn't mean that the mud is not there. It is there, but not as mud. It is a higher unity. That is why, in Buddha, you can feel neither hate nor love. That is still more difficult to understand because Buddha appears totally loving — never hating, always silent — never angry. But his silence is different from your silence. It cannot be the same.

What is your silence ? Somewhere Einstein has said that our peace is nothing but a preparation for war. Between two wars we have a gap of peace, but that peace is not really peace. It is only the gap between two wars, so it becomes a cold war. Thus, we have two types of war — hot and cold.

After the Second World War, Russia and America began a cold war. They are not at peace — just in preparation for another war. They are getting ready. Each war disturbs, destroys. You have to get ready again, so you need a gap, an interval. But if wars really disappear from the world completely, then this type of peace which means "cold war" will also disappear, because it always happens between two wars. If war disappears completely, this cold war which we call peace cannot continue.

What is your silence ? Just a preparation between two angers. When you seem at ease what is it ? Are you really relaxed, really at ease, or are you just preparing for another outburst, for another explosion ? Anger is a wastage of energy, so you also need time. When you get angry you cannot get angry again immediately. When you move into the sex act, you cannot move again immediately. You will need time, so you will need a period of *brahmacharya* (celibacy) for at least two or three days. It will depend on your age. This celibacy is not really celibacy. You are only preparing again.

Between two sex acts, there can be no *brahmacharya*. You go on calling the period between two meals a fast. That is why in the morning you say "break-fast", but where is the fast ? You were just preparing. You cannot go on thrusting food into yourself continuously. You have to have a gap, but that gap is not a fast. Really, it is only a preparation for another meal, not a fast.

So when we are silent, it is always between two angers. When we are at ease, it is always between two peaks of tension. When we are celibate, it is only between two sex acts. When we are loving, it is always between two hatreds — remember this.

So when Buddha is silent, do not think this is your silence. When your anger has disappeared, your silence has disappeared also. They both exist together; they cannot be separated. So when Buddha is a *brahmachari* — a celibate, do not think this is your celibacy. When sex has disappeared, *brahmacharya* has also disappeared. They both were part of one thing, so they both have disappeared. With a Buddha a very different being is there such as you cannot conceive. You can only conceive of the dichotomy you know. You cannot conceive of what type of man this is, of what has happened to him.

The whole energy has come to a different level, a different plane of existence. The mud has become a lotus, but it is still there. The mud has not been discarded from the lotus. It has been transformed.

So all of the energies within you are accepted by tantra. Tantra is not for discarding anything whatsoever, but for transformation. And tantra says that the first step is to accept. The first step is very difficult — to accept. You may be getting angry many times every day, but to accept your anger is very difficult. To be angry is very easy; to accept your anger is very difficult. Why? You do not feel so much difficulty in being angry, so why do you feel so much difficulty in accepting it? Getting angry seems not so bad as accepting it. Everyone thinks he is a good man and anger is just momentary. It comes and goes. It doesn't destroy your self-image. You go on remaining good. You say that it just happened. It is not destructive to your ego.

So those who are cunning will repent immediately. They will get angry and they will repent. They will ask for forgiveness. These are the cunning ones. Why do I call them cunning? Because their anger gives a trembling to their self-image. They begin to feel uneasy. They begin to feel, "I get angry? I am so bad that I get angry?" So the image of a good man trembles. He has to try and make it established again. Immediately he says, "This was bad. I will never do it again. Forgive me." By asking for forgiveness his self-image is established again. He is okay — back to his previous state when there was no anger.

197

He has cancelled his anger by asking for forgiveness. He has called himself bad just to remain good.

That is why you can go on for lives together being angry, being sexual, being possessive, being this and that, but never accepting. This is a trick of the mind. Whatsoever you do is just on the periphery. In the center, you remain good. If you accept that "I have anger", in the center you become bad. Then it is not just a question of getting angry. Then it is not momentary. Rather, then anger is part of your constitution. Then it is not that someone irritates you into anger. Even if you are alone, the anger is there. When you are not getting angry, the anger is still there, because anger is your energy, your part.

It is not that sometimes it flares up and then goes off — no! It cannot flare up if it is not always present. You can turn off this light, you can turn on this light: but the current must remain continuously there. If the current is not there, you cannot turn it on and off. The current, the anger current, is always there, the sex current is always there, the greed current is always there. You can turn it on, you can turn it off. In situations you change, but inwardly you remain the same.

"Accepting" means anger is not an act: rather, YOU are anger. Sex is not just an act: YOU are sex. Greed is not just an act: YOU are greed. Accepting this means throwing the self-image. And we all have built beautiful self-images. Everyone has built a beautiful self-image — absolutely beautiful. And whatsoever you are doing never touches it. You go on protecting it. The image is protected, so you feel good. That is why you can become angry, you can become sexual, and you are not disturbed. But if you accept and say, "I am sex, I am anger, I am greed," then your self-image falls down immediately.

Tantra says this is the first step — and the most difficult: to accept whatsoever you are. Sometimes we try to accept, but whenever we accept we again do so in a very calculated way. Our cunningness is deep and subtle, and mind has very subtle ways to deceive. Sometimes you accept and say, "Yes, I am angry." But if you accept this, you accept only when you think of how to transcend anger. Then you accept and say, "Okay, I am angry. Now tell me how to go beyond it." You accept sex only to be non-sexual. Whenever you are trying to be something else, you are able to accept, because your self-image is again maintained by the future.

You are violent and you are striving to be non-violent, so you accept and say, "Okay, I am violent. Today I am violent, but tomorrow I will be non-violent however. How will you become non-violent? You postpone this self-image into the future. You do not think of yourself in the present. You always think in terms of the ideal — of non-violence, love and compassion. Then you are in the future. This present is just to become a past. Your real self is in the future, so you go on identifying yourself with ideals. Those ideals are also ways of not accepting the reality. You are violent: that is the case. And the present is the only thing that is existential; the future is not. Your ideals are just dreams. They are tricks to postpone the mind, to focus the mind somewhere else.

You are violent: this is the case, so accept it. And do not try to be non-violent. A violent mind CANNOT become non-violent. How is this possible? Look deep into it: you are violent, so how can you be non-violent? Whatsoever you do will be done by the violent man — whatsoever! Even while striving to be non-violent, the effort will be done by the violent mind. You are violent, so by trying to be non-violent you will be violent. In the very effort to be non-violent, you will try every type of violence.

That is why you go to these strivers for non-violence: they may not be violent with others, but they are with themselves. They are very violent with themselves — murdering themselves. And the more they get mad against themselves, the more they are celebrated. When they become completely mad, suicidal, then the society says, "These are the sages." But they have only transformed the object of violence — nothing else. They were violent with someone else; now they are violent with themselves. But the violence is there. And when you are violent with someone else, the law can protect, the court can help, the society will condemn you. But when you are violent against yourself, there is no law. No law can protect you against yourself.

When man is aginst himself there is no protection. Nothing can be done. And no one cares because it is your business. No one else is involved in it: it is your business. So-called monks, so-called saints, they are violent against themselves. No one is interested. They say, "Okay! Go on doing. It is your business."

If your mind is one of greed, how can you be non-greedy? The greedy mind will remain greedy. Whatsoever is done by it to go beyond greed is not going to help. Of course, we can create new greeds. Ask a greedy mind, "What are you doing just accumulating wealth? You will die and you cannot take your wealth with you." This is the logic of the so-called religious preachers — that you cannot take your wealth with you. But if someone could take it, then the whole logic will fail. The greedy man feels the logic, of course. He asks, "How can I take wealth with me?" But he really wants to take it. That is why the priest becomes influential. He shows him that it is nonsense to accumulate things which cannot be taken beyond death. He says, "I will teach you how to accumulate things which can be taken. Virtue can be taken, *punya* (good deeds) can be taken, goodness can be taken, but not wealth. So donate the wealth."

But this is an appeal to his greed. This is telling him, "Now we will give you better things which can be carried beyond death." The appeal obtains results. The greedy man feels, "You are right. Death is there and nothing can be done about it, so I must do something which can be carried beyond. I must create some kind of bank balance in the other world also. The world, this bank balance, cannot be with me forever." He goes on talking in these terms.

Go through the scriptures: they appeal to your greed. They say, "What are you doing wasting your time in momentary pleasures!" The emphasis is on "momentary". So find some eternal pleasures; then it is okay. They are not against pleasures. They are just against their being "momentary". Look at the greed!

Sometimes it happens that you may find a non-greedy man who is enjoying momentary pleasures, but you cannot find among your saints a man who is not asking, demanding, for eternal pleasures. The greed in them is even more. You can find a non-greedy man among ordinary men, but you cannot find a non-greedy man among your so-called saints. They also want pleasures, but they are more greedy than you. You are satisfied with momentary pleasures and they are not. Their greed is bigger. Their greed can only be satisfied with eternal pleasures.

Infinite greed asks infinite pleasures — remember this. A finite greed is satisfied with finite pleasure. They will ask you, "What are you doing loving a woman! She is nothing but bones and blood. Look deep into the woman you love. What is she?" They are not against the woman. They are against the bones, against the blood, against the body. But if a woman is of gold, then it is okay. They are asking for women of gold.

They are not in this world, so they create another world. They say, "In heaven there are golden damsels — *apsaras* — who are beautiful and never aging." In the Hindu heaven, *apsaras*, the heavenly girls, remain always at sixteen. They never grow older. They are always sixteen — never less, never more. So what are you doing wasting your time on these ordinary women! Think of heaven. They are not against pleasure. Really, they are against momentary pleasure.

If, through some whim, God gives this world eternal pleasure, your whole edifice of religion will fall down immediately; the whole appeal will be lost. If somehow bank balances can be carried beyond death, no one will be interested in creating bank balances in the other world. So death is a great help to the priests.

A greedy man is always attracted by another greed. If you tell him and convince him that his greed is the cause of his misery and that if he leaves greed he will attain a blissful state, he may try because now you are not really against his greed. You are giving his greed new pastures. He can move into new dimensions of greed.

So tantra says that a greedy mind cannot become non-greedy, a violent mind cannot become non-violent. But this seems very hopeless. If this is the case, then nothing can be done. Then what does tantra stand for? If a greedy mind cannot become non-greedy, and a violent mind non-violent, and a sex-obsessed mind transformed beyond sex, if nothing can be done, then what does tantra stand for? Tantra is not saying that nothing can be done. Something can be done, but the dimension is completely different.

A greedy mind has to understand that it is greedy and accept it — not try to be non-greedy. The greedy mind has to go deep within itself to realize the depth of its greed — not moving away from it, but remaining with it; not moving in ideals — in contradictory ideals, in opposite ideals — but remaining in the present, moving into the greed, knowing the greed, understanding the greed, and not trying to escape from it in any way. If you can remain with your greed, many things will happen. If you can remain with your greed, with your sex, with your anger, your ego will dissolve. This will be the first thing — and what a great miracle it is!

Many people come to me and they go on asking how to be egoless. You cannot be egoless because you have to look at the foundations of your ego to find it. You are greedy and you think you are non-greedy: this is the ego. If you are greedy and you know and accept totally that you are greedy, then where can you allow your ego to stand? If you are angry and you say that you are angry: you do not say it to others, but you feel it deep down, you feel the helplessness, then where can your anger stand? If you are sexual, accept it. Whatsoever is there, accept it.

The non-acceptance of nature creates the ego, the non-acceptance of your suchness — your *tathata*, that which you are. If you accept it, the ego will not be there. If you do not accept it, if you reject it, if you create ideals against it, there will be ego: ideals are the stuff the ego is made of.

Accept yourself. But then you will look like an animal. You will not look like a man because your concept of man is in your ideals. That is why we go on teaching others not to be like animals, and everyone is an animal. What can you do ? You ARE an animal. Accept your animality. And the moment you accept your animality, you have done the first thing to go beyond animals — because no animal knows that it is an animal: only man can know. That is going beyond. You cannot go by denying.

Accept ! When everything is accepted, suddenly you will feel that you have transcended. Who is accepting ? Who accepts the Whole ? That which accepts has gone beyond. If you reject, you remain on the same plane. If you accept, you go beyond. Acceptance is transcendence. And if you accept yourself totally, suddenly you are thrown to your center. Then you cannot move anywhere: you cannot move from your suchness, from your nature, so you are thrown to your center.

All these tantric techniques which we are discussing and trying to understand are different ways of throwing you to your center, of throwing you from the periphery. And you are trying to escape from the center in many ways. Ideals are good escapes. Idealists are the most subtle of egoists.

Many things happen: you are violent and you create an ideal of non-violence. Then you need not go into yourself, into your violence; there is no need. Then this is the only need — to go on thinking about non-violence, reading about non-violence, and trying to practise non-violence. You say to yourself, "Do not touch violence," and you are violent. So you can escape from yourself. You can go to the periphery, but then you will never come to the center. That is one thing.

Secondly, when you create the ideal of non-violence, you can condemn others. Now it becomes very easy. You have the ideal to judge everyone, and you can say to anyone, "You are violent." India has created many ideals. That is why India continuously goes on condemning the whole world. The whole mind of India is condemnatory. It goes on condemning the whole world. Everyone else is violent, only India is non-violent. No one seems to be non-violent here, but the ideal is good for condemning others. It never changes you, but you can condemn others because you have the ideal, the criterion. And whenever you are violent, you can rationalize it. Your violence is an altogether different thing.

These past twenty-five years we have been violent many times, but we have never condemned our violence. We have always defended and rationalized it in beautiful terms. If we are violent in Bengal, in Bangladesh, then we say that it is to help the people there to obtain freedom. If we are violent in Kashmir, it is to help Kashmiris. But, you know, all those who are war-mongering say the same. If America is violent in Vietnam, it is for "those poor people". No one is violent for himself; no one ever has been. We are always violent "to help someone". Even if I kill you, it is for your own good. It is "to help you". And even if you are killed, even if I kill you, just look at "my compassion": Even "for your own good" I can kill you. So go on condemning the whole world.

When India attacked Goa, when India went to war with China, Bertrand Russell criticized Nehru, saying, "Where is your non-violence now ? You are all Gandhi-ites. Where is your non-violence now ?" Nehru replied by banning Bertrand Russell's book in India. The book Russell wrote was banned. This is our non-violent mind.

This was a good discussion. The book should have been distributed free, because he argued beautifully. He said, "you are a violent people. Your non-violence was just political. Your Gandhi was not a sage. He was just a diplomatic mind. And you all talk about non-violence, but when a moment comes for you, you become violent. When others are fighting, you stand on your high altar and you condemn the whole world as violent."

With individuals, with societies, with cultures, with nations, this happens. If you have ideals, you need not transform yourself. You can always hope to be transformed in the future by the ideals themselves. And you can condemn others very easily.

Tantra says to remain with yourself. Whatsoever you are, accept it. Do not condemn yourself, do not condemn others. Condemnation is futile. Energies are not changed by it.

The first step is to accept. Remain with the fact. This is very scientific. Remain with the fact of anger, greed and sex. And know the fact in its total "facticity". Do not just touch it from above, from the surface. Know the fact in its totality, in its total facticity. Move into it to the roots. And, remember, whenever you can move to the roots of anything, you transcend it. If you can know your sex to the very roots, you become the master of it. If you can know your anger to the very roots, you become the master of it. Then anger becomes just instrumental. You can use it.

I remember many things about Gurdjieff. Gurdjieff taught his disciples to be "rightly angry". We have heard about Buddha's words: "right meditation, right thinking and right contemplation." We have heard about Mahavir's teaching of "right vision and right knowledge". Gurdjieff taught "right anger and right greed", and the teaching was influenced by the old tantra tradition. Gurdjieff was condemned very much in the West, because in the West he was a living symbol of tantra.

He would teach "right anger": he would teach you how to be angry totally. If you were angry he would tell you, "Go on. Do not suppress it; let it come out in its totality. Move into it. Become anger. Do not withhold; do not stand aside. Take a deep jump into it. Let your whole body become a flare, a fire."

You have never moved this deeply and you have never seen anyone do so, because everyone is more or less cultured. No one is original; everyone is more or less imitating. No one is original! If you can move in anger totally, you will become just a fire — a burning. The fire will be so deep, the flames will be so deep, that the past and future both will cease immediately. You will become just a present flame. And when your every cell is burning, when every part of the body has become fiery and you have become just anger (not angry), then Gurdjieff will say,

"Now be aware. Do not suppress. Now be aware. Now suddenly be aware of what you have become, of what anger is."

In this momnt of total "presentness", one can become suddenly aware, and you can start laughing at the absurdity of the whole thing, at the foolishness, at the stupidity of the whole thing. But this is not suppression. This is laughter. You can laugh at yourself because you have transcended yourself. Never again will anger be capable of mastering you.

You have known anger in its totality, and still you could laugh and still you could go beyond it. You could see from beyond your anger. Once you have seen its totality, you know what anger is. And now you also know that even if the whole energy transforms into anger, still you can be an observer, a witness. So there is no fear. Remember this: that which is not known always creates fear. That which is dark always creates fear. You are afraid of your own anger.

So people go on saying that we suppress anger because it is not good to be angry: it may hurt others. But that is not the real cause. The real cause is that they are afraid of their anger. If they really get angry, they do not know what may happen. They are afraid of themselves. They have never known anger. It is a very fearful thing hidden inside, so they are afraid of it. That is why they fall in line with the society, with the culture, with the education, and they say, "We must not be angry. Anger is bad. It hurts others."

You are afraid of your anger, you are afraid of your sex. You have never been in sex totally. You have never been in sex so totally that you could have forgotten yourself. You were always there; your mind was always there. And if the mind is there in the sex act, then the act is just pseudo — bogus. The mind must dissolve; you must become just body. There must not be any thinking. If thinking is there, you are divided. Then the sex act is nothing but releasing overflowing energy. It is a release, nothing else. But you are afraid to be totally in sex: that is why you fall in line, why you tow the line with the society that sex is bad. You are afraid !

Why are you afraid? Because if you move into sex totally, you do not know what you can do, you do not know what can happen, you do not know what animal force may come up, you do not know what your unconscious may throw you into. You do not know! Then you will not be the master; you will not be in control. Your self-image may be destroyed. Thus you control the sex act. And the way to control it is to remain in the mind. Let the sex act be there, but local.

Try to understand this "local and general". Tantra says a sex act is local when only your sex center is involved. It is local: it is a local release. The sex center keeps on accumulating energy. When it is overflowing, you have to release it. Otherwise it will create tensions, it will create heaviness. You release it, but it is a local release. Your whole body, your whole self, is not involved. Non-local, total involvement means that every fibre of the body, every cell of the body, whatsoever you are, is in it. Your whole being has become sexual. Not only your sex center: your whole being has become sexual.

But then you are afraid because then anything is possible. And you do not know what can happen because you have never known the totality. You may do certain things of which you cannot conceive.

Your unconscious will explode. You will become not one animal, but many animals, because you have passed through many lives, through many animal bodies. You may start howling; you may start screaming; you may start roaring like a lion. You do not know.

Anything is possible: that creates fear. You need to be in control, so you never lose yourself in anything. That is why you never know anything. And unless you know, you cannot transcend.

Accept, move deep, go to the very roots. This is tantra. Tantra stands for deep experiences. Anything experienced can be transcended; anything suppressed can never be transcended.

This much for today.

9
Techniques For Centering
November 12, 1972, Bombay, India

SUTRAS:

13.   Or, imagine the five-colored circles of the peacock tail to
be your five senses in illimitable space. Now let their beauty
melt within. Similarly, at any point in space or on a wall — until
the point dissolves. Then your wish for another comes true.

14.   Place your whole attention in the nerve, delicate as the
lotus thread, in the center of your spinal column. In such be
transformed.

Man is born with a center, but he remains completely oblivious of it. Man can live without knowing his center, but man cannot be without a center. The center is the link between man and Existence. It is the root. You may not know it; knowledge is not essential for the center to be. But if you do not know it, you will lead a life that is rootless, as if rootless. You will not feel any ground; you will not feel yourself based; you will not feel at home in the universe. You will be homeless.

Of course, the center is there, but by not knowing it, your life will be just a drifting — meaningless, empty, reaching no- where. You will feel as if you are living without life — drifting, just waiting for death. You can go on postponing from one moment to another, but you know very well that that postponing will lead you nowhere. You are just passing time, and that feel- ing of deep frustration will follow you like a shadow. Man is born with a center, but not with the knowledge of the center. The knowledge has to be gained.

You have the center. The center is there; you cannot be with- out it. How can you exist without a center ? How can you exist without a bridge between you and Existence (or, if you like, the word "God") ? You cannot exist without a deep link. You have roots into the Divine. Every moment you live through those roots, but those roots are underground. Just as with any tree, the roots are underground. The tree is unaware of its own roots. You also have roots. That rootedness is your center. When I say

211

man is born with it, I mean it is a possibility that you can become aware of your rootedness. If you become aware, your life becomes actual; otherwise your life will be just like a deep sleep — a dream.

What Abraham Maslow has called "self-actualization" is really nothing but becoming aware of your inner center from where you are linked with the total universe, becoming aware of your roots — that you are not alone, that you are not atomic, that you are part of this Cosmic Whole, that this universe is not an alien world. You are not a stranger: this universe is your home. But unless you find your roots, your center, this universe remains something alien, something foreign.

Sartre says that man is as if he is thrown in the world. Of course, if you do not know your center you will feel a "thrownness", as if you have been thrown in the world. You are an outsider: you do not belong to this world and this world doesn't belong to you. Then fear, then anxiety, then anguish, are bound to result. A man as an outsider in the universe is bound to feel deep anxiety, dread, fear, anguish. His whole life will be just a fight, a struggle, and a struggle which is destined to be a failure. Man cannot succeed because a part can never succeed against the whole.

You cannot succeed against Existence. You can succeed with it, but never against it. And that is the difference between a religious man and a non-religious man. A non-religious man is against the universe, a religious man is with the universe. A religious man feels at home. He doesn't feel he is thrown in the world: he feels he has grown in the world. Remember the difference between being "thrown" and being "grown".

When Sartre says man is thrown in the world, the very word, the very formulation, shows that you do not belong. And the word, the choice of the word "thrown", means that you have been forced without your consent. So this world appears inimical. Then anguish will be the result.

It can be otherwise only if you are not thrown into the world, but you have grown as a part, as an organic part. Really, it would be better to say that you are the universe grown into a particular dimension which we call human. The universe grows in multi-dimensions — in trees, in hills, in stars, in planets: in multi-dimensions. Man is also a dimension of growth. The universe is realizing itself through many, many dimensions. Man is also a dimension along with the height and the peak. No tree can become aware of its roots; no animal can become aware of its roots. That is why there is no anxiety for them.

If you are not aware of your roots, of your center, you can never be aware of your death. Death is only for man. It exists only for man because man can become aware of his roots, aware of his center, aware of his totality and his rootedness in the universe.

If you live without a center, if you feel you are an outsider, then anguish will result. On the contrary, if you feel that you are at home, a growth, a realization of the potentiality of the Existence itself — as if Existence itself has become aware in you, as if it has gained awareness in you, if you feel that way, if you really realize that way, the result will be bliss.

Bliss is the result of an organic unity with the universe and anguish of an enmity. But unless you know the center, you are bound to feel a "thrownness", as if life has been forced upon you. This center which is there, although man is not aware of it, is the concern of these sutras which we will discuss. Before we enter into "Vigyana Bhairava Tantra" and its techniques concerning the center, two or three things more.

One: when man is born, he is rooted in a particular spot, in a particular "chakra" (center), and that is the navel. The Japanese call it *"hara"*; hence, the term *"hara-kiri"*: *"hara-kiri"* means suicide. Literally the term means killing the *"hara"* — the spine, the center. *"Hara"* is the center: destroying the center is the meaning of *"hara-kiri"*. But in a way, we have all committed *"hara-kiri"*. We have not killed the center, but we have forgotten it. Or, we have never remembered it. It is there waiting, and we have been drifting away and away from it.

When a child is born, he is rooted in the navel, in the *"hara"*.

He lives through the *"hara"*. Look at a child breathing: his navel goes up and down. He breathes with the belly, he lives with the belly — not with the head, not with the heart. But by and by he will have to drift away.

First he will develop another center — that is the heart, the center of emotion. He will learn love, he will be loved, and another center will develop. This center is not the real center: this center is a by-product. That is why psychologists say that if a child is not loved, he will never be able to love.

If a child is brought up in a non-loving situation — a situation which is cold, no one to love and give warmth — he himself will never be able in his life to love anyone because the very center will not develop. Mother's love, father's love, family, society, they help to develop a center. That center is a by-product: you are not born with it. So if it is not being helped to grow, it will not grow. Many, many persons are without the love center. They go on talking about love, and they go on believing that they love, but they lack the center, so how can they love ? It is difficult to get a loving mother — very difficult, and rare to get a loving father. Every father, every mother, thinks that he or she loves. It is not so easy. Love is a difficult growth — very difficult. But if love is not there in the beginning for the child, he himself will never be able to love.

That is why the whole humanity lives without love. You go on producing children, but you do not know how to give them a love center. Rather, on the contrary, the more society becomes civilized, the more it forces a third center which is intellect. The navel is the original center. A child is born with it; it is not a by-product. Without it life is impossible, so it is given. The second center is a by-product. If the child gets love, he responds. In this responding, a center grows in him: that is the heart center. The third center is reason, intellect, head. Education, logic and training create a third center: that too is a by-product.

But we live at the third center. The second is almost absent — or even if present, then non-functioning; or even if it functions sometimes, it functions irregularly. But the third center, the head, becomes the basic force in life because the whole life depends on this third center. It is utilitarian. You need it for reason, logic, thinking. So everyone becomes, sooner or later, head oriented: you begin to live in the head.

Head, heart, navel — these are three centers. The navel is the given center, the original one. Heart can be developed, and it is good to develop it for many reasons. Reason is necessary to develop also, but reason must not be developed at the cost of heart — because if reason is developed at the cost of the heart, then you miss the link and you cannot come to the navel again. The development is from reason to existence to being: let us try to understand it in this way.

The center of the navel is in being; the center of the heart is in feeling; the center of the head is in knowing. Knowing is the farthest from being, feeling is nearer. If you miss the feeling center, then it is very difficult to create a bridge between reason and being — really, very difficult. That is why a loving person may realize his at-homeness in the world more easily than a person who lives through intellect.

Western culture has basically emphasized the head center. That is why in the West a deep concern is felt for man. And the deep concern is with his homelessness, his emptiness, his uprootedness. Simone Weil wrote a book, "The Need for Roots." Western man feels uprooted, as if with no roots. The reason is because only the head has become the center. The heart has not been trained; it is missing.

The beating of the heart is not your heart: it is just a physiological function. So if you feel the beating, do not misunderstand that you have a heart. Heart is something else. "Heart" means the capacity to feel; "head" means the capacity to know. "Heart" means the capacity to feel, and "being" means the capacity to be one — to be one with something: the capacity to be one with something.

Religion is concerned with "the being"; poetry is concerned with the heart; philosophy and science are concerned with the head. These two centers, heart and head, are peripheral centers

— not real centers, just false centers. The real center is the navel — the *"hara"*. How to attain it again ? Or, how to Realize it ?

Ordinarily, it sometimes happens — rarely, accidently, it happens — that you come near the *hara*. That moment will become a very deep, blissful moment. For example, in sex sometimes you come near the *hara*, because in sex your mind, your consciousness, moves downwards again. You have to leave your head and fall down. In a deep sexual orgasm, sometimes it happens that you are near your *hara*. That is why so much fascination about sex. It is not really sex which gives you the blissful experience. Really, it is the *hara*.

In falling down toward sex, you pass through the *hara;* you touch it. But for modern man even that has become impossible, because for modern man even sex is a cerebral affair, a mental affair. Even sex has gone into the head; he thinks about it. That is why so many films, so many novels, so much literature, pornography and the like. Man thinks about sex, but that is absurdity. Sex is an experience; you cannot think about it. And if you start thinking about it, it will be more and more difficult to experience it because it is not a concern of the head at all. Reason is not needed.

And the more modern man feels incapable of going deep in sex, the more he thinks about it. It becomes a vicious circle. And the more he thinks about it, the more it becomes cerebral. Then even sex becomes futile. It has become futile in the West, — a repetitive thing — boring. Nothing is gained; you just go on repeating an old habit. And ultimately you feel frustrated — as if you have been cheated. Why ? Because, really, the consciousness is not falling down, back to the center.

Only when passing through the *hara* do you feel bliss. So whatsoever may be the cause, whenever you pass the *hara* you feel bliss. A warrior on the field fighting sometimes passes through the *hara*, but not modern warriors because they are not warriors at all. A person throwing a bomb on a city is sleeping. He is not a warrior; he is not a fighter; he is not a Kshatriya — not Arjuna fighting.

Sometimes when one is on the verge of death one is thrown back to the *hara*. For a warrior fighting with his sword, any moment death becomes possible. Any moment he may be no more. And when fighting with a sword you cannot think. If you think, you will be no more. You have to act without thinking because thinking needs time. If you are fighting with a sword you cannot think. If you think, then the other will win; you will be no more. There is no time to think, and the mind needs time. Because there is no time to think and thinking will mean death, consciousness falls down from the head: it goes to the *hara*. And a warrior has a blissful experience. That is why there is so much fascination about war. Sex and war have been two fascinations and the reason is this: you pass through the *hara*. You pass through it in any danger.

Nietzsche says live dangerously. Why? Because in danger you are thrown back to the *hara*. You cannot think; you cannot work things out with the mind. You have to act immediately.

A snake passes. Suddenly you see the snake and there is a jump. There is no deliberate thinking about it that "There is a snake". There is no syllogism; you do not argue within your mind, "Now there is a snake and snakes are dangerous, so I must jump." There is no logical reasoning like this. If you reason like this, then you will not be alive at all. You cannot reason. You have to act spontaneously, immediately. The act comes first and then comes thinking. When you have jumped, then you think.

In ordinary life, when there is no danger, you think first, then you act. In danger, the whole process is reversed; you act first and then you think. That action coming first without thinking throws you to your original center — the *hara*. That is why the fascination with danger.

You are driving a car faster and faster and faster, and suddenly a moment comes when every moment becomes dangerous. Any moment and there will be no life. In that moment of suspense, when death and life are just as near to each other as possible, two points just near and you in between, the mind stops: you are thrown to the *hara*. That is why so much fascination with cars, driving — fast driving, mad driving. Or, you are gambling and you have put everything you have on a stake: the mind stops; there is danger. The next moment you can become a beggar. The mind cannot function; you are thrown to the *hara*.

Dangers have their appeal because in danger your day-to-day ordinary consciousness cannot function. Danger goes deep. Your mind is not needed; you become a no-mind. YOU ARE ! You are conscious, but there is no thinking. That moment becomes meditative. Really, in gambling, gamblers are seeking a meditative state of mind. In danger, in fight, in duel, in wars, man has always been seeking dangers, meditative states.

A sudden bliss suddenly erupts, explodes in you. It becomes a showering inside. But these are sudden accidental happenings. One thing is certain: whenever you feel blissful, you are nearer the *hara*. That is certain no matter what the cause. The cause is irrelevant. Whenever you pass near the original center, you are filled with bliss.

These sutras are concerned with creating a rootedness in the *hara*, in the center, scientifically, in a planned way — not accidentally, not momentarily, but permanently. You can remain continuously in the *hara*. That can become your rootedness. How to make this so and how to create this are the concerns of these sutras.

Now we will take the first sutra which is another of the "Ways concerning the point or center". First: *"Or, imagine the five-coloured circles of the peacock tail to be your five senses in illimitable space. Now let their beauty melt within. Similarly, at any point in space or a wall — until the point dissolves. Then your wish for another comes true."*

All these sutras are concerned with how to achieve the inner center. The basic mechanism used, the basic technique used, is if you can create a center outside — anywhere: in the mind, in the heart, or even outside on a wall — and if you concentrate totally on it and you bracket out the whole world, you forget the whole world and only one point remains in your consciousness, suddenly you will be thrown to your inner center.

How does it work? First understand it. Your mind is just a vagabond, a wandering. It is never at one point. It is always going, moving, reaching, but never at any point. It goes from one thought to another, from A to B. But it is never at the A; it is never at the B. It is always on the move. Remember this: mind is always on the move, hoping to reach somewhere but never reaching. It cannot reach! The very structure of the mind is movement. It can only move. That is the inherent nature of the mind. The very process is movement. From A to B, from B to C, it goes on and on.

If you stop at A or B or any point, the mind will fight with you. The mind will say move on, because if you stop the mind dies immediately. It can be alive only in movement. The mind means a process. If you stop and do not move, mind suddenly becomes dead. It is no more there; only consciousness remains.

Consciousness is your nature; mind is your activity — just like walking. It is difficult because we think mind is something substantial; we think mind is a substance. It is not. Mind is just an activity. So it is really better to call it "minding" than mind. It is a process just like walking. Walking is a process. If you stop, there is no walking. You cannot say that now the walking is sitting. There is no walking. If you stop, there is no walking. The walking has stopped. You have legs, but no walking. Legs can walk. But if you stop, then legs will be there but there will be no walking.

Consciousness is like legs — your nature. Mind is like walking — just a process. When consciousness moves from one place to another, this process is mind. When consciousness moves from A to B, B to C, this movement is mind. If you stop movement, there is no mind. You are conscious, but there is no mind. You have legs, but no walking. Walking is a function, an activity; mind is also a function, an activity.

If you stop at any point, the mind will struggle. The mind will say, "Go on!" The mind will try in every way to push you forward or backward or anywhere, but, "Go on !" Anywhere will do, but do not stay at a point.

If you insist and if you do not obey the mind, it is difficult because you have always obeyed. You have never ordered the mind; you have never been masters. You cannot be because, really, you have never disidentified yourself from the mind. You think you are the mind. This fallacy that "you are the mind" gives the mind total freedom, because then there is no one to master it, to control it. There is no one ! Mind itself becomes the master. It may become the "master", but that mastery is just seemingly so. Try once and you can break that "mastery". It is false.

Mind is just a slave pretending to be the master, but it has pretended so long, for lives and lives, that even the master believes that the slave is the master. That is just a belief. Try the contrary and you will know that that belief was totally unfounded.

This first sutra says, "Imagine the five-coloured circle of the peacock tail to be your five senses in illimitable space. Now let their beauty melt within." Think that your five senses are five colours, and those five colours are filling the whole space. Just imagine your five senses are five colours — beautiful colours, alive, extended into infinite space. Then move within with those colours. Move within and feel a center where all these five colours are meeting within you. This is just imagination, but it helps. Just imagine these five colours penetrating within you and meeting at a point.

Of course, these five colours will meet on a point: the whole world will dissolve. In your imagination there are only five colours, just like around the tail of a peacock, spread all over space, going deep within you, meeting at a point. Any point will do, but the *hara* is the best. Think that they are meeting at your navel — that the whole world has become colours, and those colours are meeting your navel at a point. See that point, concentrate on that point, and concentrate until the point dissolves. It dissolves ! If you concentrate on the point it dissolves, because it is just imagination. Remember, whatsoever we have done is imagination. If you concentrate on it, it will dissolve. And when the point dissolves, you are thrown to your center.

The world has dissolved. There is no world for you. In this meditation there is only colour. You have forgotten the whole world; you have forgotten all the objects. You have chosen only five colours. Choose any five colours. This is particularly for those who have a very keen eye, a very deep colour sensation. This meditation will not be helpful to everyone. Unless you have a painter's eye, a colour consciousness, unless you can imagine colour, it is difficult.

Have you ever observed that your dreams are colourless ? Only one person in a hundred is capable of seeing coloured dreams. You see just black and white. Why ? The whole world coloured, and your dreams are colourless. If some one of you remembers that his dreams are coloured, this meditation is for him. If someone remembers even sometimes that he sees colours in his dreams, then this meditation will be for him. It is for him !

If you say to a person who is insensitive to colour, "Imagine the whole space filled with colours," he will not be able to imagine. Even if he will try to imagine, if he will think, "Red !" he will see the word "red": he will not see the colour. He will say, "Green !" and the word "green" will be there, but there will be no greenness.

So if you have a colour sensitivity, then try this method. There are five colours. The whole world is just colours and those five colours are meeting in you. Deep down somwhere in you, those five colours are meeting. Concentrate on that point, and go on concentrating on it. Do not move from it: remain at it. Do not allow the mind; do not try to think about green and red and yellow and about colours. Do not think. Just see them meeting in you. Do not think about them ! If you think, the mind has moved. Just be filled with colours meeting in you, and then at the meeting point, concentrate. Do not think ! Concentration is not thinking; it is not contemplation.

If you are really filled with colours and you have become just a rainbow, a peacock, and the whole space is filled with colours, it will give you a deep feeling of beauty. But do not think about it; do not say it is beautiful. Do not move in thinking. Concentrate on the point where all these colours are meeting and go on concentrating on it. It will disappear, it will dissolve, because it is just imagination. And if you force concentration, imagination cannot remain there. It will dissolve.

The world has dissolved already; there were only colours. Those colours were your imagination. Those imaginative colours were meeting at a point. That point, of course, was imaginary, and now, with deep concentration, that point will dissolve. Where are you now? Where will you be? You will be thrown to your center.

Objects have dissolved through imagination. Now imagination will dissolve through concentration. You alone are left as a subjectivity. The objective world has dissolved; the mental world has dissolved. You are there only as pure consciousness.

That is why this sutra says, "At any point in space or on a wall..." This will help. If you cannot imagine colours, then any point on the wall will help. Take anything just as an object of concentration. If it is inner, it is better, but, again, there are two types of personalities. For those who are introvert, it will be easy to conceive of all the colours meeting within. But there are extroverts who cannot conceive of anything within. They can imagine only the outside: their minds move only on the outside; they cannot move in. For them there is nothing like innerness.

The English philosopher David Hume has said, "Whenever I go in, I never meet any Self. All that I meet are only reflections of the outside world — a thought, some emotion, some feeling. I never meet the innerness: I only meet the outside world reflected in." This is the extrovert mind par excellence, and David Hume is one of the most extrovert minds.

So if you cannot feel anything within, and if the mind asks what does this innerness mean — how to go in, then try any point on the wall instead. There are persons who come to me and ask how to go in. It is a problem, because if you know only outgoingness, if you know only outward movements, it is difficult to imagine how to go in.

If you are an extrovert then do not try this point inside: try it outside. The same will be the result. Make a dot on the wall; concentrate on it. Then you will have to concentrate on it with open eyes. If you are creating a center inside, a point within, then you will have to concentrate with closed eyes.

Make a point on a wall and concentrate on it. The real thing happens because of concentration, not because of the point. Whether it is out or in is irrelevant. It depends on you. If you are looking at the outside wall, concentrating on it, then go on concentrating until the point dissolves. That has to be noted: "until the point dissolves!" Do not blink your eyes, because blinking gives a space for the mind to move again. Do not blink, because then the mind starts thinking. It becomes a gap. In the blinking, the concentration is lost. So no blinking.

You might have heard about Bodhidharma, one of the greatest Masters of meditation in the whole history of humankind. A very beautiful story is reported about him. He was concentrating on something — something outward. His eyes would blink and the concentration would be lost, so he tore his eyelids. This is a beautiful story: he tore his eyelids, threw them away and concentrated. After a few weeks, he saw some plants growing on the spot where he had thrown his eyelids. This anecdote happened on a mountain in China, and the mountain's name is "Tah" or "Ta". Hence, the name "tea". Those plants which were growing became tea, and that is why tea helps you to be awake.

When your eyes are blinking and you are falling down into sleep, take a cup of tea. Those are Bodhidharma's eyelids. That is why Zen monks consider tea to be sacred. Tea is not any ordinary thing. It is sacred — Bodhidharma's eyelids. In Japan they have tea ceremonies, and every house has a tearoom, and the tea is served with religious ceremony; it is sacred. Tea has to be taken in a very meditative mood.

Japan has created beautiful ceremonies around tea drinking. They will enter the tearoom as if they are entering a temple. Then the tea will be made, and everyone will sit silently listening to the samovar bubbling. There is the steaming, the noise, and everyone just listening. It is no ordinary thing — Bodhidharma's eyelids. And because Bodhidharma was trying to be awake with open eyes, tea helps. Because the story happened on the mountain of "Tah", it is called tea. Whether true or untrue, this anecdote is beautiful.

If you are concentrating outwardly, then non-blinking eyes will be needed, as if you have no more eyelids. That is the meaning of throwing the eyelids. You have only eyes without eyelids to close them. Concentrate until the point dissolves: it dissolves! If you persist, if you insist and do not allow the mind to move, the point dissolves. And when the point dissolves, if you were concentrated on the point and there was only this point for you in the world, if the whole world had dissolved already, if only this point remained and now the point also dissolves, then the consciousness cannot move anywhere; there is no object to move to. All the dimensions are closed. The mind is thrown to itself, the consciousness is thrown to itself, and you enter the center.

So whether in or out, within or without, concentrate until the point dissolves. This point will dissolve for two reasons. If it is within, it is imaginary: it will dissolve. If it it outside, it is not imaginary: it is real. You have made a dot on the wall and have concentrated. Then why will this dot dissolve? One can understand it dissolving inside: it was not there at all; you just imagined it. But on the wall it is there, so why will it dissolve?

It dissolves for a certain reason. If you concentrate on a point, really, the point is not really going to dissolve: the mind dissolves. If you are concentrating on an outer point, the mind cannot move. Without movement it cannot live. It dies; it stops. And when the mind stops, you cannot be related with anything outward. Suddenly all bridges are broken, because mind is the bridge. When you are concentrating on a point on the wall, constantly your mind is jumping from you to the point, from the point to you, from you to the point. There is a constant jumping; there is a process.

When the mind dissolves, you cannot see the point because, really, you never see the point through the eyes: you see the point through the mind AND through the eyes. If the mind is not there, the eyes cannot function. You may go on staring at the wall, but the point will not be seen. The mind is not there; the bridge is broken. The point is real: it is there. When the mind will come back, you will see it again; it is there. But now you cannot see it. And when you cannot see, you cannot move out. Suddenly, you are at your center.

This centering will make you aware of your existential roots. You will know from where you are joined to the Existence. In you, there is a point which is related with the total Existence — which is one with it. Once you know this center, you know you are at home. This world is not alien. You are not an outsider. You are an insider. You belong to the world. There is no need of any struggle; there is no fight. There is no inimical relationship between you and the Existence. The Existence becomes your mother.

It is the Existence that has come into you and that has become aware. It is the Existence that has flowered in you. This feeling, this Realization, this happening, and there can be no anguish again.

Then bliss is not a phenomenon; it is not something that happens and then goes. Then blissfulness is your very nature. When one is rooted in one's center, blissfulness is natural. One happens to be blissful, and by and by one even becomes unaware that one is blissful because awareness needs contrast. If you are miserable, then you can feel it when you are blissful. When misery is no more, by and by you forget misery completely. And you forget your bliss also. And only when you can forget your bliss also are you really blissful. Then it is natural. As stars are shining, as rivers are flowing, so are you blissful. Your very being is blissful. It is not something that has happened to you: now it Is YOU.

With the second sutra, the mechanism is the same, the scientific base is the same, the working structure is the same: *"Place your whole attention in the nerve, delicate as the lotus thread, in the center of your spinal column. In such be transformed."*

"Place your whole attention in the nerve, delicate as the lotus thread, in the center of your spinal column": For this sutra, for this technique of meditation, one has to close his eyes and visualize his spinal column, his backbone. It is good to look in some physiology book for the structure of the body, or to go to some medical college or hospital and look at the structure of the body. Then close your eyes and visualize your backbone. Let the backbone be straight, erect. Visualize it, see it, and just in the middle of it visualize a nerve, delicate as the lotus thread, running in the center of your spinal column. ". . .In such be transformed."

If you can, concentrate on the spinal column, and then on a thread in the middle of it — on a very delicate nerve like a "lotus thread" running through it. Concentrate on it, and this very concentration throws you to your center. Why?

The spinal column is the base of your whole body structure. Everything is joined to it. Really, your brain is nothing but one pole of your spinal column. Physiologists say it is nothing but a spinal column growth. Your brain is really a growth of your spinal column.

Your spine is connected with your whole body. Everything is connected to it. That is why it is called the spine, the base. In this spine there is really a thread-like thing, but physiology will not say anything about it because it is not material. In this spine, just in the middle, there is a silver cord — a very delicate nerve. It is not really a nerve in the physiological sense. You cannot operate and find it; it will not be found there.

But in deep meditation it is seen. It is there: it is non-material. It is energy, not matter. And, really, that energy cord in your spinal column is your life. Through that you are related to the invisible Existence, and through that also you are related to the visible. That is the bridge between the invisible and the visible. Through that thread you are related to the body, and through that thread also you are related to your soul.

First visualize the spine — and you will feel very strange. If you try visualizing the spine, you will be able to visualize it. And if you go on endeavouring, then it will not be just your imagination. You will become capable of seeing your spinal column.

I was working with a seeker on this technique. I gave him a picture of body structure to concentrate upon so that he would begin to feel how the spinal column can be visualized inside. Then he started. Within a week he came and said, "This is very strange. I tried to see the picture you gave me, but many times that picture disappeared and I saw a different spine. It is not exactly like the picture you gave to me."

So I told him, "Now you are on the right path. Forget that picture completely, and go on seeing through the spine that has become visible to you."

Man can see his own body structure from within. We have not tried it because it is very, very fearful, loathsome; because when you see your bones, blood, veins, you become afraid. So, really, we have completely blocked our minds from seeing within. We see the body from without as if someone else is looking at the body. It is just as if you go outside this room and look at it. Then you know the outer walls. Come in and look at the house: then you can look at the inner walls. You see your body from outside as if you are somebody else seeing your body. You have not seen your body from inside. We are capable of it, but because of this fear it has become a strange thing.

Indian yoga books talk about many things of the body which are found to be exactly right by new scientific research, and science is unable to explain this. How could they know ? Surgery and knowledge of the inside of the human body are very recent developments. How could they know of all the nerves, of all the centers, of all the inner structures? They knew even about the latest findings: they have talked about them; they have worked upon them. Yoga has been always aware about all the basic, significant things in the body. But they were not working, they were not dissecting bodies, so how could they know?

Really, there is another way of looking at your own body — from within. If you can concentrate within, suddenly you begin to see your body — the inner lining of the body. This is good for those who are deeply body oriented. If you feel yourself a materialist, if you feel yourself to be nothing but body, this technique will be very helpful for you. If you feel yourself to be a body, if you are a believer in Charvak or in Marx, if you believe that man is nothing but a body, this technique will be very helpful for you. Then go and see the bone structure of man.

In the old tantra and yoga schools they used many bones. Even now a tantric will always be found with some bones, with a man's skull. Really, that is to help concentration from inside. First he concentrates on that skull, then he closes his eyes and tries to visualize his own skull. He goes on trying to see the outer skull inside, and by and by he begins to feel his own skull. His consciousness begins to be focused. That outer skull, the concentration on it and the visualization, are just helps. Once you are focused inside, you can move from your toe to your head. You can move inside and it is a great universe. Your small body is a great universe.

This sutra uses the spinal column because within the spinal column there is the thread of life. This is why so much insistence on a straight backbone: because if the backbone is not straight you will not be capable of seeing the inner thread. It is very delicate, it is very subtle. It is minute. It is an energy flow. So if the spinal column is straight, absolutely straight, only then can you have glimpses of that thread.

But our spinal columns are not straight. Hindus have tried to make everyone's spinal column straight from the very childhood. Their ways of sitting, their ways of sleeping, their ways of walking were all based, basically, on a straight spinal column.

If the spinal column is not straight, then it is very difficult to see the inner core. It is delicate — and, really, it is not material. It is immaterial; it is a force. When the spinal column is absolutely straight, that thread-like force is seen easily.

"...In such be transformed": And once you can feel, concentrate and realize this thread, you will be filled with a new light. The light will be coming from your spinal column. It will spread all over your body; it may even go beyond your body. When it goes beyond,, the auras are seen.

Everyone has an aura, but ordinarily your auras are nothing but shadows with no light in them — just dark shadows around you. And those auras reflect your every mood. When you are angry, then your auras become as if blood-filled: they become filled with a red angry expression. When you are sad, dim, down, then your auras are filled with the dark threads, as if you are just near death — everything dead, heavy.

When this spinal column thread is realized, your auras become "enlightened". So a Buddha, a Mahavir, a Krishna, a Christ, are not painted with auras just as decorations. Those auras exist. Your spinal column begins to throw light. Within you become enlightened; your whole body becomes a body of light. Then it penetrates the outer. So, really, for a Buddha, for anyone who is enlightened, there is no need to ask anyone what he is. The aura shows everything. And when someone becomes enlightened the Teacher knows it, because the aura reveals everything.

I will tell you one story: Hui Neng, a Chinese Master, was working under his Guru. But when Hui Neng went to his Guru, the Guru said, "For what have you come here ? There is no need to come to me." Hui Neng couldn't understand. Hui Neng thought that he was not yet ready to be accepted, but the Teacher was seeing something else. He was seeing his growing aura. He was saying this: "Even if you do not come to me, the thing is bound to happen sooner or later, anywhere. You are already in it, so there is no need to come to me."

But Hui Neng said, "Do not reject me." So the Guru accepted him and told him just to go behind in the kitchen of the monastery. It was a big monastery of five hundred monks. The Guru said to Hui Neng, "Just go behind the monastery and help in the kitchen, and do not come again to me. Whenever it will be needed, I will come to you."

No meditation was given to Hui Neng, no scriptures to read, study or meditate upon. Nothing was taught to him. He was just thrown into the kitchen. The whole monastery was working. There were pundits, scholars, and there were meditators, and there were yogis, and the whole monastery was agog. Everyone was working and this Hui Neng was just cleaning rice and doing kitchen work.

Twelve years passed. Hui Neng didn't go again to the Guru because it was not allowed. He waited, he waited, he waited. He simply waited. He was just taken as a servant. Scholars would come, meditators would come, and no one would even pay any attention to him. And there were big scholars in the monastery.

And then the Teacher declared that his death was near, and now he wanted to appoint someone to function in his place, so he said, "Those who think they are Enlightened should compose a small poem of four lines. And in those four lines you should put all that you have gained. And if I approve any poems and indicate that the lines show that Enlightenment has happened, I will choose someone as my successor."

There was a great scholar in the monastery, so no one attempted because everyone knew that he was going to win. He was a great knower of scriptures, so he composed four lines. Those four lines were just like this — the meaning of it was like this: "Mind is like a mirror, and dust gathers on it. Clean the dust, and you are Enlightened."

But even this great scholar was afraid because the Teacher would know. He already knows who is Enlightened and who is not, though all he has written is beautiful. It is the very essence of all the scriptures. "Mind is like a mirror, and dust gathers on it. Remove the dust, and you are Enlightened." This was the whole gist of all the Vedas, but he knew that was all that it was. He had not known anything, so he was afraid. He didn't go directly to the Teacher, but in the night he went to the hut — to his Teacher's hut, and wrote all the four lines on the wall without signing — without any signature. In this way, if the Guru approved and would say, "Okay, this is right," then he would say, "I have written them." If he would say, "No! Who has written these lines?" then he would keep mum, he thought.

But the Teacher approved. In the morning the Teacher said, "Okay!" He laughed and said, "Okay! The man who has written this is an Enlightened One." So the whole monastery began to talk about it. Everyone knew who had written it. They were discussing and appreciating, and the lines were beautiful — really beautiful. Then some monks came to the kitchen. They were drinking tea and they were talking, and Hui Neng was there serving them. He heard what had happened. The moment he heard those four lines, he laughed. So someone asked, "Why are you laughing, you fool? You do not know anything. For twelve years you have been serving in the kitchen. Why are you laughing?"

No one had even heard him laugh before. He was just taken as an idiot who would not even talk. So he said, "I cannot write, and I am not an Enlightened One either, but these lines are wrong. So if someone comes with me, I will compose four lines. If someone comes with me, he can write it on the wall. I cannot write; I do not know writing."

So someone followed just as joke. A crowd came there and Hui Neng said, "Write: 'There is no mind and there is no mirror, so where can the dust gather? One who knows this is Enlightened.' "

But the Teacher came out and he said, "You are wrong" to Hui Neng. Hui Neng touched his feet and returned back to his kitchen.

In the night when everyone was asleep, the Teacher came to Hui Neng and said, "You are right, but I could not say so before those idiots — and they are learned idiots. And if I had said that you are appointed my successor, they would kill you. So escape from here! You are my successor, but do not tell it to anyone. And I knew this the day you came. Your aura was growing: that was why no meditation was given to you. There was no need. You were already in meditation. And these twelve years silence — not doing anything, not even meditation, emptied you completely of your mind, and the aura has become full. You have become a 'full moon'. But escape from here! Otherwise they will kill you.

"You have been here for twelve years, and the light has been constantly spreading from you. But no one observed it, and they have been coming to the kitchen. Everyone has been coming to the kitchen every day — thrice, four times. Everyone passes from here: that is why I posted you at the kitchen. But no one has recognized your aura, so you escape from here."

When the spinal column thread is touched, seen, realized, an aura begins to grow around you: "... In such be transformed." Be filled with that light and be transformed. This is also a centering — a centering in the spinal column. If you are body oriented, this technique will help you. If you are not body oriented, it is very difficult. It will be very difficult to visualize from the inside. Then to look at your body from the inside will be difficult.

This sutra will be more helpful for women than for men. They are more body oriented. They live more in the body; they feel more. They can visualize the body more. Women are more bodily than men. But for anyone who can feel the body — who feels the body, who can visualize, who can close his eyes and feel his body from within, this technique will be very helpful for him.

Then visualize your spinal column, and then in the middle a silver cord running through it. First it may look like imagination, but by and by you will feel that imagination has disappeared and your mind has become focused on that spinal column. And then you will see your own spine. And the moment you see the inner core, suddenly you will feel an explosion of the light within you.

Sometimes this can also happen without any effort. It happens sometimes. Again, in a deep sex act it sometimes happens. Tantra knows: In a deep sex act your whole energy becomes concentrated near the spie. Really, in a deep sex act the spine begins to discharge electricity. And sometimes, even if you touch the spine, you will get a shock. And if the intercourse is very deep and very loving and long; really, if the two lovers are just in a deep embrace — silent, non-moving, just being filled with each other, just remaining in a deep embrace; it happens. It has happened many times that a dark room will suddenly become filled with light, and both bodies will be surrounded with a blue aura.

Many, many such cases have happened. Even in some of your experiences it may have happened, but you may not have noticed that in a dark room, in deep love, suddenly you feel a light around both of your bodies, and that light spreads and fills the whole room. Many times it has happened that suddenly things drop from the table in the room without any visible cause. And now psychologists say that in a deep sex act, electricity is discharged. That electricity can have many effects and impacts. Things may suddenly drop, move or be broken, and even photographs have been taken in which light is visible. But that light is always concentrated around the spinal column.

So sometimes, in a deep sex act also (and tantra knows this well and has worked on it), you may become aware — if you can look within to the thread running in the middle of the spinal column. And tantra has used the sex act for this realization, but then the sex act has to be totally different, the quality has to be different. It is not something to be gotten over with; it is not something to be done for a release; it is not something to be finished hurriedly; it is not a bodily act then. Then it is a deep spiritual communion. Really, through two bodies it is a deep meeting of two innernesses, of two subjectivities penetrating each other.

So I will suggest to you to try this technique, when in a deep sex act. It will be easier. Just forget about sex. When in a deep embrace, remain inside. Forget the other person also. Just go inside and visualize your spinal column. It will be easier, because then more energy is flowing near the spinal column. And the thread is more visible because you are silent, because your body is at rest. Love is the deepest relaxation, but we have made love also a great tension. We have made it an anxiety, a burden.

In the warmth of love, filled, relaxed, close your eyes. But men ordinarily do not close their eyes. Ordinarily, women do close their eyes. That is why I said that women are more body oriented while men are not. In a deep embrace in the act of sex, women will close their eyes. Really, they cannot love with open eyes. With closed eyes, they feel the body more from within.

Close your eyes and feel your body. Relax. Concentrate on the spinal column. And this sutra says very simply: "In such be transformed." And you will be transformed through it.

Enough for today.

10
Fulfillment Through Becoming Centered

November 13, 1972, Bombay, India

QUESTIONS:

1. Is self-actualization a basic need?
2. Explain contemplation, concentration and meditation.
3. How does the training for the development of the navel center differ from that of the heart and head centers?
4. Are all Enlightened Ones navel centered?

There are many questions. The first: *"Is self-actualization a basic need of man?"*

First, try to understand what is meant by "self-actualization". A. H. Maslow has used this term "self-actualization". Man is born as potentiality. He is not really actual — just potential. Man is born as a possibility, not as an actuality. He may become something. He may attain actualization of his potentiality or he may not attain. The opportunity may be used or it may not be used — and nature is not forcing you to become actual. You are free. You can choose to become actual; you can choose not to do anything about it. Man is born as a seed. Thus, no man is born fulfilled — just with the possibility of fulfillment.

If that is the case (and that is the case), then self-actualization becomes a basic need — because unless you are fulfilled, unless you become what you can be or what you are meant to be, unless your destiny is fulfilled, unless you actually attain, unless your seed becomes a fulfilled tree, you will feel that you are missing something. And everyone is feeling, EVERYONE is feeling, that he is missing something. That feeling of missing is really because of this, that you are not yet actual.

It is not really that you are missing riches or position, prestige or power. Even if you get whatsoever you demand — riches, power, prestige, anything — you will feel this constant sense of something missing within you, because this "something missing" is not related with anything outward. It is related with your inner growth. Unless you become fulfilled, unless you come to a realization, a flowering, unless you come to an inner satisfaction in which you feel, "Now this is what I was meant to be," this sense of something missing will be felt. And you cannot destroy this feeling of something missing by anything else.

So self-actualization means a person who has become what he was to become. He was born as a seed and now he has flowered. He has come to the complete growth, an inner growth, to the inner end. The moment you feel that all your potentialities have become actual, you will feel the peak of life, of love, of existence itself.

Abraham Maslow who has used this term "self-actualization" has also coined another term: "peak experience." When one attains to oneself, he reaches a peak — a peak of bliss. Then there is no hankering after anything. He is totally content with himself. Now nothing is lacking: there is no desire, no demand, no movement. Whatsoever he is, he is totally content with himself. Self-actualization becomes a peak experience, and only a self-actualized person can attain peak experiences. Then whatsoever he touches, whatsoever he is doing or not doing, even just existing, is a peak experience for him; just to be is blissful. Then bliss is not concerned with anything outside. It is just a by-product of the inner growth.

A Buddha is a self-actualized person: that is why we picture Buddha, Mahavir and others — that is why we have made sculptures, pictures, depictions of them — sitting on a fully blossomed lotus. That fully blossomed lotus is the peak of flowering inside. Inside they have flowered and have become fully blossomed. That inner flowering gives a radiance, a constant showering of bliss from them. All those who come even within their shadows, all those who come near them, feel a silent milieu around them.

There is an interesting report about Mahavir. It is a myth, but myths are beautiful and they say much which cannot be said otherwise. It is reported that when Mahavir would move, all around him, in an area of about 24 miles, all flowers would bloom. Even if it was not the season for the flowers, they would bloom. This is simply a poetic expression, but even if one was not self-actualized, if one were to come in contact with Mahavir his flowering would become infectious, and one would feel an inner flowering in oneself also. Even if it was not the right season for a person, even if he was not ready, he would reflect. He would feel an echo. If Mahavir would be near someone, that person would feel an echo within himself, and he would have a glimpse of what he could be.

Self-actualization is the basic need. And when I say "basic", I mean that if all your needs are fulfilled, all except self-realization, self-actualization, you will feel unfulfilled. On the contrary, if self-actualization happens and nothing is fulfilled, still you will feel a deep, total fulfilment. That is why Buddha was a beggar, but yet an emperor.

Buddha came to Kashi when he became Enlightened. The king of Kashi came to see him and he asked, "I do not see anything with you. You are just a beggar, but yet I feel myself a beggar in comparison to you. You do not have anything, but the way you walk, the way you look, the way you laugh, makes it seem as if the whole world is your kingdom — and you have nothing visible — nothing ! So where is the secret of your power ? You look like an emperor. Really, no emperor has ever looked like that — as if the whole world belongs to you. You are the king, but where is your power, the source ?"

So Buddha said, "It is in me. My power, my source of power, whatsoever you feel around me, is really within me. I do not have anything except myself, but it is enough. I am fulfilled; now I do not desire anything. I have become desireless."

Really, a self-actualized person will become desireless. Remember this: ordinarily we say that if you become desireless, you will know yourself. The contrary is more true. If you know yourself, you will become desireless. And the emphasis of tantra is not on being desireless, but on becoming self-actualized. Then desirelessness follows. "Desire" means you are not fulfilled within. You are missing something, so you hanker after it. You go on from one desire to another in search of fulfillment. That search never ends because one desire creates another desire. Really, one desire creates ten desires. If you go in search of a desireless state of bliss through desires, you will never reach. But if you try something else — methods of self-actualization, methods of realizing your inner potentiality, of making them actual — then the more you will become actual and the less and less desires will be felt, because, really, they are felt only because you are empty inside. When you are not empty within, desiring ceases.

What to do about self-actualization? Two things have to be understood. One: self-actualization doesn't mean that if you become a great painter or a great musician or a great poet you will be self-actualized. Of course, a part of you will be actualized, and even that gives much contentment. If you have a potentiality of being a good musician, and if you fulfill it and you become a musician, a part of you will be fulfilled — but not the total. The remaining humanity within you will remain unfulfilled. You will be lopsided. One part will have grown, and the remaining will have remained just like a stone hanging on your neck.

Look at a poet. When he is in his poetic mood he looks like a Buddha: he forgets himself completely. The ordinary man in the poet is as if no more there. So when a poet is in his mood, he has a peak — a partial peak. And sometimes poets have glimpses which are only possible with Enlightened Buddha-like minds. A poet can speak like Buddha. For example, Khalil Gibran: he speaks like a Buddha, but he is not a Buddha. He is a poet — a great poet.

So if you see Khalil Gibran through his poetry, he looks like Buddha, Christ or Krishna. But if you go and meet the man Khalil Gibran, he is just ordinary. He talks about love so beautifully, even a Buddha may not talk so beautifully. But Buddha knows love with his total being. Khalil Gibran knows love in his poetic flight. When he is on his poetic flight, he has glimpses of love — beautiful glimpses. He expressed them with rare insight. But if you go and see the real Khalil Gibran, the man, you will feel a disparity. The poet and the man are far apart. The poet seems to be something which happens to this man sometimes, but this man is not the poet.

That is why poets feel that when they are creating poetry, someone else is creating; they are not creating. They feel as if they have become instruments of some other energy, some other force. They are no more. This feeling comes because, really, their totality is not actualized — only a part of it is, a fragment.

You have not touched the sky. Only your one finger has touched the sky, and you remain rooted on the earth. Sometimes you jump, and for a moment you are not on the earth. You have deceived gravity. But the next moment you are on the earth again. If a poet is fulfilled, he will have glimpses — partial glimpses. If a musician is fulfilled, he will have partial glimpses.

It is said of Beethoven that when he was on the stage, at the rostrum, he was a different man, altogether different. Goethe has said that when Beethoven was on stage directing his group, his orchestra, he looked like a god. It could not be said that he was an ordinary man. He was not a man at all: he was superhuman. The way he looked, the way he raised his hands, was all superhuman. But when back from the stage he was just an ordinary man. The man on the stage seemed to be possessed by something else, as if Beethoven was no more there and some other force had entered in him. Back down from the stage, he was again Beethoven, the man.

Because of this, poets, musicians, great artists, creative people, are more tense: because they have two types of being. Ordinary man is not so tense because he always lives in one. He lives on earth, but poets, musicians, great artists they jump. They go beyond gravity. In certain moments they are not on this earth, they are not part of humanity. They become part of the Buddha world — the land of the Buddhas. Then again they are back here. They have two points of existence; their personalities are split.

So every creative artist, every great artist, is in a certain way insane. The tension is so much! The rift, the gap between these two types of existences, is so great — unbridgeably great! Sometimes he is just an ordinary man; sometimes he becomes Buddha-like. Between these two points he is divided, but he has glimpses.

When I say "self-actualization", I do not mean that you should become a great poet or you should become a great musician. I mean that you should become a total man. I do not say a great man because a great man is always partial. Greatness in anything is always partial. One moves and moves and moves in one direction, and in all other dimensions, all other directions, one remains the same — lopsided.

When I say become a total man, I do not mean become a great man. I mean create a balance, be centered, be fulfilled as a man — not as a musician, not as a poet, not as an artist, but fulfilled as a man. What does it mean to be fulfilled as a man? A great poet is a great poet because of great poetry. A great musician is great because of great music. A great man is a great man because of certain things he has done: he may be a great hero. A great man is partial in any direction. Greatness is partial — fragmentary. That is why great men have to face more anguish than ordinary men.

What is a total man? What is meant by being a whole man — a total man? It means, firstly, be centered, be "centralized." Do not exist without a center. This moment you are something, the next moment something else. People come to me, and I ask them generally, "Where do you feel your center — in the heart, in the mind, in the navel — where? In the sex center? Where? Where do you feel your center?"

Generally, they say, "Sometimes I feel it in the head, sometimes in the heart, sometimes I do not feel it at all." So I tell them to close their eyes before me and feel it just now. This is the majority; in the majority of cases this happens. They say, "Just now, for a moment, I feel that I am centered in the head." But the next moment they are not there. They say, "I am in the heart." And the next moment the center has slipped. It is somewhere else — at the sex center or somewhere else.

Really, you are not centered. You are momentarily centered. Each moment has its own center, so you go on shifting. When mind is functioning you feel that head is the center. When you are in love, you feel it is the heart. When you are not doing anything particularly, you are confused. Where the center is you cannot find out, because you can find this out only when you are working, doing something. Then a particular part of the body becomes the center. But YOU are not centered. If you are not doing anything, you cannot find where your center of being is.

A total man is centered. Whatsoever he is doing, he remains in the center. If his mind is functioning, he is thinking. Thinking goes on in the head, but he remains centered in the navel. The center is never missed. He uses head, but he never moves to the head. He uses heart, but he never moves to the heart. All these things become instruments, and he remains centered.

Secondly, he is balanced. Of course, when one is centered one is balanced. His life is a deep balance. He is never one-sided; he is never on any extreme. He remains in the middle. Buddha has called this the middle path. He remains always in the middle.

A man who is not centered will always move to the extreme. If he will eat, he will eat much: he will overeat. Or, he can fast, but right eating is impossible for him. Fasting is easy, overeating is okay. He can be in the world, committed, involved, or he can renounce the world — but he can never be balanced. He can never remain in the middle, because if you are not centered you do not know what "middle" means.

A person who is centered is always in the middle, never at any extreme, in everything. Buddha says his eating is right eating: it is neither overeating, nor fasting. His labour is right labour: never too much, never too little. Whatsoever he is, he is always balanced.

First thing: a self-actualized person will be centered; second thing: balanced. Thirdly, if these two things happen — centering, balance — many things will follow. Thirdly, he will always be at ease. Whatsoever the situation, the at-easeness will not be lost. I say whatsoever the situation, unconditionally, the at-easeness will not be lost, because one who is at the center is always at ease. Even if death comes, he will be at ease. He will receive death as one receives any other guest. If misery comes, he will receive it. Whatsoever happens, it cannot dislodge him from his center. That at-easeness is also a by-product of being centered.

For such a man, nothing is trivial, nothing is great. Everything becomes sacred, beautiful, holy — everything! Whatsoever he is doing, whatsoever, it is of ultimate concern — as if of ultimate concern. Nothing is trivial. He will not say that "this" is trivial, "this" is great. Really, things are not great; neither are they small and trivial. The touch of the man is significant. A self-actualized person, a balanced, centered person, changes everything. The very touch makes it great.

If you observe a Buddha, you will see that he walks and he loves walking. If you go to Bodh Gaya where Buddha attained Enlightenment, to the bank of Niranjana — to the place where he was sitting under the Bodhi Tree, you will see that the place of his steps has been marked. He would meditate for one hour, then he would walk around. In Buddhist terminology, this is called "chakraman". He would sit under the Bodhi Tree, then he would walk. But he would walk with a serene attitude — as if in meditation.

Someone asked Buddha, "Why do you do this? Sometimes you sit with closed eyes and meditate, then you walk." Buddha said, "Sitting in order to be silent is easy, so I walk. But I carry the same silence within. I sit, but inside I am the same — silent. I walk, but inside I am the same — silent."

The inner quality is the same. He meets an emperor, he meets a beggar, but Buddha is the same: he has the same inner quality. When meeting a beggar he is not different, when meeting an emperor he is not different. He is the same. The beggar is not a nobody and the emperor is not a somebody. And, really, while meeting a Buddha emperors have felt like beggars and beggars have felt like emperors.

The touch, the man, the quality, remains the same. When he was alive, every day in the morning he would say to his disciples, "If you have to ask anything, ask." The day he was dying, that morning it was the same. He called his disciples and said, "Now if you want to ask anything, you can ask, and remember that this is the last morning. Before this day ends, I will be no more." He was the same. That was his daily question in the morning. He was the same! The day was the last, but he was the same. Just as on any day, he said, "Okay, if you have to ask anything, you can ask — but this is the last day."

There was no change of tone, but the disciples began to weep. They forgot to ask anything. Buddha said, "Why are you weeping? If you would have wept on another day, it would have been okay. But this is the last day. I will be no more by the evening, so do not waste time in weeping. Another day it would be okay; you could have wasted time. Do not waste your time in weeping. Why are you weeping? Ask if you have anything to ask." He was the same in life and death.

So, thirdly, the man is at ease: life and death are the same; bliss and misery are same. Nothing disturbs; nothing dislocates him from his home, from his centeredness. To such a man you cannot add anything. You cannot take anything out of him, you cannot add anything into him. He is fulfilled. His every breath is a fulfilled breath — silent, blissful. He has attained. He has attained to Existence, to Being. He has flowered as a total man.

This is not a partial flowering. Buddha is not a great poet. Of course, whatsoever he says is poetry. He is not a poet at all, but even if he moves, walks, it is poetry. He is not a painter, but whenever he speaks, whatsoever he says, becomes a painting. He is not a musician, but his whole being is music par excellence. The man as a totality has attained. So now, whatsoever he is doing or not doing, when he is sitting in silence, not doing anything, even in silence his presence works, creates: it becomes creative.

Tantra is concerned not with any partial growth. It is concerned with you as a total being. So three things are basic: you must be centered, rooted, balanced: that is, always in the middle — of course, without any effort. If there is effort you are not balanced. You must be at ease — at ease in the universe, at home in the Existence, and then many things follow. This is a basic need, because, really, unless this need is fulfilled you are a man only in name, you are a man as a possibility. You are not actually man. You can be; you have the potentiality. But the potentiality has to be made actual.

The second question: *"Kindly explain contemplation, concentration and meditation."*

"Contemplation" means thinking — directed thinking. We all think: that is not contemplation. That thinking is undirected, vague, leading nowhere. Really, our thinking is not contemplation, but what Freudians call "association". One thought leads to another without any direction from you. The thought itself leads to another because of association.

You see a dog crossing the street: the moment you see the dog, your mind starts thinking about dogs. The dog has led you, and then the mind has many associations. When you were a child, you were afraid of a particular dog. That dog comes to the mind and the childhood comes to the mind. Then dogs are forgotten. Then just by association you begin to daydream about your childhood. Then the childhood goes on being connected with other things, and you move in circles.

Whenever you are at ease, try to go back from your thinking to where the thoughts came. Go back; retrace the steps. Then you will see that another thought was there, and that led to this. And they are not logically connected, because how is a dog on the street connected with your childhood?

There is no logical connection — only association in your mind. If I was crossing the street, the same dog will not lead me to my childhood. It will lead to something else. In a third person, it will lead to still something else. Everyone has associated chains in the mind. With any one chain, any happening, any accident, leads to the chain. Then the mind begins to function like a computer. Then one thing leads to another, another leads to another, and you go on, and the whole day you are doing that.

Write down on a sheet of paper whatsoever comes to your mind honestly; then you will be just amazed. What is happening in your mind! There is no relation between two thoughts, and you go on doing this type of thinking. You call this thinking. This is just association of one thought to another, and they lead themselves. You are led.

Thinking becomes contemplation when it moves not through association, but is directed. You are working on a particular problem, then you bracket out all associations. You move on that problem only: you direct your mind. The mind will try to escape from any by-path to any sideway — to some association. You cut off all the sideways. On only one road, you direct your mind.

A scientist working on a problem is in contemplation. A logician working on a problem, a mathematician working on a problem, is in contemplation. A poet contemplates a flower: then the whole world is bracketed out, and only that flower remains and the poet, and he moves with the flower. Many things from the sideways will attract. He does not allow his mind to move anywhere. Mind moves in one line, directed. This is contemplation.

Science is based on contemplation. Any logical thinking is contemplation: thought is directed, thinking guided. Thinking, ordinary thinking is absurd. Contemplation is logical, rational.

Then there is concentration: concentration is staying at one point. It is not contemplation. It is not thinking; it is not contemplation. It is, really, being at one point, not allowing the mind to move at all. In thinking mind moves as a madman — in ordinary thinking. In contemplation the madman is led, directed; he cannot escape anywhere. In concentration the mind is not allowed to move; in ordinary thinking, it is allowed to move anywhere. In contemplation, it is allowed to move only somewhere; in concentration, it is not allowed to move. It is only allowed to be at one point. The whole energy, the whole movement, stops, sticks to one point.

Yoga is concerned with concentration, ordinary man with undirected thinking, the scientific mind with directed thinking. The yogic mind has its thinking, focused, fixed at one point: no movement is allowed. And then, meditation. In ordinary thinking, mind is allowed to move anywhere; in contemplation, it is allowed only in one direction: all other directions are cut off. In concentration, it is not allowed to move even in one direction. It is allowed only to concentrate on one point. And in meditation, mind is not allowed at all. Meditation is "no-mind". These are four stages — ordinary thinking, contemplation, concentration, meditation.

Meditation means no-mind: not even concentration is allowed. Mind itself is not allowed to be! That is why meditation cannot be grasped by mind. Up to concentration mind has a reach, an approachable reach. Mind can understand concentration. But mind cannot understand meditation. Really, mind is not allowed at all. In concentration, mind is allowed to be at one point. In meditation, even that point is taken away. In ordinary thinking, all directions are open. In contemplation, only one direction is open. In concentration, only one point is open — no direction. In meditation, even that point is not open: mind is not allowed to be.

Ordinary thinking is the ordinary state of mind, and meditation is the highest possibility. The lowest one is ordinary thinking — association, and the highest, the peak, is meditation — no-mind.

And with the second question, it is also asked : *"Contemplation and concentration are mental processes. How can mental processes help in achieving a state of no-mind?"*

The question is significant. Mind asks how can mind itself go beyond mind ? How can any mental process help to achieve something which is not of the mind ? It looks contradictory. How can your mind try, make effort, to create a state which is not of mind ?

Try to understand. When mind is, what is there ? A process of thinking ! When no-mind is meant, what is there ? No process of thinking ! If you go on decreasing your process of thinking, if you go on dissolving your thinking, by and by, slowly, you are reaching no-mind. Mind means thinking; no mind means non-thinking. And mind can help. Mind can help in committing suicide. You can commit suicide, but you never ask how a man who is alive can help himself to be dead. You can help yourself to be dead. Everyone is trying to help. You can help yourself to be dead, and you are alive. Mind can help to be no-mind. How can mind help ?

If the process of thinking becomes more and more dense, then you are proceeding from mind to more mind. If the process of thinking becomes less dense, is decreased, is slowed down, you are helping yourself toward no-mind. It depends on you. And mind can be a help, because, really, mind is what you are doing with your consciousness this very moment. If you leave your consciousness without doing anything with it, it becomes meditation.

So there are two possibilities: either slowly, gradually, you decrease your mind, by and by. If one percent is decreased, then you have ninety-nine percent mind and one percent no-mind within you. It is as if you are removing furniture from your room, as if you have removed some furniture. Then some space is created there. Then you remove more furniture, and more space is created there. When you have removed all the furniture, the whole room becomes space.

Really, space is not created by removing the furniture: space was already there. It is only that the space was occupied by the furniture. When you remove the furniture, no space comes in from outside. The space was there occupied by furniture. You have removed the furniture, and the space is recovered, reclaimed. Deep down mind is space occupied, filled, by thoughts. If you remove some thoughts, space is created or discovered or reclaimed. If you go on removing your thoughts, by and by you go on regaining your space. This space is meditation.

Slowly it can be done, suddenly also. There is no need to go on for lives together removing the furniture by and by because there are problems. When you remove the furniture, one percent space is created and ninety-nine percent space is occupied. That ninety-nine percent occupied space will not feel good about the unoccupied space; it will try to fill it. So one goes on slowly decreasing thoughts and then again creating new thoughts.

In the morning you sit for meditation for some time: you slow down your process of thought. Then you go to the market, and again there is a rush of thoughts: the space is filled again. The next day you again do this, and you go on doing this — throwing out, inviting in again.

Suddenly also you can throw all the furniture out. It is your decision. It is difficult because you have become accustomed to the furniture. You may feel uncomfortable without the furniture; you will not know what to do with that space. You may become afraid even to move in that space. You have never moved in such freedom.

Mind is a conditioning. We have become accustomed to thoughts. Have you ever observed — or if you have not observed, then observe — that you go on repeating the same thoughts every day. You are like a gramophone record, and then too, not a fresh, new one — old. You go on and on repeating the same things. Why ? What is the use of it ? Only one use — just a long habit. You feel you are doing something.

You are lying on your bed just waiting for sleep to come: why are you doing this every day ? The same things are repeated. But it helps in a way. Old habits help as a conditioning. A child needs a toy. If the toy is given to him, he will fall into sleep; then you can take away the toy. But if the toy is not there, the child cannot fall into sleep. It is a conditioning. The moment the toy is given to him, it triggers something in his mind. Now he is ready to fall into sleep.

The same is happening with you. The toys may differ. One person cannot fall into sleep unless he starts chanting, "Ram-Ram-Ram." He cannot fall into sleep! This is a toy. If he chants "Ram-Ram-Ram," the toy is given to him; he can fall into sleep.

You feel difficulty in falling asleep in a new room. If you are accustomed to sleeping in particular clothes, then you will need those particular clothes every day. Psychologists say that if you sleep in a nightgown and it is not given to you, you will feel difficulty in falling asleep. Why? If you have never slept naked and you are told to sleep naked, you will not feel at ease. Why? There is no relationship between nakedness and sleep, but for you there is a relationship, an old habit. With old habits one feels at ease, comfortable. Thinking patterns are also just habits. You feel comfortable — the same thought every day, the same routine. You feel everything is okay.

You have investments in your thoughts: that is the problem. Your furniture is not just rubbish to be thrown; you have invested many, many things in it. All the furniture can be thrown immediately: it can be done! There are sudden methods of which we will speak. There are sudden methods! Immediately, this very moment, you can be freed of your whole mental furniture. But then you will be suddenly vacant, empty, and you will not know who you are. Now you will not know what to do because for the first time your old patterns are no more. The shock may be too sudden. You may even die or you may go mad.

That is why sudden methods are not used. Unless one is ready, sudden methods are not used. One may go suddenly mad because one may miss all the moorings. The past drops immediately — and when past drops immediately — you cannot conceive of the future, because the future was always conceived of in terms of the past.

Only the present remains, and you have never been in the present. Either you were in the past or in the future. So when you are just in the present for the first time, you will feel you have gone berserk, mad. That is why sudden methods are not used unless you are working in a school, unless you are working with a teacher in a group, unless you are totally devoted, unless you have dedicated your whole life for meditation.

So gradual methods are good. They take a long time, but by and by you become accustomed to space. You begin to feel the space and the beauty of it, and the bliss of it, and then your furniture is removed by and by.

So from ordinary thinking it is good to become contemplative: that is the gradual method. From contemplation it is good to concentrate: that is the gradual method. And from concentration it is good to take a jump into meditation. Then you are moving slowly, feeling the ground, every step. And when you are really rooted in every step, only then do you begin to go for the next one. It is not a jump: it is a gradual growth. So these four things — ordinary thinking, contemplation, concentration, meditation — are four steps.

The third question: *"Is the development of the navel center exclusively free and separate from the growth of the heart and head centers, or does the navel center develop simultaneously with the growth of the heart and the head? And also, please explain in which way the training and techniques for the navel center will differ from the training and techniques for the development of the heart and head centers."*

One basic thing to be understood: the heart and head centers are to be developed, not the navel center. The navel center is just to be discovered: it is not to be developed. The navel center is already there. You have to uncover or discover it. It is there fully developed: you are not to develop it. The heart center and the head center are developments. They are not there to be discovered: they have to be developed. Society, culture, education, conditioning, helps to develop them.

But you are born with a navel center. Without the navel center you cannot be. You can be without the heart center, you can be without the head center. They are necessities; it is good to

252

have them. But you can be without them. It will be very inconvenient, but you can be without them. However, without the navel center you cannot be. It is not a necessity: it is your life.

So there are techniques for how to develop the heart center, how to grow love, how to grow in sensitivity, how to become a more sensitive mind. There are methods and techniques how to become more rational, more logical. Reason can be developed; emotion can be developed. But existence cannot be developed. It is already there; it has to be discovered.

Many things are implied in this. One: it may not be possible for you to have a mind, a reasoning faculty, like an Einstein. It may not be possible for you, but you can become a Buddha. Einstein is a mind center functioning at its perfection. Or someone else, a lover, a Majanu, is functioning at his heart center in its perfection. You may not be able to become a Majanu, but you can become a Buddha because Buddhahood is not to be developed in you: it is already there. It is concerned with the basic center, the original center — the navel. It is already there! You are already a Buddha, only unaware.

You are not already an Einstein. You will have to try, and then too it is not a guarantee that you will become one. There is no guarantee because, really, it seems impossible. Why does it seem impossible? Because the head of Einstein needs the same growth, the same milieu, the same training, as was given to Einstein. It cannot be repeated because it is unrepeatable. You will have to find the same parents first, because the training begins in the womb. It is difficult to find the same parents — impossible. How can you find the same parents, the same date of birth, the same home, the same associates, the same friends? You will have to repeat the life of Einstein exactly — ditto! If even one point is missing, you will be a different man.

So that is impossible. One individual is born only once in this world because the same situation cannot be repeated. The same situation is such a big phenomenon. It means there must be the same world in the same moment! It is not possible: it is impossible. And you are already here, so whatsoever you do your past will be in it. You cannot become an Einstein. Individuality cannot be repeated.

Buddha is not an individual: Buddha is a phenomenon. No individual factors are meaningful; just your being is enough to be a Buddha. The center is already there functioning: you have to discover it. So the techniques for developing the heart are techniques for "developing" something, and the techniques concerning the navel center are concerned with "uncovering". You have to uncover. You are already a Buddha: you only have to know the fact.

So there are two types of persons — Buddhas who know that they are Buddhas and Buddhas who do not know that they are Buddhas. But ALL are Buddhas. As far as Existence is concerned, everyone is the same. Only in Existence is there "communism": in everything else communism is absurd. No one is equal; inequality is basic in everything else. So it may look like a paradox if I say that only religion leads to communism, but I mean this communism: this deep equality of Existence, of Being. Then you are equal to Buddha, to Christ, to Krishna, but in no other way are two individuals equal. Inequality is basic as far as outer life is concerned; equality is basic as far as inner life is concerned.

So these 112 methods are not really for developing the navel center. They are for uncovering it. That is why instantly sometimes one becomes a Buddha: because there is no question of creating something. If you can look at yourself, if you can go deep down into yourself, all that you need is already there: it is already the case. So the only question is how to be thrown to that point where you are already a Buddha. Meditation doesn't help you to be a Buddha. It only helps you to become aware of your Buddhahood.

One question more: *"Are all Enlightened Ones navel centered? For example, is Krishnamurti head or navel centered? Was Ramakrishna heart or navel centered?"*

Every Enlightened One is navel centered, but the expression of each Enlightened One may flow through other centers.

Understand the distinction clearly. Every Enlightened One is navel centered; there is no other possibility. But the expression is a different thing.

Ramakrishna expresses himself from the heart. He uses his heart as the vehicle of his message. Whatsoever he has found at the navel, he expresses through his heart. He sings, he dances: that is his way of expressing his bliss. The bliss is found at the navel, nowhere else. He is centered at the navel. But how to say to others that he is centered at the navel? He uses his heart for the expression.

Krishnamurti uses his head for that expression: that is why their expressions are contradictory. If you believe in Ramakrishna you cannot believe in Krishnamurti. If you believe in Krishnamurti, you cannot believe in Ramakrishna, because belief is always centered in the expression, not in the experience. Ramakrishna looks childish to a man who thinks with reason. What is this nonsense — dancing, singing? What is he doing? Buddha never danced, and this Ramakrishna is dancing. He looks childish.

To reason, heart always looks childish, but to the heart reason looks useless, superficial. Whatsoever Krishnamurti says is the same: the experience is the same as it was for Ramakrishna or Chaitanya or Meera. But if the person is head centered, his explanation, expression is rational. If Ramakrishna will see Krishnamurti, he will say, "Come on and let us dance. Why waste your time? Through dance it can be expressed more easily, and it goes deeper." Krishnamurti will say, "Dance? One gets hypnotized through dance. Do not dance. Analyze! Reason! Reason it out, analyze, be aware."

These are different centers used for expression, but the experience is the same. One can paint the experience. Zen Masters have painted their experience. When they became Enlightened, they would paint it. They would not say anything: they would just paint it. The *Rishis* (sages) of the Upanishads have created beautiful poetry. When they became Enlightened they would create poetry. Chaitanya used to dance; Ramakrishna used to

255

sing. Buddha used the head, Mahavir used the head, reason, to explain, to say, whatsoever they had experienced. They created great systems of thought to express their experience.

But the experience is neither rational nor emotional: it is beyond both. There have been few persons, very few, who could express through both the centers. You can find many Krishnamurtis, you can find many Ramakrishnas. But only sometimes does it happen that a person can express through both the centers. Then the person becomes confusing. Then you are never at ease with that man because you cannot conceive of any relationship between the two: they appear contradictory.

So if I say something, when I say it I must say it through reason. So I attract many people who are rationalistic, head oriented. Then one day they see that I allow singing and dancing. Then they become uncomfortable. What is this ? There is no relationship. But to me there is no contradiction. Dancing is also a way of speaking — and sometimes a deeper way. Reason is also a way of speaking — and sometimes a very clear way. So both are ways of expression.

If you see Buddha dancing, you will be in difficulty. If you see Mahavir playing on a flute standing naked, then you will not be able to sleep. What happened to Mahavir ? Has he gone mad ? With Krishna the flute is okay, but with Mahavir it is absolutely unbelievable. A flute in the hand of Mahavir ? Inconceivable ! You cannot even imagine it. But the reason is not that there is any contradiction between Mahavir and Krishna, Buddha and Chaitanya: it is due to difference of expression. Buddha will attract a particular type of mind — the head-oriented mind, and Chaitanya and Ramakrishna will attract quite the opposite — the heart-oriented mind.

But difficulties arise: a person like me creates difficulties. I attract both — and then no one is at ease, because whenever I am talking, then the head-oriented person is at ease. But whenever I allow the other type of expression, the head-oriented one becomes uneasy. And the same happens to the other. When some emotional method is used, the heart-oriented one feels at ease.

But when I discuss, when I reason out something, then he is absent; he is not here. He says, "This is not for me."

One lady came just a day before, and she said, "I was at Mount Abu, but then there was difficulty. The first day when I heard you, it was beautiful. It appealed to me; I was just thrilled. But then I saw *kirtan* (devotional chanting), dancing, so I decided to leave immediately; that was not for me. I went to the bus station, but then there was a problem. I wanted to hear you talk, so I came back. I didn't want to miss what you were saying." She must have been in difficulty. She said to me, "It was so contradictory."

It appeared so because these centers are contradictory, and this contradiction is in YOU. Your head is not at ease with your heart. They are in conflict. Because of your inner conflict, Ramakrishna and Krishnamurti appear to be in conflict. Create a bridge between your head and your heart, and then you will know that these are mediums.

Ramakrishna was absolutely uneducated: no development of reason. He was pure heart. Only one center was developed — heart. Krishnamurti is pure reason. He was in the hands of some of the most vigorous rationalists — Annie Besant, Leadbeater and the Theosophists. They were great system-makers of this century. Really, Theosophy is one of the greatest systems ever created — absolutely rational. He was brought up by rationalists. He is pure reason. Even if he talks about heart and love, the very expression is rational.

Ramakrishna is different. Even if he talks about reason, he is absurd. Totapuri came to him, and he began to learn Vedanta from him. So Totapuri said, "Leave all this devotional nonsense. Leave this Kali, the Mother, absolutely. Unless you leave all this I am not going to teach you, because Vedanta is not devotion. It is knowledge." So Ramakrishna said, "Okay, but allow me one moment so that I can go and ask Mother if I may leave everything, this whole nonsense. Allow me one moment to ask the Mother."

This is a heart-oriented man. Even to leave Mother he will have to ask her. "And," he said, "She is so loving, she will allow me, so you do not bother." Totapuri could not understand what he said. He said, "She is so loving, she has never said 'no' to me at anytime. If I say, 'Mother, I am to leave you because now I am learning Vedanta and I cannot do this devotional nonsense, so allow me please,' she will allow. She will give me total freedom to dispose of it."

Create a bridge between your head and heart, and then all those who have ever become Enlightened will speak the same thing. Only their languages may differ.

11
Techniques To Penetrate
The Inner Centers

November 14, 1972, Bombay, India

SUTRAS:

15.   Closing the seven openings of the head with your hands,
a space between your eyes becomes all inclusive.

16.   Blessed one, as senses are absorbed in the heart, reach
the center of the lotus.

17.   Unminding mind, keep in the middle — until.

Man is as if he were a circle without a center. His life is superficial; his life is only on the circumference. You live on the outside: you never live within. You cannot unless a center is found. I discovered that you cannot live within. Really, you have no "within" without a center. You have only the "without". That is why we go on talking about the within, about how to go in, how to know oneself, how to penetrate inwards, but these words do not carry any authentic meaning. You know the meaning of the words, but you cannot FEEL what they mean because you are never in. You have never been in!

Even when you are alone, in your mind you are in a crowd. When no one is there outside, still you are not within. You go on thinking of others; you go on moving outwards. Even while asleep you are dreaming of others. You are not within. Only in very deep sleep, when there is no dreaming, are you within, but then you become unconscious. Remember this fact: when you are conscious you are never within, and when you are within in deep sleep, you become unconscious. So your whole consciousness consists of the without. And whenever we talk about going within, the words are understood but the meaning is not — because the meaning is not carried by the words: the meaning comes through experience.

Words are without meaning. When I say "within", you understand the word — but only the word, not the meaning. You do not know what "within" is, because consciously you have never been within. Your mind is constantly outgoing. You do not have any feel of what the "inner" means or what it is.

That is what I mean when I say that you are a circle without a center – a circumference only: the center is there, but you drop into it only when you are not conscious. Otherwise, when you are conscious you move outwards, and because of this your life is never intense; it cannot be. It is just lukewarm. You are alive as if dead, or both simultaneously. You are deadly alive – living a dead-like life. You are existing at the minimum – not at the maximum peak, but at the minimum. You can say, "I am" – that is all. You are not dead: that is what you mean by being alive.

But life can never be known at the circumference. Life can be known only at the center. On the circumference only lukewarm life is possible. So, really, you live a very inauthentic life, and then even death becomes inauthentic – because one who has not really lived cannot really die. Only authentic life can become authentic death. Then death is beautiful: anything authentic is beautiful. And even life, if it is inauthentic, is bound to be ugly. And your life is ugly – just rotten. Nothing happens. You simply go on waiting, hoping that something will happen somewhere, someday.

At this very moment there is just emptiness, and every moment has been like that in the past – just empty. You are just waiting for the future, hoping that something will happen someday – just hoping. Then every moment is lost. It has not happened in the past, so it is not going to happen in the future either. It can happen only in this moment, but then you will need an intensity – a penetrating intensity. Then you will need to be rooted in the center. Then the periphery will not do. Then you will have to find your moment.

Really, we never think about what we are, and whatsoever we think is just hocum. Once I lived with a professor on a university campus. One day he came and he was very upset, so I asked, "What is the matter?" He said, "I feel feverish." I was reading something, so I said to him, "Go to sleep. Take this blanket and rest." He went to the bed, but after a few minutes, he said, "No, I am not feverish. Really, I am angry. Someone has insulted me, and I feel much violence against him."

So I said, "Why did you say that you are feeling feverish?" He said, "I couldn't acknowledge the fact that I was angry, but really I am angry. There is no fever." He threw off the blanket. Then I said, "Okay, if you are angry, then take this pillow. Beat it and be violent with it. Let your violence be released. And if the pillow is not enough, then I am available. You can beat me, and let this anger be thrown out."

He laughed, but the laughter was false — just painted on his face. It came on his face and then disappeared. It never penetrated in. It never came from within: it was just a painted smile. But the laughter, even false laughter, created a gap. He said, "Not really: I am not really angry. Someone had said something before others, and I felt very much embarrassed. Really, this is the thing."

So, I said to him, "You have changed your statement about your own feelings three times within half an hour. You said you are feeling feverish, then you said you are angry, and now you say that you are not angry but just embarrassed. Which one is real?" He said, "Really, I am embarrassed." I said, "Which? When you said you were feverish, you were also certain about that. When you said you were angry, you were also certain about that. And you are also certain about this. Are you one person or many persons? For how long a time is this certainty going to continue?"

So the man said, "Really, I do not know what I am feeling. What it is, I do not know. I am simply disturbed. Whether to call it anger or embarrassment or what, I do not know. And this is not the moment to discuss it with me." He said, "Leave me alone. You have made my situation philosophical. You are discussing what is real, what is authentic, and I am feeling very much disturbed."

This is not only with some other person — X, Y or Z. It is with you. You are never certain, because certainty comes from being centered. You are not even certain about yourself. It is impossible to be certain about others when you are never certain about yourself. There is just a vagueness, a cloudiness. Nothing is certain.

Someone was here just a few days ago, and he said to me, "I am in love with someone, and I want to marry her." I looked into his eyes deeply for a few minutes without saying anything. He became restless and he said, "Why are you looking at me? I feel so awkward." I continued looking. He said, "Do you think that my love is false?" I didn't say anything. I just continued looking. He said, "Why do you feel that this marriage is not going to be good?" He said by himself, "I had not really thought it over very much, and that is why I have come to you. Really, I do not know whether I am in love or not."

I had not said a single word. I was just looking into his eyes. But he became restless, and things which were inside began to come up, to bubble up.

You are not certain; you cannot be certain about anything: neither about your love, nor about your hate, nor about your friendships. There is nothing which you can be certain about because you have no center. Without a center there is no certainty. All your feelings of certainty are false and momentary. One moment you will feel that you are certain, but the next moment the certainty will have gone because in each moment you have a different center. You do not have a permanent center, a crystallized center. Each moment is an atomic center, so each moment has its own self.

George Gurdjieff used to say that man is a crowd. Personality is just a deception because you are not a person: you are many persons. So when one person speaks in you, that is a momentary center. The next moment there is another. With every moment, with every atomic situation, you feel certain, and you never become aware that you are just a flux — many waves without any center. Then in the end you will feel that life has been just a wastage. It is bound to be. There is just a wastage, just a wandering — purposeless, meaningless.

Tantra, yoga, religion, their basic concern is how first to discover the center — how first to be an individual. They are concerned with how to find the center which persists in every situation. Then, as life goes on moving without, as the flux of life goes on and on, as waves come and go, the center persists inside. Then you remain one — rooted, centered.

These sutras are techniques to find the center. The center is already there because there is no possibility of being a circle without a center. The circle can exist only with a center, so the center is only forgotten. It is there, but we are not aware. It is there, but we do not know how to look at it. We do not know how to focus the consciousness on it.

The third technique about centering: *"Closing the seven openings of the head with your hands, a space between your eyes becomes all inclusive."*

This is one of the oldest techniques — and very much used, and one of the simplest also: Close all the openings of the head — eyes, ears, nose, mouth — ALL the openings of the head. When all the openings of the head are closed, your consciousness, which is continuously flowing out, is stopped suddenly: it cannot move out.

You may not have observed, but even if you stop your breathing for a moment, suddenly your mind will stop — because with breathing mind moves on. That is a conditioning with the mind. You must understand what "conditioning" means. Then only will this sutra be easy to understand.

Pavlov, one of the most famous Russian psychologists, has made this term "conditioning" — or "conditioned reflex" — a day-to-day word all over the world. Everyone who is acquainted with psychology even a little knows the word. Two processes of thought — any two processes — can become so associated, that if you start with one, the other is also triggered.

This is the famous Pavlovian example: Pavlov worked with a dog. He found that if you put dog food before a dog, its saliva begins to flow. The tongue of the dog comes out and he begins to get ready, prepared, for eating. This is natural. When he is seeing the food, or even imagining the food, saliva starts flowing. But Pavlov conditioned this process with another. Whenever the saliva would start to flow and the food was there, he would do some other things. For example: he would ring a bell, and the dog would listen to the bell ringing. For fifteen days, whenever the food was placed, the bell would ring. Then on the sixteenth day food was not placed before the dog. Only the bell was rung, but still the saliva started flowing and the tongue came out, as if the food was there.

But there was no food — only the bell ringing. There is no natural association between the bell ringing and saliva. The natural association is with food. But now the continuous ringing of the bell had become associated with it, and even the ringing of the bell would start the process.

According to Pavlov (and he is right), our whole life is a conditioned process. The mind is a conditioning. Thus, if you stop something in the conditioning, every other associated thing also stops.

For example, you have never thought without breathing. Thinking has always been with breathing. You are not conscious of breathing, but breathing is there — continuously, day and night. Every thought, every thinking process, is associated with breathing. If you stop your breathing suddenly, thought will also stop. And if all the seven holes — the seven openings of the head — are closed, your consciousness suddenly cannot move out. It remains in, and that "remaining in" creates a space between your eyes. That space is known as the third eye.

If all the openings of the head are closed, you cannot move out, because you have always been moving out from these openings. You remain in, and with that remaining in your consciousness becomes concentrated between these two eyes, between these two ordinary eyes. It remains in between these two, focused. That spot is known as the third eye.

This space "becomes all inclusive": This sutra says that in this space everything is included. The whole Existence is included. If you can feel the space, you have felt all. Once you can feel inside this space between the two eyes, then you have known Existence — the totality of it — because this inner space is all inclusive. Nothing is left out of it.

The Upanishads say, "Knowing the One, one knows all." These two eyes can only see the finite. The third eye sees the infinite. These two eyes can only see the material. The third eye sees the immaterial — the spiritual. By these two eyes you can never feel the energy, you can never see the energy: you can see only matter. But with the third eye, energy as such is seen.

This closing of the openings is a way of centering, because once the stream of consciousness cannot flow out it remains at its source. That source of consciousness is the third eye. If you are centered at the third eye, many things happen. The first is discovering that the whole world is in you.

Swami Ram use to say that "The sun moves in me, the stars move in me, the moon rises in me. The whole universe is in me." When he said this for the first time, his disciples throught he had gone crazy. How can stars be in Ramteerth ?

He was talking about the third eye, the inner space. When for the first time the inner space becomes illumined, this is the feeling. When you see that everything is in you, you become the universe.

The third eye is not part of your physical body. It is NOT part of your physical body ! The space between our two eyes is not a space which is confined in your body. It is the infinite space which has penetrated in you. Once this space is known, you will never be the same person again. The moment you know this inner space, you have known the deathless. Then there is no death.

When you know this space for the first time, your life will be authentic, intense, for the first time really alive. Now no security is needed. Now no fear is possible. Now you cannot be killed. Now nothing can be taken away from you. Now the whole universe belongs to you: you are the universe. Those who have known this inner space, they have cried in ecstacy, *"Aham Brahmasmi:* I am the universe, I am the Existence."

The Sufi mystic Mansoor was murdered only because of this experience of the third eye. When for the first time he became aware of this inner space, he started crying, "I am God." In India, he would have been worshipped, because India has known many, many persons who have come to know this inner space of the third eye. But in a Mohammedan country it was difficult. And Mansoor's statement that "I am God — *Anal-hak, Aham Brahmasmi"* — was taken to be something anti-religious, because Mohammedanism cannot conceive that man and God can become one. Man is man — the created, and God is the Creator. So how can the created become the Creator ? So this statement of Mansoor's, "I am God," could not be understood. Thus, he was murdered. But when he was being murdered, killed, he was laughing. So someone asked, "Why are you laughing, Mansoor ?"

Mansoor is reported to have said, "I am laughing because you are not killing me, and you cannot kill me. You are deceived by this body, but I am not this body. I am the Creator of this universe, and it was my finger which moved this whole universe in the beginning."

In India he would have been understood easily. The language has been known for centuries and centuries. We have known that a moment comes when the inner space is known. Then one simply goes mad. And this realization is so certain that even if you kill a Mansoor he will not change his statement — because, really, you cannot kill him as far as he is concerned. Now he has become the Whole. There is no possibility of destroying him.

After Mansoor, Sufis learned that it is good to be silent, so in Sufi tradition after Mansoor, it has been consistently taught to disciples, "Whenever you come to the third eye, remain silent and do not say anything. Whenever this happens, then keep quiet. Do not say anything or just go on formally saying things which people believe."

So Islam has now two traditions: one, just the ordinary, the outward, the exoteric; another, the real Islam, is Sufism — the esoteric. But Sufis remain silent because since Mansoor they have learned that to talk in that language which comes when the third eye opens is to be unnecessarily in difficulty — and, it helps no one.

This sutra says: "Closing the seven openings of the head with your hands, a space between your eyes becomes all inclusive." Your inner space becomes all the space.

The fourth technique: *"Blessed one, as senses are absorbed in the heart, reach the center of the lotus."*

Every technique is useful for a certain type of mind. The technique we have been discussing, the third — closing of the openings of the head — can be used by many. It is very simple and not very dangerous. You can use it very easily, and there is also no need to close the openings with your hands. Closing is needed, so you can use ear plugs and you can use a mask for the eyes. The real thing is to close the openings of your head completely for a few moments — for a few moments or for a few seconds. Try it. Do not practise it. Only suddenly is it helpful: when it is sudden it is helpful. When lying in your bed, suddenly close all your openings for a few seconds, and see within what is happening.

When you feel suffocated, go on — unless it becomes absolutely unbearable — because breathing will be closed. Go on — unless it becomes absolutely unbearable. And when it is absolutely unbearable, you will not be able to close the openings any more, so you need not worry. The inner force will throw all the openings open. So as far as you are concerned, continue. When the suffocation comes, that is the moment — because the suffocation will break the old associations. If you can continue for a few moments more, it would be good. It will be difficult and arduous, and you will feel that you are going to die — but do not be afraid, because you cannot die. You cannot die just by closing the openings. But when you feel now you are going to die, that is the moment.

If you can persist in that moment, suddenly everything will be illumined. You will feel the inner space which goes on spreading, and the Whole is included in it. Then open your openings. Then go on trying it again and again. Whenever you have time, try it. But do not practise it. You can practise stopping the breath for a few moments: you can practise ! But practice will not help. A sudden jerk is needed. In that jerk, the flow into your old channels of consciousness stops, and a new thing becomes possible.

Many practise even today — many persons all over India. But they practise it, and it is a sudden method. If you practise, then nothing will happen. NOTHING will happen ! If I throw you out of this room suddenly, your thoughts will stop. But if we practise it daily, then nothing will happen. It will become a mechanical habit. So do not practise it. Just try it whenever you can. Then suddenly, by and by, you will become aware of an inner space. That inner space comes only to your consciousness when you are on the verge of death. When you are feeling, "Now I cannot continue for a single moment; now death is near," that is the right moment. Persist ! Do not be afraid. Death is not so easy. At least up until now not a single person has died doing this method.

There are built-in securities: that is why you cannot die. Before death one becomes unconscious. If you are conscious and feeling that you are going to die, do not be afraid. You are still conscious, so you cannot die. And if you become unconscious, then your breath will start. Then you cannot prevent it. So you can use ear plugs, etc. Hands are not necessary. Hands were used only because of this, that if you are falling into unconsciousness, the hands will become loose and the life process will become outgoing again by itself.

You can use plugs for the ears, a mask for the eyes, but do not use any plugs for the nose or for the mouth, because then it CAN become fatal. At least the nose should remain open. Close it with your hands. Then, when you are actually falling into unconsciousness, the hands will become loose and the breathing will come in. So there is a built-in security. This method can be used by many.

The fourth method is for those who have a very developed heart, who are loving, feeling types, emotional. "Blessed one, as senses are absorbed in the heart, reach the center of the lotus": This method can be used only by heart-oriented persons. Therefore, understand first what is a heart-oriented person. Then this method can be understood.

With one who is heart-oriented, everything leads to the heart — everything! If you love him, his heart will feel your love, not his head. A head-oriented person, even when loved, feels it cerebrally, in the head. He thinks about it; he plans about it. Even his love is a deliberate effort of the mind.

A feeling type lives without reasoning. Of course, the heart has its own reasons, but it lives without reasoning. If someone asks you, "Why do you love?" if you can answer why, then you are a head-oriented person. And if you say, "I do not know; I just love," you are a heart-oriented person.

Even if you say that someone is beautiful and "that is why I love", it is a reason. For a heart-oriented person, someone is beautiful "because I love him". The head-oriented person loves someone because he is beautiful or she is beautiful. The reason comes first, and then comes love. For the heart-oriented, love comes first and then everything else follows. The feeling type is centered in the heart, so whatsoever happens touches his heart.

Just observe yourself. In your life, many things are happening every moment. Where do they touch you? You are passing, and a beggar crosses the street. Where are you touched by the beggar? Do you start thinking about economic conditions? Do you start thinking about how beggings should be stopped by law or about how a socialist society should be created so that there are no beggars? This is a head-oriented man. This beggar becomes just a datum for him. His heart is not touched. Only his head is touched. He is not going to do something for this beggar here and now — no! He will do something for communism, he will do something for the future, for some utopia. He may even devote his whole life, but he cannot do anything just now.

The mind is always doing in the future; the heart is always here and now. A heart-oriented person will do something now for this beggar. This beggar is an individual, not a datum. But

271

for a head-oriented man, this beggar is just a mathematical figure. For him, how begging should be stopped is the problem, not that this beggar should be helped: that is irrelevant. So just watch yourself. In many situations, watch how you act. Are you concerned with the heart or are you concerned with the head?

If you feel that you are a heart-oriented person, then this method will be very helpful to you. But know well that everyone is trying to deceive himself that he is heart-oriented. Everyone tries to feel that he is a very loving person, a feeling type — because love is such a basic need that no one can feel at ease if he sees that he has no love, no loving heart. So everyone goes on thinking and believing, but belief will not do. Observe very impartially, as if you are observing someone else, and then decide — because there is no need to deceive yourself and it will be of no help. Even if you deceive yourself, you cannot deceive the technique. So when you do this technique, you will feel that nothing is happening.

People come to me, and I ask them to what type they belong. They do not know really. They have never thought about it — about what type they are. They have just vague conceptions about themselves, and those conceptions are really just imagination. They have certain ideals and self-images, and they think — or, rather, they wish — that they were those images. They are not, and often it happens that they prove to be just the contrary.

There is a reason for it. A person who insists that he is a heart-oriented person may be insisting only because he feels the absence of heart, and he is afraid. He cannot become aware of the fact that he has no heart.

Look at the world! If everyone is right about his heart, then this world cannot be so heartless. This world is our total, so somewhere, something is wrong. Heart is not there. Really, it was never trained to be there. Mind is trained, so it is there. There are schools, colleges, universities to train the mind, but there is no place to train the heart. And the training of the mind pays, but the training of the heart is dangerous because if your heart is trained you will become absolutely unfit for this world — because the whole world is run through reason.

If your heart is trained, you will just be absurd in the whole pattern. When the whole world will be moving to the right, you will be moving to the left. Everywhere you will feel difficulty. Really, the more man becomes civilized, the less and less is the heart trained. We have really forgotten about it — that it exists, or that there is any need for its training. That is why such methods which can work very easily never work.

All the religions, most of the religions, are based on heart-oriented techniques — Christianity, Islam, Hinduism and many others. They are based on the heart-oriented persons. The older the religion, the more it is based on heart-oriented persons. Really, when the Vedas were written and Hinduism was developing, there were people who were heart-oriented. And to find a mind-oriented person then was really difficult. But now the reverse is a problem. You cannot pray because prayer is a heart-oriented technique. That is why even in the West, where Christianity (which is a religion of prayer) prevails, prayer has become difficult. Particularly, the Catholic Church is prayer oriented.

There exists no such thing as meditation for Christianity, but now, even in the West, people are becoming crazy about meditation. No one is going to church — and even if someone is going, it is just a formal thing, just Sunday religion — because the heart-oriented prayer has become absolutely unrelated with man as he is in the West.

Meditation is more mind oriented, prayer is more heart oriented. Or, we can say that prayer is a technique of meditation for heart-oriented persons. This technique is also for heart-oriented persons: "Blessed one, as senses are absorbed in the heart, reach the center of the lotus."

So what is to be done in this technique? "As senses are absorbed in heart..." Try! Many ways are possible. You touch someone: if you are a heart-oriented person the touch immediately goes to your heart, and you can feel the quality. If you take the hand of a person who is head oriented, the hand will be cold — not just cold, but the very quality will be cold. A deadness, a certain deadness, will be in the hand. If the person is heart oriented, then there is a certain warmth. Then his hand will really melt with you. You will feel a certain thing flowing from his hand to you, and there will be a meeting — a communication of warmth.

This warmth comes from the heart. It can never come from the head because the head is always cool, cold, calculative. The heart is warm — non-calculative. The head always thinks about how to take more; the heart always feels how to give more. That warmth is just a giving — a giving of energy, a giving of inner vibrations, a giving of life. That is why you feel a different quality in it. If the person really embraces you, you will feel a deep melting with him.

Touch! Close your eyes; touch anything. Touch your beloved or your lover, touch your child or your mother, or your friend, or touch a tree or a flower, or just touch the earth. Close your eyes and feel a communication from your heart to the earth, or to your beloved. Just feel that your hand is just your heart stretched out to touch the earth. Let the feeling of touch be related to the heart.

You are listening to music: do not listen to it from the head. Just forget your head and feel that you are headless. There is no head at all. It is good to have your own picture in your bedroom without the head. Concentrate on it: you are without the head; do not allow the head to come in. While listening to music, listen to it from the heart. Feel the music coming to your heart; let your heart vibrate with it. Let your senses be joined to the heart, not to the head. Try this with all the senses, and feel more and more that every sense goes into the heart and dissolves into it.

"Blessed one, as senses are absorbed in the heart, reach the center of the lotus": The heart is the lotus. Every sense is just the opening of the lotus, the petals of the lotus. Try to relate your senses to the heart first. Secondly, always think that every sense goes deep down into the heart and becomes absorbed in it. When these two things become established, only then will your senses begin to help you: they will lead you to the heart, and your heart will become a lotus.

This lotus of the heart will give you a centering. Once you know the center of the heart, it is very easy to fall down into the navel center. It is very easy! Really, this sutra does not even mention this; there is no need. If you are really absorbed in the heart totally, and reason has stopped working, then you will fall down. From the heart, the door is opened toward the navel. Only from the head is it difficult to go toward the navel. Or, if you are between the two, between the heart and the head, then too it is difficult to go to the navel. Once you are absorbed in the navel, you have suddenly fallen beyond the heart. You have fallen into the navel center which is the basic one — the original.

That is why prayer helps. That is why Jesus could say, "Love is God." It is not exactly right, but love is the door. If you are deeply in love — with anyone: it doesn't matter who (love matters: the object of love doesn't matter), if you are in deep love with anyone, so much in love that there is no relationship from the head, if just the heart is functioning, then this love will become prayer and your beloved or your lover will become Divine.

Really, the eye of the heart cannot see anything else, and that is why it happens with ordinary love also. If you fall in love with someone, that someone becomes Divine. It may not prove to be very lasting and it may not prove to be a very deep thing, but in the moment the lover or the beloved becomes Divine. The head will destroy the whole thing sooner or later, because the head will come in and try to manage everything. Even love has to be managed. And once the head manages, everything is destroyed.

If you can be in love without the head's management coming in, your love is bound to become prayer and your beloved will become the door. Your love will make you centered in the heart — and once you are centered in the heart, you automatically fall down deep into the navel center.

The fifth technique: *"Unminding mind, keep in the middle — until."*

"Unminding mind, keep in the middle — until": This much is the sutra. Just like any scientific sutra, it is short, but even these few words can transform your life totally. "Unminding mind, keep in the middle — until. Keep in the middle..."

Buddha developed his whole technology of meditation on this sutra. His path is known as *"majjhim nikaya"* — the middle path. Buddha says, "Remain always in the middle — in everything."

One Prince Shrown took initiation: Buddha initiated him into Sannyas. That prince was a rare man, and when he took Sannyas, when he was initiated, his whole kingdom was just amazed. The kingdom couldn't believe it: the people couldn't believe that Prince Shrown could become a sannyasin. No one had ever even imagined it, as he was a man of this world — indulging in everything, indulging to the extreme. Wine and women were his whole milieu.

Then suddenly Buddha came to the town, and the prince went to see him for a *darshan* (spiritual encounter). He fell at Buddha's feet and he said, "Initiate me. I will leave this world." Those who had come with him were not even aware. This was so sudden, so they asked Buddha, "What is happening? This is a miracle. Shrown is not that type of man, and he has lived very luxuriously. Up to now we couldn't even imagine that Shrown is going to take Sannyas, so what has happened? You have done something."

Buddha said, "I have not done anything. Mind can move easily from one extreme to the other. That is the way of the mind — to move from one extreme to another. So Shrown is not doing something new. It is to be expected. Because you do not know the law of the mind, that is why you are so much taken back."

The mind moves from one extreme to another; that is the way of the mind. So it happens every day: a person who was mad after wealth renounces everything, becomes a naked fakir. We think, "What a miracle!" But it is nothing — just the ordinary law. A person who was not mad after wealth cannot be expected to renounce, because only from one extreme can you move to another — just like a pendulum, from one extreme to the other.

So a person who was after wealth, mad after wealth, will become mad against it, but the madness will remain: that is the mind. A man who was just for sex may become a celibate, may move into isolation, but the madness will remain. Before he was living only for sex, now he will be living only against sex — but the attitude, the approach, remains the same.

So a *brahmachari* (a celibate) is not really beyond sex: his whole mind is sex oriented. He is against, but not beyond. The way of "beyond" is always in the middle: it is never at the extreme. So Buddha says, "This could have been expected. No miracle has happened. This is how mind works."

Shrown became a beggar, a sannyasin. He became a *bhikkhu* (monk), and soon other disciples of Buddha observed that he was moving to the other extreme. Buddha never asked anyone to be naked, but Shrown became naked. Buddha was not for nakedness. He said, "That is just another extreme."

There are persons who live for clothes as if that is their life, and there are other persons who become naked — but both believe in the same thing. Buddha never taught nakedness, but Shrown became naked. He was Buddha's only disciple who was naked. He became very, very self-torturing. Buddha allowed one meal every day for the sannyasins, but Shrown would take only one meal on alternate days. He became lean and thin. While all other disciples would sit for meditation under trees, under the shade, he would never sit under any tree. He would always remain in the hot sun. He was a beautiful man and he had a very lovely body, but within six months no one could recognize that he was the same man. He became ugly, dark, black, burned.

Buddha went to Shrown one night and asked him, "Shrown, I have heard that when you were a prince, before initiation, you used to play on a *veena* (sitar) and you were a great musician. So I have come to ask you one question. If the strings of the *veena* are very loose, what happens?" Shrown said, "If the strings are very loose, then no music is possible." And then Buddha said, "And if the strings are very tight, too much tight, then what happens?" Shrown said, "Then too music cannot be produced. The strings must be in the middle — neither loose nor tight, but just exactly in the middle." Shrown said, "It is easy to play the *veena,* but only a master can set these strings right in the middle."

So Buddha said, "This much I have to say to you after observing you for the last six months — that in life also the music comes only when the strings are neither loose nor tight, but just in the middle. So to renounce is easy, but only a master knows how to be in the middle. So, Shrown, be a master, and let these strings of life be just in the middle — in everything. Do not go to this extreme, do not go to that one — and everything has two extremes. But you remain just in the middle."

But the mind is very unmindful. That is why the sutra says, "Unminding mind..." You will hear this, you will understand this, but the mind will not mind. The mind will always go on choosing extremes.

The extreme has a fascination for the mind. Why? Because in the middle mind dies. Look at a pendulum: if you have any old clock, look at the pendulum. The pendulum can go on moving the whole day if goes to the extremes. When it goes to the left, it is gathering momentum to go to the right. When it goes toward the right, do not think that it is going toward the right. It is accumulating momentum to go toward the left. So the extremes are right-left, right-left.

Let the momentum stay in the middle! Let the pendulum stay in the middle! Then the whole momentum is lost. Then the pendulum has no energy, because the energy comes from one of the extremes. Then that extreme throws it toward another, then again, and it is a circle: the pendulum goes on moving. Let it be in the middle, and the whole movement will then stop.

Mind is just like a pendulum, and every day, if you observe, you will come to know this. You decide one thing on one extreme, and then you move to another. You are angry; then you repent. You decide, "No, this is enough. Now I will never be angry. But you do not see the extreme."

"Never" is an extreme. How are you so certain that you will never be angry? What are you saying? Think once more. Never? Then go to the past and remember how many times you have decided that "I will never be angry". When you say, "I will never be angry," you do not know that by being angry you have accumulated momentum to go to the other extreme. Now you are feeling repentant, you are feeling bad. Your self-image is disturbed, shaken. Now you cannot say you are a good man, you cannot say that you are a religious man. You have been angry, and how can a religious man be angry? How can a good man be angry? So you repent to regain your goodness again. At least in your own eyes you can feel at ease that you have repented and you have decided that now there will be no more anger. The shaken image has come back to the old status quo. Now you feel at ease: you have moved to another extreme.

But the mind that says, "Now I will never be angry," will again be angry. And when you are again angry, you will forget completely your repentance, your decision — everything. After anger, again the decision will come and the repentance will come, and you will never feel the deception of it. This has been so always.

Mind moves from anger to repentance, from repentance to anger. Remain in the middle. Do not be angry and do not repent. If you have been angry, then, please, at least do this: do not repent. Do not move to the other extreme. Remain in the middle. Say, "I have been angry and I am a bad man — a violent man. I have been angry. This is how I am." But do not repent; do not move to the other extreme. Remain in the middle. If you can remain, you will not gather the momentum, the energy, to be angry again.

So this sutra says, "Unminding mind, keep in the middle — until." And what is meant by "until"? Until you EXPLODE. Keep in the middle until the mind dies. Keep in the middle until there is no mind. So, "Unminding mind, keep in the middle until there is no mind." If mind is at the extremes, then the middle will be "no-mind".

But this is the most difficult thing in the world to do. It looks easy, it looks simple. It may appear as if you can do this. And you will feel good if you think that there is no need for any repentance. Try this, and then you will know that when you are angry the mind will insist on repenting.

Freud says that husbands and wives continue to quarrel, and for centuries and centuries there have been counsellors, advisors, great men, who have been teaching how to live and love. But they go on quarreling. For the first time, Freud became aware of the phenomenon that whenever you are in love (so-called love), you are also in hate. In the morning it is love, in the evening it is hate, and the pendulum goes on moving. Every husband, every wife, knows this, but Freud has a very uncanny insight. Freud says that if a couple has stopped fighting, know well that love has died.

That love which existed with hate and fight cannot remain, so if you see a couple never fighting, do not think that this is the ideal couple. It means no couple at all. They are living parallel, but not with each other. They are parallel lines never meeting anywhere, not even to fight. They are both alone together — alone together, parallel.

Mind has to move to the opposite, so psychology now gives better advice. The advice is better, more deep, more penetrating. It says that if you really want to love (with the mind), then do not be afraid to fight. Really, you must fight authentically so you can move to the other extreme of authentic love. So when you are fighting with your wife, do not avoid it; otherwise the love will also be avoided. Do not avoid it! When the time for fight is there, fight until the end. Then by evening you will be able to love: the mind will have gathered momentum. The ordinary love cannot exist without fight because there is a movement of mind. Only a love which is not of the mind can exist without fight, but then it is a different thing altogether.

A Buddha loving: that is a different thing altogether. But if Buddha comes to love you, you will not feel good because there will be no fault in it. It will be simply sweet and sweet and sweet — and boring — because the fault comes from fight. A Buddha cannot be angry: he can only love. You will not feel his love because you can feel only the opposites. You can feel it only in the contrast.

When Buddha came back to his home town after twelve years, his wife wouldn't come to receive him. The whole city gathered to receive him except his wife. Buddha laughed and he said to his chief disciple Ananda, "Yashodhara has not come. I know her well. It seems she still loves me. She is proud, and she feels hurt. I was thinking that twelve years is a long time and she might not be in love now. But it seems she is still in love — still angry. She has not come to receive me. I will have to go to the house."

So Buddha went. Ananda was with him. It was a condition with Ananda. When Ananda took initiation, he made a condition with Buddha in which Buddha agreed that he would always remain with him. He was an elder cousin-brother, so Buddha had to concede.

Ananda followed him into the house, into the palace, so Buddha said, "At least for this, you remain behind and do not come with me, because she will be furious. I am coming back after twelve years, and I just ran away without even telling her. She is still angry, so do not come with me. Otherwise she will feel that I have not even allowed her to say anything. She must be feeling to say many things, so let her be angry. Do not come with me."

Buddha went in. Of course, Yashodhara was just on a volcano. She erupted, exploded. She started crying and weeping and saying things. Buddha stayed there, waited there, and by and by she cooled down and realized that Buddha had not even uttered a single word. She wiped her eyes and looked at Buddha, and Buddha said, "I have come to say that I have gained something, I have known something, I have Realized something. If you become cool, I can give you the message — the Truth that I have Realized. I have waited so much in order that you could go through a catharsis. Twelve years is a long affair. You must have gathered many wounds and your anger is understandable; I expected this. That shows that you are still in love with me. But there is a love beyond this love, and only because of that love have I come back to tell you something."

But Yashodhara could not feel that love. It is difficult to feel it because it is so silent. It is so silent, it is as if absent. When mind ceases, then a different love happens. But that love has no opposite to it. When mind ceases, really, whatsoever happens has no opposite to it. With the mind, there is always the polar opposite, and mind moves like a pendulum. This sutra is wonderful, and miracles are possible through it: "Unminding mind, keep in the middle — until."

So try it. And this sutra is for your whole life. You cannot practise it sometimes. You have to be aware continuously. Doing, walking, eating, in relationship, everywhere, remain in the middle. Try at least, and you will feel a certain calmness developing, a tranquillity coming to you, a quiet center growing within you.

Even if you are not successful in being exactly in the middle, try to be in the middle. By and by you will have the feel of what "middle" means. Whatsoever may be the case — hate or love, anger or repentance — always remember the polar opposites and remain in between. And sooner or later you will stumble upon the exact middle point.

Once you know it you can never forget it again because that middle point is beyond the mind. That middle point is all that spirituality means.

12
Beyond Mind To The Source

November 15, 1972, Bombay, India

QUESTIONS:

1. Explain the functions of the navel center, the third-eye center and the spinal cord.
2. Buddha's ascetism seems the opposite of worldly life and not the middle path. Please explain.
3. What are some practical ways to develop the heart center?
4. Should one love in the middle-path way, or be intense in both the love and hate poles?

There are many questions. The first question: *"Last night you said that with the dawn of Enlightenment, the space between the two eyebrows, the third eye, becomes all inclusive. The other day you said that all Enlightened Ones are centered in their navel, and on still another day you have explained about the silver cord in the middle of the spine. Thus, we know about three basic things as the roots of man. Please. explain the relative significance and relative functions of these three things: the navel center, the. third eye and the siver cord."*

The basic thing to be understood about these centers is this: whenever you are centered within, the moment you are centered, whatsoever may be the center, you fall down to the navel. If you are centered at the heart, the heart is irrelevant: centering is meaningful. Or, if you are centered at the third eye, the third eye is not basic: the basic point is that your consciousness is centered. So whatsoever may be the point of centering, once you are centered — anywhere — you will fall down to the navel.

The basic existential center is the navel, but your functional center may be anywhere. From that center you will fall down automatically. There is no need to think about it. And this is not so only with the heart center or the third-eye center. If you are really centered in reason, in the head, you will also fall down to the navel center.

Centering is the thing, but it is very difficult to be centered in reason, in the head. There are problems. The heart center is based on love, faith, surrender. The head is based on doubt and negation.

To be totally negative is really impossible; to be totally in doubt is impossible. But it has happened sometimes, because the impossible also happens. Sometimes, if your doubt comes to such an intensity that nothing remains which is believed, not even the doubting mind is believed, if the doubt turns upon itself and everything becomes doubt, then you will fall down to the navel center immediately. But this is a very rare phenomenon.

Trust is easier. You can trust totally more easily than you can doubt totally. You can say "yes" totally more easily than you can say "no". So even if you are centered at the head, the CENTERING is what is basic: you will fall down to your existential roots. So be centered anywhere. The spine will do; the heart will do; the head will do. Or, you can also find other centers in the body.

Buddhists talk about nine "chakras" — nine dynamic centers in the body: Hindus talk about seven chakras — seven dynamic centers in the body; Tibetans talk about thirteen centers in the body. You can find your own also. There is no need to study about these.

Any point in the body can be made an object of centering. For example, tantra uses the sex center for centering. Tantra works with bringing your consciousness to it totally. The sex center will do.

Taoists have used the big toe as the center. Move your consciousness down to the big toe; remain there; forget the whole body. Let your whole consciousness go to the toe. That will do, because, really, on what you are centering is irrelevant. You are centering: that is what is basic. The thing happens because of centering, not because of the center — remember this. The center is not significant. CENTERING is significant.

So do not be puzzled because in so many methods, in 112 methods, many centers will be used. Do not become puzzled over which center is more important or which is real: any center will do. You can choose according to your own liking.

If your mind is very sexual, it is good to choose the sex center. Use it, because your consciousness is naturally flowing toward it. Then it is better to choose it. But it has become difficult to choose the sex center. That is one of the most natural centers: your consciousness is attracted toward it biologically. Why not use this biological force toward inner transformation? Make it the point of your centering.

But social conditioning, sex-repressive teachings, moralizing, they have done a deep harm. You are disjoined from your sex center. Really, our image of our real selves excludes the sex center. Imagine your body: you will leave your sex organs out of it. That is why many people feel as if their sex organs are something different from them, that they are not part of them. That is why there is so much hiding, so much becoming unconscious.

If someone should come from space, from some other planet, and he should see you, he will not be able to conceive that you have any sex center. If he should listen to your talk, he will not be able to understand that there exists anything like sex. If he moves in your society, in the formal world, he will not know that anything like sex is happening.

We have created a division. A barrier is there, and we have cut off the sex center from ourselves. Really, because of sex we have divided the body into two. The upper means "higher" in our minds and the lower means "lower": it is condemned. So "lower" is not just some information about the location of the bottom half: it is an evaluation also. You yourself do not think that the lower body is you.

If someone asks you, "Where are you in your body?" you will point to your head because that is the highest. That is why Brahmins in India will say, "We are the head and Sudras (the 'Untouchables'), they are the feet." The feet are lower than the head. Really, you are the head, and the feet and the other parts only belong to you: they are not you. To divide this, we have made clothes in two parts — some for the upper body and some for the lower body. This is only to divide the body in two. There is a subtle division.

The lower body is not part of you. It hangs on you: that is another thing. That is why it is difficult to use the sex center for centering. But if you can use it, that is the best, because biologically your energy is flowing toward that center. Concentrate on it. Whenever you feel any sexual urge, close your eyes and feel your energy flowing toward the sex center.

Make it a meditation; feel yourself centered in the sex center. Then suddenly you will feel a change of quality in the energy. Sexuality will disappear, and the sex center will become illumined, full of energy, dynamic. You will feel life at its peak, at this center. And if you are centered, sex will really be forgotten completely at that moment. And from the sex center you will feel energy flowing all over the body, even transcending the body and going into the Cosmos. If you are totally centered at the sex center, suddenly you will be thrown to your basic root at the navel.

Tantra has used the sex center, and I think tantra has been one of the most scientific approaches toward human transformation, because to use sex is very scientific. When the mind is already flowing toward it, why not use this natural flow as a vehicle?

That is the basic difference between tantra and so-called moralist teachings. Moralist teachers can never use the sex center for transformation: they are afraid. And one who is afraid of sex energy will really find it very, very difficult to transform himself or herself because he is fighting against the current, unnecessarily flowing against the river.

It is easy to flow with the river. Float! And if you can float without any conflict, you can use this center for centering. Any center will do.

You can create your own centers: no need to be traditional. All centers are devices — devices for centering. When you are centered you will come down to your navel automatically. A centered consciousness goes back to the original source.

The second question: *"Buddha inspired a large number of persons to become sannyasins — sannyasins who would beg for their meals and live away from society, business and politics. Buddha himself lived an ascetic life. This monastic life seems to be the other extreme of the worldly life. This doesn't seem to be the middle path. Can you explain this?"*

It will be difficult to understand because you are not aware of what is the other end of worldly life. The other end of life is always death. There have been teachers who said that suicide is the only path. And not only in the past: even now, in the present, there are thinkers who say that life is absurd. If life as such is meaningless, then death becomes meaningful. Life and death are the polar opposites, so the opposite to life is death. Try to understand it. And it will be helpful, very helpful, for you to find out the way for yourself.

If death is the polar opposite of life, then mind can move to death very easily — and it happens. When someone commits suicide, have you ever observed that the person who commits suicide was attached too much to life? Only those who are too much attached to life can commit suicide.

For example, you are too attached to your husband or to your wife and you think you cannot live without him or her. Then the husband or the wife dies, and you commit suicide. The mind has moved to the other end because it was too attached to life. When life frustrates, the mind can move to the other end.

Suicides are of two types — wholesale suicide and gradual suicide. You can commit gradual suicide — by withdrawing yourself from life, cutting yourself off, cutting your moorings in life by and by, dying slowly, gradually.

In Buddha's time there were schools who preached suicide. These were the real opposites to life, to worldly life. There were schools who were teaching that to commit suicide was the only way out of this nonsense which we call life, the only way out of this suffering. If you are alive, you will have to suffer, they said, and there is no way of going beyond misery while alive. So "Commit suicide. Destroy yourself". When you hear this it looks

289

like too extremist a view, but try to understand it deeply. It carries some meaning.

Sigmund Freud, after forty years of constant work with the human mind, one of the longest researches one individual can do, came to conclude that man as he is cannot be happy. The very way mind functions creates misery, so at the most less misery or more misery can be the choice. No misery cannot be the choice. If you adjust your mind, you will be less miserable: that is all. It looks very hopeless.

The existentialists — Sartre, Camus and others — say that life can never be blissful. The very nature of life is dread, anguish, suffering, so the most one can do is to face it bravely, with no hope. You can only face it bravely, and that is all — with no hope. The situation as such is hopeless. Camus asks, "Well, if this is the situation, then why not commit suicide ? If there is no way to go beyond in life, then why not leave this life ?"

One of Dostoevsky's characters in one of the greatest novels of the world, "The Brothers Karamazov," says, "I am trying to find out where your God is just to return to Him the entrance ticket — the entrance ticket to life. I don't want to be here. And if there is any God, He must be very violent and cruel," the character says, "because without asking me He has thrown me into life. It has never been my choice. Why am I alive without my choice ?"

There were many schools in Buddha's time. Buddha's time was one of the most intellectually dynamic periods in human history. For example, there was Ajit Kesh Kambal. You may not have heard the name because it is difficult to create a following around those who preach suicide. So no sect exists around Ajit Kesh Kambal, but he said continuously for fifty years that suicide alone is the only way.

It is reported that someone asked Ajit, "Then why have you not committed suicide up to now ?" He said, "Just to preach, I have to suffer life. I have a message to give to the world. If I commit suicide, then who will preach ? Who will teach this message ? Just to give this message, I am here. Otherwise, life is not worth living." This is the opposite extreme of life, of this so-called life which we live.

Buddha's was the middle path. Buddha said neither death nor life. That is what sannyas means: neither attachment to life nor repulsion, but just being in the middle. So Buddha says that sannyas is to be just in the middle. Sannyas is not negation of life. Rather, sannyas is the negation of both life and death. When you are concerned with neither life nor death, then you become a sannyasin.

If you can see the polar opposites of life and death, then Buddha's initiation into sannyas is just an initiation in the middle path. So a sannyasin is not really against life. If he is, then he is not a sannyasin. Then, really, he is a neurotic: he has gone to the other extreme. A sannyasin has a very balanced consciousness — balanced just in the middle.

If life is misery, the mind says, "Then move to the other end." But to Buddhists life is misery because you are at the extreme: that is the Buddhist idea. Life is a misery because it is at one extreme, and death will also be a misery because it is another extreme. Bliss is just in the middle; bliss is balance.

A sannyasin is a balanced being — neither leaning to the right — nor to the left, neither a leftist nor a rightist: just in the middle — silent, unmoving, not choosing this nor that, in a non-choice, remaining in the center.

So do not choose death: CHOICE is misery. If you choose death you have chosen misery, if you choose life you have chosen misery, because life and death are two extremes. And remember: they are two extremes of one thing. They are not really two — only one thing which has two poles: life and death.

If you choose one, you will have to go against the other pole. That creates misery because death is implied in life. You cannot choose life without choosing death. How can you ? The moment you choose life, you have chosen death. That creates misery because as a result of your having chosen life, death will be there. You have chosen happiness: simultaneously, without your knowing, you have chosen unhappiness because that is part of it.

If you have chosen love, then you have chosen hate. The other is intrinsic in it; it is hidden there. And one who chooses love will suffer, because then he will hate — and when he comes to hate he will suffer.

Do not choose: be in the middle. In the middle is the Truth. At one end is death, at the other end is life. But this energy moving between these two in the middle is the Truth. Do not choose, because choice means choice of one thing against another thing. To be in the middle means being choiceless. Then you will leave the whole thing. And when you have not chosen, you cannot be made miserable.

Man is made miserable through choice. Do not choose. Just be! It is arduous, it appears impossible — but try it. Whenever you have two opposites, try to be in the middle. By and by you will know the "hunch", the feel. And once you know the feel of how to be in the middle (and it is a delicate thing — very delicate: the most delicate thing in life), once you have the feel, nothing can disturb you, nothing can make you suffer. Then you exist without suffering.

That is what a sannyasin means: to exist without suffering. But to exist without suffering you have to exist without choice, so be in the middle. And Buddha has tried for the first time, so consciously, to create a path of being always in the middle.

The third question: *"Enlighten us about a few practical points for the opening and development of the heart center."*

The first point: try to be headless. Visualize yourself as headless; move headlessly. It sounds absurd, but it is one of the most important exercises. Try it, and then you will know. Walk, and feel as if you have no head. In the beginning it will be only "as if". It will be very weird. When the feeling will come to you that you have no head, it will be very weird and strange. But by and by you will settle down at the heart.

There is one law. You may have seen that someone who is blind has more keen ears, more musical ears. Blind men are more musical; their feeling for music is deeper. Why? The energy that ordinarily moves through the eyes now cannot move through them, so it chooses a different path: it moves through the ears.

Blind men have a deeper sensitivity of touch. If a blind man touches you, you will feel the difference, because we ordinarily do much work with touch through our eyes: we are touching each other through our eyes. A blind man cannot touch through the eyes, so the energy moves through his hands. A blind man is more sensitive than anyone who has eyes. Sometimes it may not be so, but generally it is so. Energy starts moving from another center if one center is not there.

So try this exercise I am talking about — the exercise in headlessness and suddenly you will feel a strange thing: it will be as if for the first time you are at the heart. Walk headlessly. Sit down to meditate, close your eyes and simply feel that there is no head. Feel, "My head has disappeared." In the beginning it will be just "as if", but by and by you will feel that the head has really disappeared. And when you feel that your head has disappeared, your center will fall down to the heart — immediately ! You will be looking at the world through the heart and not through the head.

When for the first time Westerners reached Japan, they couldn't believe that Japan has traditionally been thinking for centuries that they think through the belly. If you ask a Japanese child (if he is not educated in Western ways), "Where is your thinking ?" he will point to his belly.

Centuries and centuries have passed, and Japan has been living without the head. It is just a concept. If I ask you, "Where is your thinking going on ?" you will point toward the head, but a Japanese will point to the belly, not to the head — and one of the reasons why the Japanese mind is more calm, quiet and collected is this.

Now this is disturbed because the West has spread over everything. Now there exists no East. Only in some individuals here and there who are like islands does the East exist. Geographically, the East has disappeared. Now the whole world is Western.

Try headlessness. Meditate standing before your mirror in the bath. Look deep into your eyes and feel that you are looking from the heart. By and by the heart center will begin to function. And when the heart functions, it changes your total personality, the total structure, the whole pattern, because the heart has its own way.

So the first thing: try headlessness. Secondly, be more loving, because love cannot function through the head. Be more loving! That is why, when someone is in love, he loses his head. People say that he has gone mad. If you are not mad and in love, then you are not in love really. The head must be lost. If the head is there unaffected, functioning ordinarily, then love is not possible, because for love you need the heart to function — not the head. It is a function of the heart.

It happens that when a very rational person falls in love, he becomes stupid. He himself feels what stupidity he is doing, what silliness. What is he doing! Then he makes two parts of his life. He creates a division. The heart becomes a silent, intimate affair. When he moves out of his house, he moves out of his heart. He lives in the world with the head and only comes down to the heart when he is loving. But it is very difficult. It is VERY difficult, and ordinarily it never happens.

I was staying in Calcutta at a friend's house, and the friend was a justice of the High Court. His wife told me, "I have only one problem to tell you. Can you help me ?" So I said, "What is the problem ?" She said, "My husband is your friend. He loves you and respects you, so if you say something to him it may be helpful." So I asked her. "What is to be said ? Tell me ?" She said, "He remains a High Court judge even in the bed. I have not known a lover, a friend or a husband. He is a High Court judge twenty-four hours a day."

It is difficult: it is difficult to come down from your pedestal. It becomes a fixed attitude. If you are a business man, you will remain a business man in the bed also. It is difficult to accommodate two persons within, and it is not easy to change your pattern completely, immediately, anytime you like. It is difficult, but if you are in love you will have to come down from the head.

So for this meditation try to be more and more loving. And when I say be more loving, I mean change the quality of your relationship: let it be based on love. Not only with your wife or with your child or with your friend, but toward life as such become more loving. That is why Mahavir and Buddha have talked about non-violence: it was just to create a loving attitude toward life.

When Mahavir moves, walks, he remains aware not even to kill an ant. Why? Really, the ant is not concerned. He is coming down from the head to the heart. He is creating a loving attitude toward life as such. The more your relationship is based on love — all relationships — the more your heart center will function. It will start working; you will look at the world through different eyes: because the heart has its own way of looking at the world. The mind can never look in that way: that is impossible for the mind. The mind can only analyze! The heart synthesizes; the mind can only dissect, divide. It is a divider. Only the heart gives unity.

When you can look through the heart the whole universe looks like one unity. When you approach through the mind, the whole world becomes atomic. There is no unity: only atoms and atoms and atoms. The heart gives a unitary experience. It joins together and the ultimate synthesis is God. If you can look through the heart, the whole universe looks like one. That oneness is God.

That is why science can never find God. That is impossible, because the method applied can never reach to the ultimate unity. The very method of science is reason, analysis, division. So science comes to molecules, atoms, electrons, and they will go on dividing. They can never come to the organic unity of the Whole. The Whole is impossible to look at through the head.

So be more loving. Remember, whatsoever you are doing the quality of love must be there. This has to be a constant remembering. You are walking on the grass: feel that the grass is alive. Every blade is as much alive as you are.

Mahatma Gandhi was staying with Ravindranath Tagore in Shanti Niketan, and look at their different approaches! Gandhi's non-violence was a mind affair. He was always reasoning about it, rational about it. He thought about it, he struggled over it, he pondered, contemplated and then he concluded. He experimented, then he concluded. If you have read his autobiography, you will recall that he has named the book, "Experiments with Truth." The very word "Experiments" is scientific, of the reason, a lab word.

He was staying with Ravindranath the poet, and they both went for a walk in the gardens. The land was green, alive, so Gandhi said to Ravindranath, "Come out to the lawn." Ravindranath said, "That is impossible. I cannot walk over the lawn. Every blade is as much alive as I am. I cannot step over so alive a phenomenon."

And Ravindranath was not a preacher of non-violence — not at all. He never talked about non-violence, but his approach was through the heart. He feels the grass. Gandhi pondered over what he said, and then answered, "You are right." This is a mind approach. This is a MIND APPROACH!

Be loving. Even with things, be loving. If you are sitting on a chair, be loving. Feel the chair; have a feeling of gratitude. The chair is giving comfort to you. Feel the touch, love it, have a loving feeling. The chair itself is not important. If you are eating, eat lovingly.

Indians say that food is Divine. The meaning is that when you are eating, the food is giving you life, energy, vitality. Be grateful; be loving to it.

Ordinarily we eat food very violently — as if we are killing something. Not as if we are absorbing: as if we are killing. Or, very indifferently you go on throwing things into your belly without any feeling. Touch your food lovingly, with gratitude: it is your life. Take it in, taste it, enjoy it. Do not be indifferent and do not be violent.

Our teeth are very violent because of our animal heritage. Animals have no other weapons: nails and teeth are the only weapons of violence. Your teeth are basically a weapon, so people go on killing with their teeth: they kill their food. That is why, the more violent you are, the more you will need food.

But there is a limit to food, so one goes on smoking or one goes on chewing gum. That is violence. You enjoy it because you are killing something with your teeth, grinding something with your teeth, so one goes on chewing gum or *pan* (betel nut leaves — commonly used in India). This is a part of violence. Do whatsoever you are doing, but do it lovingly. Do not be indifferent. Then your heart center will start functioning, and you will come down deep into the heart.

First: try headlessness, secondly: try love, thirdly: be more and more aesthetic — sensitive toward beauty, toward music, toward all that touches the heart. If this world can be trained more for music and less for mathematics, we will have a better humanity; if we can train the mind more for poetry and less for philosophy, we will have a better humanity: because while you are listening to music or playing music, the mind is not needed — you drop from the mind.

Be more aesthetic, more poetic, more sensitive. You may not be a great musician or a great poet or a great painter, but you can enjoy, and you can create something in your own right: there is no need to be a Picasso. You can paint your house yourself; you can paint some pictures.

No need to be a maestro — an Alauddin Khan (a great Indian musician): you can play something in your house. You can play on a flute, no matter how amateurish. But do something which is concerned with the heart. Sing, dance, do something which is concerned with the heart. Be more sensitive to the world of the heart — and not much is needed to be sensitive.

Even a poor man can be sensitive: riches are not needed. You may not have a palace where you can be sensitive. If you are just lying on the beach, it is enough to be sensitive. You can be sensitive to the sand, you can be sensitive to the sun, you can be sensitive to the waves, to the wind, to the trees, to the sky. The whole world is there for you to be sensitive to it. Try to be more sensitive, alive — and ACTIVELY sensitive, because the whole world has become passive.

You go to a cinema hall: someone else is doing something and you just sit there and see. Someone else is loving on the screen and you are seeing: you are just a voyeur — passively dead, not doing anything. You are not a participant. Unless you are a participant, your heart center will not function. So it is better sometimes to dance.

You are not going to be a great dancer. There is no need. Howsoever awkward, just dance. That will give you the feeling of the heart. While you are dancing, your center will be the heart: it can never be at the mind. Jump, play like children. Sometimes forget completely your name, your prestige, your degree. Forget them completely; be childlike. Do not be serious. Sometimes take life as a fun, and the heart will develop. The heart gathers energy.

And when you have a heart that is alive, your mind's quality will also change. Then you can go to the mind; you can function through the mind. But then the mind will become just an instrument: you can use it. Then you are not obsessed with it, and you can move away from it any moment you like. Then you are a master. The heart will give you a feeling that you are a master.

And another thing: you will come to know that you are neither the head nor the heart, because you can move from heart to head, from head to heart. Then you know that you are something else — X. If you remain in the head and never move anywhere, you become identified with the head. You do not know that you are different. This movement from heart to head and from head to heart will give you the feeling that you are totally different. Sometimes you are at the heart and sometimes you are at the head, but you are neither heart nor head.

This third point of awareness will lead you to the third center — to the navel. And the navel is not really a center.

There, YOU ARE! That is why it cannot be developed: it can only be discovered.

The third question: *"You said that Western psychologists now say it is better not to avoid fighting in a love relationship and that facing it when it comes makes the love more intense. Then you spoke of Buddha's middle path which excludes both extremes. For those who have not yet transcended into the love that is beyond the two poles, which way is preferable for lovers in your opinion?"*

Some basic points: Firstly, the mind's love is bound to be a movement between two polar opposites of hate and love. With mind, duality is bound to be there. So if you are loving to someone with your mind, you cannot escape the other pole. You can hide it, you can suppress it, you can forget about it: the so-called "cultured" are always doing that. But then they become numb, dead.

If you cannot fight with your lover, if you cannot be angry, then the authenticity of the love is lost. If you suppress your anger, that suppressed anger will become a part of you, and that suppressed anger will not allow you total let-go while in love. It is always there. You are withholding it; you have suppressed it.

If I am angry and I have suppressed it, then when I am loving the suppressed anger is there, and that will make my love dead. If I have not been authentic in my anger, I cannot be authentic in my love. If you are authentic, then you are authentic in both. If you are not authentic in one, you cannot be authentic in the other.

So-called teachings all over the world, civilization, culture, they have deadened love completely — and IN THE NAME OF LOVE this has happened. They say if you love someone, then do not be angry — that your love is false if you are angry. Then do not fight. Then do not hate.

Of course, it looks logical. If you are in love, how can you hate? So we cut out the hate part. But with the hate part cut, the love becomes impotent. It is as if you have cut off one leg of a man and then you say, "Now you move! Now you can run: you are free to run." But you have cut off a leg, so the man cannot move.

Hate and love are two poles of one phenomenon. If you cut hate, love will be dead and impotent. That is why every family has become impotent. And then you become afraid of letting go. When you are in love, you cannot let go completely because you are afraid. If you let go completely, the anger, the violence, the hate that is hidden and suppressed, may come out. Then you have to force it down continuously. Deep down you have to fight it continuously. And in fighting it you cannot be natural and spontaneous. Then you just pose that you are loving. You pretend, and everyone knows, your wife knows, that you are pretending. And you know that your wife is pretending. Everyone is pretending. Then the whole life becomes false.

Two things have to be done in order to go beyond mind: go into meditation, and then touch the level of no-mind within you. Then you will have a love that will not have any polar opposite. But then in that love there will be no excitement, no passion. That love will be silent — a deep peace with not even a ripple on it.

A Buddha, a Jesus, they also love. But in that love there is no excitement, no fever. The fever comes from the polar opposite; the excitement comes from the polar opposite. Two polar opposites create tension. But their love is a silent phenomenon, so only those who have reached to the state of no-mind can understand their love.

Jesus was passing, and it was a hot noon. He was tired, so he just rested under a tree. He didn't know to whom the tree belonged. It belonged to Mary Magdalene. Mary was a prostitute.

She looked from her window and saw this very beautiful man — one of the most beautiful ever born. She felt attracted — and not only attracted: she felt passion. She came out and she asked Jesus, "Come into my house. Why are you resting here? You are welcome." Jesus saw in her eyes passion, love — "so-called love". Jesus said, "Next time, when I will be tired again while passing here, I will come to your house. But just now the need is fulfilled. I am ready to move again, so thank you."

Mary felt insulted. This was rare. Really, she had never invited anyone before. People would come from far away just to have a look at her. Even kings would come to her, and here was this beggar refusing her. Jesus was just a beggar, a vagabond — just a "hippie", and he refused her. So Mary said to Jesus, "Can't you feel my love ? This is a love invitation. So come ! Do not reject me. Don't you have any love in your heart ?"

Jesus said to her in reply, "I also love you — and, really, all those who come pretending that they love you, they do not love you." He said, "Only I can love you." And he was right. But that love has a different quality. That love does not have the polar opposite, the contrast. Thus, the tension is missing; the excitement is missing. He is not excited about love, not feverish. And love is not a relationship for him: it is a state of being.

Go beyond mind; reach to a level of no-mind. Then love flowers, but that love has no opposite to it. Beyond mind there is no opposite to anything. Beyond mind everything is one. Within mind, everything is divided into two. But if you are within mind, it is better to be authentic than to be false.

So be authentic when you feel angry toward your lover or your beloved. Be authentic while you are in anger, and then, with no repression, when the moment of love will come, when the mind will move to the other extreme, you will have a spontaneous flow. So with mind take fighting as part of it. It is the very dynamism of the mind to work in polar opposites. So be authentic in your anger, be authentic in your fight. Then you will be authentic in your love also.

So for lovers, I would like to say be authentic. And if you are really authentic, a unique phenomenon will happen. You will become weary of the whole nonsense of moving in polar opposites. But be authentic: otherwise you will never become weary.

A repressed mind never becomes really aware that he is gripped in polar opposites. He is never really angry, he is never really in love, so he has no real experience of the mind. Thus, I suggest be authentic. Do not be false. BE REAL! And authenticity has its own beauty. Your lover, you beloved, will understand when you are really angry — authentically angry. Only a false anger or a false non-anger cannot be forgiven. Only a false face cannot be forgiven. Be authentic, and then you will be authentic in love also. That authentic love will compensate, and through this authentic living you will become wearied. You will come to wonder what you are doing — why you are just a pendulum moving from one pole to another. You will be bored, and then only can you decide to move beyond mind and beyond polarity.

Be an authentic man or be an authentic woman. Do not allow any falsity; do not pretend. Be real and suffer reality. Suffering is good. Suffering is really a training, a discipline. Suffer it! Suffer anger and suffer love and suffer hate. Remember only one thing: never be false. If you do not feel love, then say that you do not feel love. Do not pretend; do not try to show that you are loving. If you are angry, then say that you are angry and be angry.

There will be much suffering, but suffer it. Through that suffering a new consciousness is born. You become aware of the whole nonsense of hate and love. You hate the same person and you also love the same person, and you go on moving in a circle. That circle will become crystal clear for you, and it becomes crystal clear only through suffering.

Do not escape suffering. You need a REAL suffering. It is like a fire: it will burn you. And all that is false will burn and all that is real will be there. This is what existentialists call authenticity. Be authentic, and then you cannot be any more in the mind. Be non-authentic, and you will be for lives and lives in the mind.

You will get bored of the duality. But how can one get bored of the duality unless one is really in the duality, not pretending? Then you will know that the so-called love of the mind is nothing but a disease.

Have you observed that a lover cannot sleep? He is not at ease: he is feverish. If you examine him, he will show many symptoms of many diseases. This love, the so-called love of mind and body, is really a disease, but one remains occupied: that is the function of it. Otherwise you will feel unoccupied, as if not doing anything in this world. Your whole life will seem vacant, so love is good to fill it.

Mind itself is the disease, so whatsoever belongs to the mind is going to be a disease. Only beyond mind, where you are not divided in duality, where you are one, only there, does a different love flower.

Jesus calls it love, Buddha calls it compassion. This is just to make a distinction. It makes no difference what you call it.

There is a possibility of a love which has no opposite to it, but that love can come only when you go beyond this love. And to go beyond, I suggest that you be authentic — authenticity — to be AUTHENTIC.

In hate, in love, in anger, in everything, be authentic, real, not pretending, because only a reality can be transcended. You cannot transcend unreal things.

13
Entering The Inner Centering

November 16, 1972, Bombay, India

SUTRAS:

18.   *Look lovingly at some object. Do not go to another object. Here in the middle of the object — the blessing.*

19.   *Without support for feet or hands, sit only on the buttocks. Suddenly, the centering.*

20.   *In a moving vehicle, by rhythmically swaying, experience. Or in a still vehicle, by letting yourself swing in slowing invisible circles.*

21.   *Pierce some part of your nectar-filled form with a pin, and gently enter the piercing and attain to the inner purity.*

The human body is a mysterious mechanism. Its working is two-dimensional. In order to go to the outside, your consciousness goes through the senses to meet the world, to meet matter. But this is only one dimension of your body's functions. Your body has another dimension also: it leads you in. If consciousness goes out, then whatsoever you know is matter; if consciousness goes in, then whatsoever you know is non-matter.

In reality, there is no division: matter and non-matter are one. But this reality — "X" — if looked at through the eyes, the senses, appears as matter. This same reality, the "X", looked at from within — not through the senses, but through centering — looks like non-matter. The reality is one, but you can look at it in two ways. One is through the senses; another is not through the senses. All these techniques of centering are really to lead you to a point in yourself where senses are not working — where you go beyond senses.

Three things have to be understood first before we enter the techniques. Firstly, when you see through the eyes, the eyes are not seeing: they are only openings to see. The seer is behind the eyes. That which looks through the eyes is not the eyes. That is why you can close your eyes and still see dreams, visions, images. The seer is behind the senses; he moves through the senses to the world. But if you close your senses, the seer remains within.

If the seer, this consciousness, is centered, suddenly he becomes aware of himself. And when you are aware of yourself you are aware of the total Existence, because you and Existence are not two. But to become aware of oneself one needs centering, and by "centering" I mean your consciousness not being divided in many directions, your consciousness not moving anywhere — remaining in itself, non-moving, rooted, without any direction — just remaining there: in.

It looks difficult to remain in, because for our minds even this thinking of how to remain in becomes a going out. We start thinking: the "how" starts thinking. To think about the in, the inner, is also a thought for us — and every thought as such belongs to the outer, never to the inner, because in the innermost center you are simply consciousness.

Thoughts are like clouds. They have come to you, but they do not belong to you. Every thought comes from the outside — from without. You cannot produce a single thought inside — within. Every thought comes from the out; there is no possibility of creating a thought within. Thoughts are like clouds coming to you. So whenever you are thinking, you are not in — remember. Thinking is to be out. So even if you are thinking about the inner, the soul, the Self, you are not in.

All these thoughts about the Self, about the inner, about the within, have come from without: they do not belong to you. To you belongs only simple consciousness, sky-like, without the clouds.

So what to do? How to gain this simple consciousness inside? Some devices are used because directly you cannot do anything. Some devices are needed through which you are thrown in, thrown to it. This center always needs an indirect approach. You cannot approach it directly. Understand this clearly because this is very basic.

You are playing, and later on you report that it was very blissful, that "I was feeling very happy, and I enjoyed it". A subtle happiness has been left behind. Someone listens to you. He is also after happiness — everyone is. He says, "Then I must play, because if through playing happiness is achieved, then I must achieve." He plays also, but he is directly concerned with happiness, with bliss, with enjoyment. Happiness is a by-product. If you are totally in your play, absorbed, happiness results, but if you are constantly hankering for happiness nothing happens. The play is the start.

You are listening to music. Someone says, "I feel very blissful." But if constantly you are directly concerned with bliss, you will not even be able to listen. That concern, that greed for bliss, will become a barrier. Bliss is a by-product. You cannot grab it directly. It is so delicate a phenomenon that you have to approach it only indirectly. Do something else and it happens. You cannot do it directly.

Whatsoever is beautiful, whatsoever is eternal, is so delicate that if you try to grab it directly it is destroyed. That is what is meant by techniques and devices. These techniques go on telling you to do something. That which you are doing is not significant: that which results is significant. But your mind must be concerned with doing, with technique — not with the result. The result happens: it is bound to happen. But it always happens indirectly. So do not be concerned with the result. Be concerned with the technique. Do it as totally as possible, and forget the result. It happens, but you can become a barrier to it.

If you are concerned only with the result, then it will never happen. And then it becomes very strange. People come to me. They say, "You said that if we do meditation, 'this' will happen, but we are doing it and 'this' is not happening." And they are right, but they have forgotten the condition. You have to forget about the result. Only then does it happen.

You have to be in the act totally. The more you are in the act, the sooner the result happens. But it is always indirect. You cannot be aggressive about it; you cannot be violent about it. It is so delicate a phenomenon, it cannot be attacked. It only comes to you while you are engaged somewhere else so totally that your inner space is vacant. These techniques are all indirect. There is no direct technique for spiritual happening.

Now, the technique — the sixth technique (for centering):
"Look lovingly on some object. Do not go on to another object.
Here in the middle of the object — the blessing.

I should repeat it: "Look lovingly on some object. Do not go
on to another": do not move to another object. "Here in the
middle of this object — the blessing."

"Look lovingly on some object . . ." "Lovingly" is the key.
Have you ever looked lovingly at any object? You may say
"yes" because you do not know what it means to look lovingly
at an object. You may have looked lustfully at an object: that is
another thing. That is totally different — diametrically opposite.
So first, the difference: try to feel the difference.

A beautiful face, a beautiful body — you look at it, and you
feel that you are looking at it lovingly. But why are you looking
at it? Do you want to get something out of it? Then it is a
lust, not love. Do you want to exploit it? Then it is lust, not
love. Then, really, you are thinking of how to use this body,
how to possess it, how to make this body an instrument for
your happiness.

Lust means how to use something for your happiness; love
means your happiness is not at all concerned. Really, lust means
how to get something out of it and love means how to give
something. They are diametrically opposite.

If you see a beautiful face and you feel love toward the face,
the immediate feeling in your consciousness will be how to do
something to make this face happy, how to do something to
make this man or this woman happy. The concern is not with
yourself: the concern is with the other.

In love the other is important; in lust you are important. In
lust you are thinking how to make the other your instrument;
in love you are thinking how to become an instrument yourself.
In lust you are going to sacrifice the other; in love you are
going to sacrifice yourself. Love means giving; lust means
getting. Love is a surrender; lust is an aggression.

What you say is meaningless. Even in lust you talk in terms
of love. Your language is not very meaningful, so do not be

deceived. Look within, and then you will come to understand that you have not once in your life looked lovingly toward someone or some object.

The second distinction to be made: this sutra says, "Look lovingly on some object." Really, even if you look lovingly at something material, insentient, the object will become a person. If you look lovingly at it, your love is the key to transform anything into a person. If you look lovingly at a tree, the tree becomes a person.

Just the other day, I was talking with Vivek (a close disciple), and I told her that when we move to the new Ashram we will name every tree, because every tree is a person. Have you ever heard of anyone naming a tree? No one names a tree because no one feels love for it. If the case were otherwise a tree would become a person. Then it is not just one in a crowd: it becomes unique.

You name dogs and cats. When you name a dog and you call it Tiger or something else, the dog becomes a person. Then it is not just one dog amidst other dogs: it has a personality. You have created a person. Whenever you look lovingly at something, it becomes a person.

And the contrary is also true: whenever you look with lustful eyes toward a person, the person becomes an object, a thing. That is why lustful eyes are repulsive — because no one likes to become a thing. When you look at your wife with lustful eyes — or at any other woman, or man, with lustful eyes — the other feels hurt. What are you doing really? You are changing a person, a living person, into a dead instrument. You are thinking of how to "use", and the person is killed.

That is why lustful eyes are repulsive, ugly. When you look at someone with love, the other is raised. He becomes unique. Suddenly he becomes a person.

A person cannot be replaced; a thing can be replaced. A "thing" means that which is replaceable; a "person" means that which cannot be replaced: there is no possibility of replacing him or her. A person is unique; a thing is not unique.

Love makes anything unique. That is why without love you never feel like a person. Unless someone loves you deeply, you never feel that you have any uniqueness. You are just one in a crowd — just a number, a datum. You can be changed.

For example, if you are a clerk in an office or a teacher in a school or a professor in a university, your "professor-hood" is replaceable. Another professor will replace you: he can replace you at any moment because you are just used there as a professor. You have a functional meaning and significance.

If you are a clerk, someone else is easily able to do the work. The work will not wait for you. If you die this moment, the next moment someone will replace you and the mechanism will continue. You were just a figure: another figure will do. You were just a utility.

But then someone falls in love with this clerk or this professor. Suddenly the clerk is no more a clerk: he has become a unique person. If he dies, then the beloved cannot replace him. He is irreplaceable. Then the whole world may go on in the same way, but the one who was in love cannot be the same. This uniqueness, this being a person, happens through love.

This sutra says, "Look lovingly on some object." It makes no distinction between an object and a person. There is no need, because when you look lovingly anything will become a person. The very look changes — transforms.

You may or may not have observed what happens when you drive a particular car, say a Fiat. There are thousands and thousands and thousands of Fiats exactly similar, but your car, if you are in love with it, becomes unique — a person. It cannot be replaced. A relationship is created. Now you feel this car as a person. If something goes wrong — a slight sound, you feel it. And cars are very temperamental. You know the temper of your car — when it feels good and when it feels bad. The car becomes, by and by, a person.

Why? If there is a love relationship, anything becomes a person. If there is a lust relationship, then a person will become

a thing. And this is one of the most inhuman acts man can do —
to make someone a thing.

"Look lovingly on some object ..." So what is one to do ?
When you look lovingly, what are you to do ? The first thing:
forget yourself. Forget yourself completely! Look at a flower
and forget yourself completely. Let the flower be. You become
completely absent. Feel the flower, and a deep love will flow
from your consciousness toward the flower. And let your consciousness be filled with only one thought — how you can help
this flower to flower more, to become more beautiful, to become
more blissful. What can you do ?

It is not meaningful whether you can do or not; that is not
relevant. The feeling of what you can do — this pain, this deep
ache over what you can do to make this flower more beautiful,
more alive, more flowering — is meaningful. Let this thought
reverberate into your whole being. Let every fibre of your body
and mind feel it. You will be transfixed in an ecstasy, and the
flower will become a person.

"Do not go onto another object..." You cannot go. If you
are in a love relationship, you cannot go. If you love someone
in this group, then you forget the whole crowd; only one face
remains. Really, you do not see anyone else: you see only one
face. All the others are there, but they are subliminal — just on
the periphery of your consciousness. They are NOT. They are
just shadows. Only one face remains. If you love someone then
only that face remains, so you cannot move.

Do not go to another object: remain with one. Remain with
a rose flower or remain with a beloved's face. Remain there loving, flowing, with just one heart, with the feeling of "What can
I do to make the loved one happier, blissful".

". . . Here in the middle of this object — the blessing." And
when this is the case, you are absent, not concerned with yourself at all, not selfish, not thinking in terms of your pleasure, your
gratification. You have forgotten yourself completely, and you
are just thinking in terms of the other. The other has become
the center of your love; your consciousness is flowing toward

313

the other. With deep compassion, with a deep feeling of love, you are thinking, "What can I do to make the loved one blissful?" In this state, suddenly, "Here in the middle of the object — the blessing." Suddenly, as a by-product, the blessing comes to you. Suddenly you become centered.

This looks paradoxical because this sutra says to forget yourself completely, not to be self-centered, to move to the other completely. Buddha is reported to have said continuously that whenever you are praying, pray for others — never for yourself. Otherwise the prayer is just useless.

One man came to Buddha and he said, "I accept your teaching, but only one thing is very difficult to accept. You say that whenever we do prayer we are not to think about ourselves, we are not to ask anything about ourselves. We have to say, 'Whatsoever may be the result of my prayer, let that result be distributed to all. If blessing happens, let it be distributed to all.'"

The man said, "This is okay, but can I make only one exception? Not to my immediate neighbour: he is my enemy. Let this blessing be distributed to all except to my immediate neighbor."

The mind is self-centered, so Buddha said, "Your prayer is useless. Nothing will result out of it unless you are ready to give all, to distribute all, and then all will be yours."

In love you are to forget yourself. Then it looks paradoxical: then when and how will the centering happen? By being totally concerned with the other, with the other's happiness, when you forget yourself completely and only the other remains there, suddenly you are filled with bliss — the blessing.

Why? Because when you are not concerned with yourself you become vacant, empty. The inner space is created. When your mind is totally concerned with the other, you become mindless within. Then there are no thoughts inside. And then this thought ("How can I be helpful? How can I create more bliss? How can the other be more happy?") cannot continue any more, because, really, there is nothing you can do. This thought becomes a stop. There is nothing you can do. What can you do?

If you think you can do, you are still thinking in terms of yourself — ego.

With the love object one becomes totally helpless, remember this. Whenever you love someone you feel totally helpless. That is the agony of the love: one cannot feel what he can do. He wants to do everything, he wants to give the whole universe to the lover or beloved — but what can he do ? If you think that you can do this or that, you are still not in a love relationship. Love is very helpless — absolutely helpless, and that helplessness is the beauty because in that helplessness you are surrendered.

Love someone and you will feel helpless; hate someone and you can do something. Love someone and you are absolutely helpless — because what can you do ? Whatsoever you can do seems insignificant, meaningless. It is never enough. Nothing can be done. And when one feels that nothing can be done, one feels that he is helpless. When one wants to do everything and feels nothing can be done, mind stops. In this helplessness surrender happens. You are empty. That is why love becomes a deep meditation.

Really, if you love someone no other meditation is needed. But because no one loves, 112 methods are needed — and even they may not be enough.

Someone was here the other day. He was telling me, "It gives much hope. I have heard for the first time from you that there are 112 methods. It gives much hope, but somewhere a depression also comes into the mind. Only 112 methods ? And if these 112 don't work for me, then is there no 113th ?"

And he is right. He is right ! If these 112 methods do not work for you, then there is no go. So as he suggests, a depression also follows hope. But, really, methods are needed because the basic method is missing. If you can love, no method is needed.

Love itself is the greatest method, but love is difficult — in a way impossible. Love means putting yourself out from your consciousness, and in the same place, where your ego has been

in existence, putting someone else. Replacing yourself by someone else means love — as if now you are not and only the
other is.

Jean Paul Sartre says that the other is the hell, and he is right.
He is right because the other creates only hell for you. But he
is wrong also because if the other can be hell, the other can be
heaven. If you live through lust, the other is a hell because then
you are trying to kill that person. You are trying to make that
person a thing. Then that person will also react and will try to
make you a thing, and that creates hell.

So every husband and every wife, they are creating hell for
each other because each one is trying to possess the other. Possession is possible only with things — never with persons. You
can only be possessed by a person, but you can never possess a
person. A thing can be possessed, but you try to possess persons.
Through that effort persons become things. If I make you into
a thing, you will react. Then I am your enemy. Then you will
try to make a thing out of me. That creates hell.

You are sitting in your room alone, and then suddenly you
become aware that someone is peeping through the keyhole.
Observe minutely what happens. Have you felt any change ?
And why do you feel angry about this peeping Tom ? He is not
doing anything to you — just peeping. Why do you feel angry ?
He has changed you into a thing. He is observing; he had made
you into a thing — into an object. That gives you an uneasiness.

And the same will happen to him if you come near the keyhole and look through it. The other will become shattered,
shocked. He was a subject just a moment before: he was the
observer and you were the observed. Now suddenly he has been
caught. He has been observed observing you, and now he has
become a thing.

Suddenly you feel your freedom has been disturbed, destroyed,
when someone is observing you. That is why, unless you are
in love with someone, you cannot stare. That stare becomes
ugly and violent — unless you are in love. If you are in love,
then a stare is a beautiful thing because your stare is not chang-

ing the other into a thing. Then you can look directly into the eyes; then you can go deep into the eyes of the other. You are not changing him into a thing. Rather, through your love your look is making him a person. That is why only stares of lovers are beautiful; otherwise stares are ugly.

Psychologists say there is a time limit, and you all know — observe and you will come to know what the time limit is — for how long you can stare into someone's eyes if he is a stranger. There is a time limit. One moment more, and the other will become angry. Just a passing look can be pardoned in public because it seems as if you were just seeing, not looking.

A look is a deep thing. If I just see you when passing, no relationship is created. Or I am passing and you look at me — just while passing: no offence is meant so it is okay. But if you suddenly stand and look at me, you become an observer. Then your look will disturb me and I feel insulted. What are you doing? I am a person, not a thing. This is not the way to look.

Because of this clothes have become so meaningful. Only when you love someone can you be easily naked, because the moment you are naked your whole body becomes an object. The WHOLE body becomes an object. Someone can look at your whole body, and if he is not in love with you his eyes will turn your whole body, your whole being, into an object. But when you are in love with someone you can be naked without feeling that you are naked. Rather, you would like to be naked because you would like this transforming love to transform your whole body into a person.

Whenever you are turning someone into a thing, that act is immoral. But if you are filled with love, then in that love-filled moment, with any object, this phenomenon, this blessing, is possible — it happens.

"In the middle of the object — the blessing." Suddenly you have forgotten yourself. The other was there. Then when the right moment comes, when you are no longer present, absolutely absent, the other will also become absent. And between

317

the two the blessing happens. That is what lovers feel. That blessing is also because of an unknown unconscious meditation.

When two lovers are there, by and by they both become absent. A pure existence remains without any egos, without any conflict — just a communion. In that communion one feels blissful. It is wrongly inferred that the other has given that bliss to you. That bliss has come because unknowingly you have fallen into a deep meditative technique.

You can do it consciously — and when you do it consciously it goes deeper because then you are not obsessed with the object. This is happening every day. If you love someone, you feel blissful not because of him or her, but because of love. And why because of love? Because this phenomenon happens — this sutra happens.

But then you become obsessed. Then you think because of "A", because of "A's" proximity — nearness, because of "A's" love, this blessing happens. Then you think, "I must possess A because without A being present I may not be able to get this blessing again." You become jealous. If someone else possesses "A", then he will be blissful and you will feel miserable, so you want to take away all possibilities of "A" being possessed by anyone else. "A" should be possessed only by you because you have glimpsed at a different world through him. Then, the moment you try to possess, you will destroy the whole beauty and the whole phenomenon.

When the lover is possessed, love is gone. Then the lover is just a thing. You can use it, but the blessing will never come again because that blessing was coming when the other was a person. The other was made, created: you created the person in the other, and the other created the person in you. No one was an object. Both were subjectivities meeting — two persons meeting, not one person and one thing.

But the moment you possess, this will become impossible. And mind will try to possess because mind thinks in terms of greed: "One day bliss has happened, so it must happen to me every day. So I must possess." But the bliss happens because there is no possession. And the bliss happens not because of the other, really, but because of you. Remember this, the bliss happens because of you. Because you are so absorbed in the other, the bliss happens.

It can happen with a rose flower, it can happen with a rock, it can happen with the trees, it can happen with anything. Once you know the situation in which it happens, it can happen anywhere. If you know that you are not and with a deep love your consciousness has moved to the other — to the trees, to the sky, to the stars, to anyone, when your total consciousness is addressed to the other: it leaves you, it moves away from you; in that absense of the self, THE BLESSING.

The seventh technique: *"Without support for feet or hands, sit only on buttocks. Suddenly, the centering."*

This technique has been used by Taoists in China for centuries, and it is a wonderful technique — one of the easiest. Try this: "Without support for feet or hands sit only on buttocks. Suddenly, the centering."

What is to be done? You will need two things — first, a very sensitive body, which you do not have. You have a dead body. It is just a burden to be carried — not sensitive. First you will have to make your body sensitive; otherwise this technique will not do. So first I will tell you something about how to make your body sensitive, and particularly your buttocks, because, ordinarily, your buttocks are the most insensitive part in your body. They have to be. They have to be because you are sitting the whole day on your buttocks. If they are too sensitive, it will be difficult.

So your buttocks are insensitive: they need to be. Just like the soles of the feet, they are insensitive. Continuously sitting on them, you never feel you are sitting on your buttocks. Have you ever felt it before this? Now you can feel you are sitting on your buttocks, but you have never felt it before — and you have been sitting on your buttocks your whole life, never aware. Their function is such that they cannot be very sensitive.

So first you have to make them sensitive. Try one very easy method, and this method can be done to any part of the body. Then the body will become sensitive. Just sit on a chair relaxed. Close your eyes. Just sit on a chair relaxed and close your eyes. Feel your left hand or your right hand — either one. Feel your left hand. Forget the whole body and just feel the left hand. The more you feel, the more the left hand will become heavy.

Go on feeling the left hand. Forget the whole body. Just go on feeling the left hand as if you are just the left hand. The hand will go on becoming more and more and more heavy. As it goes on becoming heavy, go on feeling it becoming more heavy. Then try to feel what is happening in the hand. Whatever the sensation, note it down: any sensation, any jerk, any slight movement — note down in the mind that this is happening. And go on doing it every day for at least three weeks. At any time during the day, do it for ten minutes, fifteen minutes. Just feel the left hand and forget the whole body.

Within three weeks you will feel a new left hand with you or a new right hand. It will be so sensitive, so touchy. And you will become aware of very minute and delicate sensations in the hand.

When you succeed with the hand, then try with the buttocks. Then try: close your eyes and feel that only two buttocks exist; you are no more. Let your whole consciousness go to the buttocks. It is not difficult. If you try, it is wonderful. And the feeling of aliveness that comes in the body is in itself very blissful. Then, when you can feel your buttocks and they can become very sensitive, when you can feel anything happening inside — a slight movement, a slight pain or anything — then you can observe and you can know. Then your consciousness is joined to the buttocks.

First try it with the hand. Because the hand is very sensitive, it is easy. Once you gain the confidence that you can sensitize your hand, this confidence will help you to sensitize your buttocks. Then do this technique. So you will need at least six weeks before you can enter this technique — three weeks with your hand and then three weeks with your buttocks — just making them more and more sensitive.

Lying on the bed, forget the whole body. Just remember that only two buttocks are left. Feel the touch — the bedsheet, the coldness or the slowly coming warmth: feel it. Lying down in your tub bath, forget the body. Remember only the buttocks — feel. Stand against a wall with your buttocks touching the wall: feel the coldness of the wall. Stand with your beloved, with your wife or husband, buttock to buttock: feel the other through the buttocks. This is just to "create" your buttocks, to bring them to a situation where they start feeling.

Then do this technique: "Without support for feet or hands. . ." sit on the ground. Without support for feet or hands, sit only on the buttocks. The Buddha posture will do: *padmasana* will do. Or, *siddhasana* will do or any ordinary *asana,* but it is good not to use your hands. Just remain on the buttocks: sit only on buttocks. Then what to do? Just close your eyes. Feel the buttocks touching the ground. And because the buttocks have become sensitive, you will feel that one buttock is touching more. You are leaning on one buttock, and the other is touching less. Then move the leaning to the other. Immediately, move to the other, then come to the first. Go on moving from one to other, and then by and by, balance.

Balancing means that both of your buttocks are feeling the same. Your weight on both of the buttocks is exactly the same. And when your buttocks will be sensitive, this will not be difficult: you will feel it. Once both your buttocks are balanced, suddenly, the centering. With that balance, suddenly you will be thrown to your navel center, and you will be centered inside. You will forget the buttocks, you will forget the body. You will be thrown to the inner center.

That is why I say centers are not meaningful, but centering is — whether it happens at the heart or at the head or at the buttocks or anywhere. You have seen Buddhas sitting. You may not have imagined that they may be balancing their buttocks. You go to a temple and see Mahavir sitting, Buddha sitting:

you may never have imagined that this sitting may be just a balancing on the buttocks. It is — and when there is no imbalance, suddenly that balance gives you the centering.

The eighth technique: *"In a moving vehicle, by rhythmically swaying, experience. Or in a still vehicle, by letting yourself swing in slowing invisible circles."*

It is the same in a different way. "In a moving vehicle..." You are travelling by a train, or in a bullock cart (when this technique was developed there was only the bullock cart). You are moving in a bullock cart on an Indian road (even today the road is the same). But when you are moving, your whole body is moving. Then it is useless.

"In a moving vehicle, by rhythmically swaying . . ." Sway rhythmically. Try to understand: this is very minute. Whenever you are in a bullock cart or in any vehicle, you are resisting. The bullock cart sways to the left, but you resist it: you sway to the right in order to balance; otherwise you will fall down. So you are constantly resisting. Sitting in a bullock cart, you are fighting its movements. It moves to this side, and you have to move to that.

That is why when sitting in a train you become tired. You have not been doing anything. Why do you become so tired? You have been doing much unknowingly. You were fighting the train continuously; there was resistance. Do not resist: this is the first thing. If you want to do this technique, do not resist. Rather, move with the movements, sway with the movements. Become part of the bullock cart: do not resist it. Whatsoever the bullock cart is doing on the road, become part of it. That is why children are never tired of journeying.

Poonam (a disciple) has just come from London with her two children, and she was afraid there — that they may get ill, that they may get tired because of such a long journey. She became tired, and they came laughing. She became completely tired when she came here. The moment she entered my room she was dead tired, and the two children started playing right then and there. An eighteen-hour long journey from London to

Bombay and they were not a bit tired. Why? Because they do not know how to resist yet.

So a drunkard can sit in a bullock cart for the whole night, and in the morning he will be as fresh as ever, but you will not be. It is because a drunkard cannot resist. He moves with the cart; there is no fight. The fighting is not there. He is one.

"In a moving vehicle, by rhythmically swaying..." So do one thing: do not resist. And the second thing, create a rhythm: create a rhythm in your movements. Make it a beautiful harmony. Forget about the road; do not curse the road and the government: forget them. Do not curse the bullock and the bullock cart, or the driver: forget them. Close your eyes: do not resist. Move rhythmically and create a music in your movement. Make it as if it is a dance. "In a moving vehicle by rhythmically swaying, experience": the sutra says the experience will come to you.

"Or in a still vehicle..." Do not ask where to get a bullock cart; do not deceive yourself: because the sutra says, "Or in a still vehicle, by letting yourself swing in slowing invisible circles." Just sitting here, swing in a circle. Swing in a circle! First take a big circle, then go on slowing it, slowing, slowing, making it smaller and smaller and smaller, until your body is not visibly moving, but inside you feel a subtle movement.

Start with a bigger circle, with closed eyes. Otherwise, when the body will stop you will stop. With closed eyes make big circles; just sitting, swing in a circle. Go on swinging, making the circle smaller and smaller and smaller. Visibly you will stop; no one will be able to detect that you are still moving. But inside you will feel a subtle movement. Now the body is not moving, only mind. Go on making it slower and slower and experience: that will become a centering. In a vehicle, in a moving vehicle, a non-resisting rhythmical movement will create a centering within you.

Gurdjieff created many dances for such techniques. He was working on this technique. All the dances he was using in his school were, really, swaying in circles. All the dances were in circles — just whirling but remaining aware inside, by and by making the circles smaller and smaller. A time comes when the body stops, but the mind inside goes on moving, moving, moving.

If you have been traveling in a train for twenty hours, after you have come home, after you have left the train, if you close your eyes you will feel that you are still traveling. Still you are traveling. The body has stopped, but the mind is still feeling the vehicle. So just do this technique.

Gurdjieff created phenomenal dances, very beautiful. In this century he worked miracles — not miracles like Satya Sai Baba: those are not miracles; any street magician can do them. But Gurdjieff really created miracles. He prepared a group of a hundred people for meditative dancing, and he was showing that dance to an audience in New York for the first time. A hundred dancers were on the stage whirling. Those who were in the audience, even their minds began whirling: there were a hundred white-robed dancers just whirling.

When he indicated with his hand movements, they would whirl, and the moment he would say stop there would be a dead silence. That was a stop for the audience, not for dancers — because the body can stop immediately, but the mind then takes the movement inside: it goes on and on. It was beautiful even to look at, because a hundred persons suddenly became dead statues. It created a sudden shock in the audience also, because a hundred movements — beautiful movements, rhythmical movements — suddenly stopped. You would be looking at them moving, whirling, dancing, and suddenly the dancers stopped. Then your thought would also stop.

Many in New York felt that it was a weird phenomenon: their thoughts stopped immediately. But for the dancers, the dance continued inside, and the inside whirling circles became smaller and smaller until they became centered.

One day it happened that they were coming just to the edge of the stage dancing. It was expected, supposed, that Gurdjieff would stop them just before they danced down the stage on the audience. A hundred dancers were just on the edge of the stage. One step more and they would all fall down in the hall. The whole hall was expecting that suddenly Gurdjieff would say stop, but he turned his back to light his cigar. He turned his back to the dancers to light his cigar, and the whole group of a hundred dancers fell down from the stage upon the floor — on a naked stone floor.

The whole audience stood up. They were screaming, shouting, and they were thinking that many must have broken their bones: it was such a crash. But not a single one was hurt; not even a single bruise was there.

They asked Gurdjieff what had happened. No one had been hurt, and the crash was such that it seemed impossible. The reason was only this: they were really not in their bodies at that moment. They were slowing down their inner circling. And when Gurdjieff saw that now they were completely oblivious of their bodies, he allowed them to fall down.

If you are completely oblivious of your body, there is no resistance, and a bone is broken because of resistance. If you are falling down, you resist: you go against the pull of gravity. That going against, that resistance, is the problem — not gravity. If you can fall down with gravity, if you can cooperate with it, then no possibility of hurt will arise.

This sutra: "In a moving vehicle, by rhythmically swaying, experience. Or in a still vehicle, by letting yourself swing in slowing invisible circles." You can do it. There is no need of a vehicle. Just whirl like children do. When your mind goes crazy, and you feel that now you will fall down, do not stop: go on! Even if you fall down, do not worry about it. Close your eyes and whirl. Your mind will get whirled, and you will fall down. When your body has fallen down, inside, feel! The whirling will continue. And it will come nearer and nearer and nearer, and suddenly you will be centered.

Children enjoy this very much because they get a deep kick. Parents never allow their children to whirl. It is not good: they should be allowed — rather, encouraged. And if you can make them aware of inner whirling also, you can teach them meditation through their whirling. They enjoy it because they have a bodiless feeling. When they whirl, suddenly children become aware that their body is whirling, but they are not. Inside they feel a centering which we cannot feel so easily because their bodies and souls are still a bit apart. There is a gap.

When you get into your mother's womb, you cannot immediately get totally in the body; it takes time. When a child is born, then too he is not absolutely fixed. His soul is not absolutely fixed to the body: there are gaps. That is why there are many things which he cannot do. His body is ready to do it, but he cannot do it.

If you have observed, you may have noticed that newly born children cannot see with two eyes: they always see with one eye. If you observe, then you will see that when they observe and see anything, they cannot see with two eyes. They always look with one eye: one eye gets bigger. The pupil of one eye will become bigger, and the other pupil will remain small. They are not yet fixed: the consciousness of a newborn is not yet fixed: it is loose. By and by it will be fixed, and then they will look with two eyes.

They cannot yet feel their own body and others' bodies as different. It is difficult. They are not yet fixed, but fixation will come by and by.

Meditation is again trying to create a gap. You have become fixed, solidly fixed in your body. That is why you feel, "I am the body." If a gap can be created, then only can you feel that you are not the body but something beyond the body. Swaying and whirling are helpful: they create the gap.

The ninth technique: *"Pierce some part of your nectar-filled form with a pin, and gently enter the piercing and attain to the inner purity."*

This sutra says, "Pierce some part of your nectar-filled form. . ." Your body is not just a body: it is filled with you, and that "you" is the nectar. Pierce your body. When you are piercing your body, you are not pierced: only the body is pierced. But you feel the pierce as if you have been pierced: that is why you feel pain. If you can become aware that only the body is pierced, that you are not pierced, instead of pain you will feel bliss. There is no need to do it with a pin. Many things happen every day; you can use those situations for meditation. Or, you can create a situation.

Some pain is there in your body. Do one thing: forget the whole body. Just concentrate on the part of the body which is painful. And then a strange thing will be noted. When you concentrate on the part of the body which is painful, you see that that part is shrinking. First you feel that the pain aches on your whole leg. When you concentrate, then you feel it is not on the whole leg. It was exaggerated. It is just at the knee.

Concentrate more, and you will feel it is not on the whole knee but just on a pinpoint. Concentrate more on the pinpoint; forget the whole body. Just close your eyes and go on concentrating in order to find where the pain is. It will go on shrinking; the area will become smaller and smaller. Then a moment will come when it will be just a pinpoint. Go on staring at the pinpoint, and suddenly the pinpoint will disappear and you will be filled with bliss. Instead of pain you will be filled with bliss.

Why does this happen? Because you and your body are two: they are not one. The one who is concentrating is you. The concentration is being done on the body: that is the object. When you concentrate, the gap is broadened, the identification is broken. Just to have concentration you move inside, away from the body. To bring the spot of pain in perspective, you have to move away. That moving away creates the gap. And when you are concentrating on the pain, you forget the identification, you forget that "I am feeling pain".

Now you are the observer and the pain is somewhere else. You are observing the pain, not feeling the pain. This change from feeling to observation creates the gap. And when the gap is bigger, suddenly you forget the body completely: you are aware only of consciousness.

THE BOOK OF THE SECRETS

You can try this technique also: "Pierce some part of your nectar-filled body with a pin, and gently enter the piercing." If there is pain, then first you will have to concentrate on the whole area; then by and by it will come to a pinpoint. No need to wait.

You can use a pin. Use a pin on any part which is sensitive. On the body many spots are blind spots; they will not be useful. You may not have heard about blind spots on the body.

Then give a pin to anyone, to your friend, and then sit and tell your friend to pierce the pin in your back on many points. On many points you will feel no pain. You will say, "No, you have not pierced yet. I am not feeling any pain." Those are blind spots. Just on your cheeks there are two blind spots which can be tested.

If you move to Indian villages, many times in religious festivals they will pierce their cheeks with an arrow. It looks like a miracle, but it is not. The cheeks have two blind spots. If you pierce through these blind spots, no blood will come out and there will be no pain. In your back there are thousands of dead spots: you cannot feel any pain. So your body has two types of spots — sensitive, alive ones and those that are dead.

So find a sensitive spot where you can feel even a slight touch. Then pierce the pin and enter the piercing: that is the thing; that is meditation. And "gently" enter the piercing. As the pin moves inside into your skin and you feel the pain, you also enter. Do not feel that the pain is entering you; do not feel the pain; do not be identfiied with it. Enter with the pin. Pierce with the pin.

Close your eyes; observe the pain. As the pain is piercing in, you also pierce you. And with the pin piercing you, your mind will become easily concentrated. Use that point of pain, of intense pain, and observe it: that is what is meant by "gently enter the piercing".

"And attain to the inner purity": if you can enter observing, unidentified, aloof, standing far away, not feeling that the pain is piercing you, but observing that the pin is piercing the body and you are an observer, you will attain to the inner purity; the inner innocence will be revealed to you. For the first time you will become aware that you are not the body. And once you know that you are not the body, your life is changed completely — because your whole life is around the body. Once you know you are not the body, you cannot continue this life. The center is being missed.

When you are not the body, then you have to create a different life. That life is the sannyasin's life. It is a different life: the center is different now. Now you exist in the world as a soul, as an '"Atman", not as a body. If you exist as a body, then you have created a different world of material gain, greed, gratification, lust, sex. You have created a world around you; this is the body-oriented world.

Once you know you are not the body, your whole world disappears. You cannot support it any more. A different world arises which is around the soul — a world of compassion, of love, of beauty, of truth, of goodness, of innocence. The center is shifted and it is not in the body now. It is in the consciousness.

Enough for today.

14
Changing The Direction Of Energy

November 17, 1972, Bombay, India

QUESTIONS:

1. Why is Cosmic Consciousness (Samadhi) called centering?
2. Explain further how "love alone can be enough" without meditation.
3. Why is man insensitive?

The first question: *"If Enlightenment and Samadhi mean total Consciousness, Cosmic Consciousness, all-pervading Consciousness, then it seems very strange to call this state of Cosmic Consciousness centering, as the word 'centering' implies one-pointedness. Why is Cosmic Consciousness (or Samadhi) called centering?"*

Centering is the path, not the goal. Centering is the method, not the result. Samadhi is not called centering. Centering is the technique to Samadhi. Of course, they look contradictory because when one Realizes, becomes Enlightened, there is no center left.

Jacob Boehme has said that when one comes to the Divine it can be described in two ways: either the center is everywhere now, or the center is nowhere; both mean the same thing. So the word "centering" seems contradictory, but the path is not the goal and the method is not the result. And method can be contradictory. So we have to understand it because these 112 methods are methods of centering.

But once you become centered you will explode. Centering is just to gather yourself totally at one point. Once you are gathered at one point, crystallized at one point, that point explodes automatically. Then there is no center — or, then the center is everywhere. So centering is a means to explode.

Why does centering become the method? If you are not centered your energy is unfocused. It cannot explode. It is spread out; it cannot explode. Explosion needs great energy.

Explosion means that now you are not spread out: you are at one point. You become atomic; you become, really, a spiritual atom. And only when you are centered enough to become an atom can you explode. Then there is an atomic explosion.

That explosion is not talked about because it cannot be, so only the method is given. The result is not talked about. It cannot be talked about. If you do the method the result will follow, and there is no way to express it.

So remember this: basically, religion never talks about the experience itself. It talks only about the method. It shows the "how", not the "what". The "what" is left to you. If you do the "how", the "what" will come to you. And there is no way to convey it. One can know it, but he cannot convey it. It is such an infinite experience that language becomes useless. The vastness is such that no word is capable of expressing it. So only the method is given.

Buddha is reported to have said continuously for forty years, "Do not ask me about the Truth, about the Divine, about Nirvana, Liberation. Do not ask me anything about such things. Just ask me how to reach there. I can show you the path, but I cannot give you the experience, not even in words." The experience is personal; method is impersonal. Method is scientific, impersonal; experience is always personal and poetic.

What do I mean when I differentiate in this way? Method is scientific. If you can do it, centering will result. That centering is bound to result if the method is done. If the centering is not resulting, then you can know that you are missing the point somewhere. Somewhere you have missed the method; you have not followed it. Method is scientific, centering is scientific — but when the explosion comes to you, it is poetic.

By poetic I mean everyone of you will experience it in a different way. Then there is no common ground. And everyone will express it in a different way. Buddha says something, Mahavir says something. Krishna something else, and Jesus, Mohammed, Moses and Lao Tse, they all differ — not in methods, but in the way they express their experience. Only in one thing do they all agree, that whatsoever they are saying is not expressing that which they have felt. Only on that one point do they agree.

Still, they try. Still, they try to convey somehow, to hint. It seems impossible, but if you have a sympathetic heart something may be conveyed. But that needs a deep sympathy and love and reverence. So, really, whenever something is conveyed, it doesn't depend on the conveyer. It depends on you. If you can receive it in deep love and reverence, then something reaches you. But if you are critical about it, then nothing reaches. Firstly, it is difficult to express. And even if it is expressed, you are critical. Then the message becomes impossible; there is no communication.

The communication is very delicate. That is why, in all these 112 methods, it has been left out completely — only hinted at. Shiva says so many times, "Do this, and the experience," and then he becomes silent; "Do this and the blessing," and then he becomes silent.

"The blessing, the experience, the explosion": beyond them there is personal experience. With that which cannot be expressed, it is better not to express it — because if expression is tried with that which cannot be expressed, it will be misunderstood. So Shiva is silent. He is talking simply of methods, techniques, of how to do it.

But centering is not the end: it is just the path. And why does centering happen, develop, grow into an explosion? Because if much energy is centered at one point, the point will explode. The point is so small and the energy is so great, the point cannot contain it; hence, the explosion.

This bulb can contain a particular quantity of electricity. If there is more electricity, the bulb will explode. That is why centering: the more you are centered, the more energy is at your center. The moment there is more energy, the center won't be able to contain it. It will explode.

So it is scientific: it is just a scientific law. And if the center is not exploding, that means you are still not centered. Once you are centered, immediately the explosion follows. There is no time gap. So if you feel that the explosion is not coming, it means that you are still not focused, still you do not have one center, still you have many centers, still you are divided, still your energy is dissipated, still your energy is moving out.

When the energy moves out, you are just being emptied of energy, dissipated. Ultimately you will become impotent. Really, when death comes you have already died: you are just a dead cell. You have been constantly throwing energy outward — so whatsoever may be the quantity of energy, within a period you will become empty. Outgoing energy means death. You are dying every moment; your energy is being emptied; you are throwing your energy, dissipating it.

They say that even the sun which has been there for millions and millions of years, such a great reservoir of energy, is being emptied constantly. And within four thousand years, it will die. The sun will die simply because there will be no energy to radiate. Every day it is dying because the rays are carrying its energy toward the boundaries of the universe, if there are any boundaries. The energy is going out.

Only man is capable of transforming and changing the direction of energy. Otherwise death is a natural phenomenon: everything dies. Only man is capable of knowing the immortal, the deathless.

So you can reduce this whole thing into a law. If energy is moving out, death will be the result and you will never know what life means. You can only know a slow dying. You can never feel the intensity of being alive. If energy moves out, then death is the automatic result — of anything, whatsoever. If you can change the direction of energy — energy not moving out, but moving in — then a mutation, a transformation, happens.

Then this energy coming in becomes centered at one point in you. That point is just near the navel because, really, you are born as a navel. You are connnected with your mother at the navel. The life energy of the mother is being poured in you through the navel. And once the navel is cut, separated from the mother, you become an individual. Before that you are not an individual — just part of your mother.

So real birth takes place when the navel cord is cut. Then the child takes its own life, becomes its own center. That center is bound to be just at the navel, because through the navel life energy comes to the child. That was the connecting link. And, still, whether you are aware or not, your navel remains the center.

If energy begins to pour in, if you change the direction of the energy so that it comes in, it will hit the navel. It will go on in and become centered at the navel. When it is so much that the navel cannot contain it, that the center cannot contain it any longer, the center explodes. In that explosion, again you are no longer an individual. You were not an individual when you were connected with your mother; again you will not be an individual.

A new birth has taken place. You have become one with the Cosmos. Now you do not have any center; you cannot say "I". Now there is no ego. A Buddha, a Krishna, they go on talking and using the word "I". That is simply formal; they do not have any ego. They are NOT.

Buddha was dying. The day he was to die, many, many people, disciples, sannyasins, gathered, and they were sad: they were weeping and crying. So Buddha asked, "Why are you weeping?" Someone said, "Because soon you will be no more." Buddha laughed and said, "But I have been no more for forty years. I died the day I became Enlightened. The center has not been there for forty years. So do not weep; do not be sad. No one is dying now. I am no more! But still the word 'I' has to be used even to denote that I am no more."

Energy moving in is the whole of all religion, is what is meant by the religious search. How to move the energy, how to create a total about-turn? These methods help. So remember, centering is not Samadhi, centering is not the experience. Centering is the door to the experience. And when there is the experience there is no centering. So centering is just a passage.

You are not centered now: you are multi-centered really. That is why I say you are not centered now. Then when you become centered, there is only one center. Then the energy that has been moving to multi-centers has come back; it is a homecoming. Then you are at your center; then, explosion. Again the center is no more, but then you are not multi-centered. Then there is no center at all. You have become one with the Cosmos. Then Existence and you mean one and the same thing.

For example, one iceberg is floating in the sea. The iceberg has a center of its own. It has a separate individuality; it is separate from the ocean. Deep down it is not separate because it is nothing but water at a particular degree of temperature. The difference between the ocean water and the iceberg water is not in their nature. Naturally, they are the same. The difference is only of temperature. And then the sun rises, and the atmosphere becomes hot, and the iceberg begins to melt. Then there is no iceberg: it has melted. Now you cannot find it because there is no individuality, no center in it. It has become one with the ocean.

In you and in Buddha, in those who were crucifying Jesus and in Jesus, in Krishna and in Arjuna, there is no difference in nature. Arjuna is like an iceberg and Krishna is like an ocean. There is no difference in nature. They both are one and the same, but Arjuna has a form, a name, an individual, isolated existence. He feels, "I am."

Through these methods of centering, the temperature will change, the iceberg will melt, and then there will be no difference. That oceanic feeling is Samadhi; that being an iceberg is mind. And to feel oceanic is to be a no-mind.

Centering is just the passage, the point of transformation from which the iceberg will be no more. Before it there was no ocean — only an iceberg. After it there will be no iceberg — only ocean. The oceanic feeling is Samadhi: it is to feel oneself one with the Whole.

But I am not saying to think oneself one with the Whole. You can think, but thinking is before centering. That is not Realization. You do not know: you have only heard; you have read. You wish that someday this may happen to you also, but you have not Realized. Before centering you can go on thinking, but that thinking is of no use. After centering there is no thinker. You know! It has happened! You are no more; only the ocean is. Centering is the method; Samadhi is the end.

Nothing has been said about what happens in Samadhi because nothing can be said. And Shiva is very scientific. He is not interested at all in telling. He is telegraphic; he will not use a single extra word. So he simply hints: "the experience, the blessing, the happening." Not only this: sometimes he will simply say, "then." He will say, "Be centered between two breaths and 'then'." And then he will stop. Then sometimes he will simply say, "Be in the middle, just in the middle between two extremes, and 'that'."

These are indications — "that, then, the experience, the blessing, the happening, the explosion." But then he stops completely. Why? We would like him to say something more.

Two reasons. One: "that" cannot be explained. Why can it not be explained? Because there are thinkers, for example, modern positivists, language analysts and others in Europe, who say that that which can be experienced can be explained. And they have a point to make. They say if you can experience it, then why can you not tell of it. After all what is an experience? You have understood it, so why can you not make it understood for others? So they say that if there is any experience, then it can be expressed. And if you cannot express, it shows simply that there is no experience. Then you are a muddlehead — confused, blurred. And if you cannot even express, then there is no possibility that you will be able to experience.

Because of this standpoint, they say religion is all hokum. Why can you not express if you can say you have experienced? Their point appeals to many, but their argument is baseless. Leave aside religious experiences: ordinary experiences also cannot be explained and expressed — very simple experiences.

I have a pain in my head, and if you have never experienced a headache, I cannot explain to you what a headache means. That doesn't mean that I am muddleheaded; that doesn't mean that I am only thinking and I am not experiencing. The headache is there. I experience it in its totality, in its full painfulness. But if you have not experienced a headache, it cannot be explained, it cannot be expressed to you. If you also have experienced it, then, of course, there is no problem: it can be expressed.

Buddha's difficulty is this: that he has to talk with non-Buddhas — not non-Buddhists, because non-Buddhists can also be Buddhas. Jesus is a non-Buddhist, but he is a Buddha. Because Buddha is to communicate with those who have not experienced, there is a difficulty. You do not know what a headache is. There are many who have not known headaches. They have only heard the word; it means nothing to them.

You can talk with a blind man about light, but nothing is conveyed. He hears the word "light", he hears the explanation. He can understand the whole theory of light — but still the word "light" conveys nothing to him. Unless he can experience, communication is impossible. So note it: communication is possible only if two persons are communicating who have had the same experience.

We are able to communicate in ordinary life because our experiences are similar. But even then, if one is going to split hairs, then there will be difficulties. I say the sky is blue and you also say the the sky is blue, but how are we to decide that my experience of blue and your experience of blue is the same? There is no possible way to decide.

I may be looking at a different shade of blue and you may be looking at a different shade of blue, but what I am looking at inside, what I am experiencing, cannot be conveyed to you. I can simply say "blue". You also say "blue", but "blue" has a thousand shades — and not only shades: "blue" has thousands of meanings. In my pattern of mind, "blue" may mean one thing. To you it may mean something else because "blue" is not the meaning. The meaning is always in the pattern. So even in common experiences it is difficult to communicate.

Moreover, there are experiences which are of the beyond. For example, someone has fallen in love. He experiences something. His whole life is at stake, but he cannot explain what has happened to him, what is happening to him. He can weep, he can sing, he can dance: these are indications that something is happening in him. But what is happening in him? When love happens to someone, what is happening really? And love is not very uncommon. It happens to everyone in some way or the other. But, still, we have not been able to express yet what happens inside.

There are persons who feel love as a fever, as a sort of disease. Rousseau says that youth is not the peak of human life, because youth is prone to the disease called love. Unless one becomes so old that love loses all meaning, mind remains muddled and puzzled. So wisdom is possible only in very, very old age. Love will not allow you to be wise — that is his feeling.

There are others who may feel differently. Those who are really wise will become silent about love. They will not say anything — because the feeling is so infinite, so deep, that language is bound to betray it. And if it is expressed, then one feels guilty because one can never do justice to the feeling of the Infinite. So one remains silent: the deeper the experience, the lesser the possibility of expression.

Buddha remained silent about God not because there is no God. And those who are very much vocal about God really show they have no experience. Buddha remained silent. Whenever he would go to any town, he would declare, "Please, do not ask anything about God. You can ask anything, but not about God."

Scholars, pundits, who had no experience really, but only knowledge, started talking about Buddha and creating rumors, saying, "He is silent because he doesn't know. If he knows then why will he not say?"

And Buddha would laugh, and that laughter could be under-stood only by very few. If love cannot be expressed, then how can God be expressed ?

And then any expression is harmful — that is one thing. That is why Shiva is silent about the experience. He goes to the point from where a finger can be used as an indication — "then, that, the experience," and then he becomes silent.

Secondly, even if it can be expressed in a certain way, even if it cannot be expressed fully — only partially, it can be ex-pressed. Even if it cannot be expressed, really, then too some parallels can be created to help. But those too Shiva is not using, and there is a reason: it is because our minds are so greedy that whenever something is said about that experience the mind clings to it. And then the mind forgets the method and remembers only the experience, because method needs effort — a long effort which is sometimes tedious, sometimes dangerous. A long sustained effort is needed.

So we forget about the method. We remember the result and we go on imagining, wishing, desiring, the result. And one can fool oneself very easily. One can imagine that the result has been achieved.

Someone was here a few days before. He is a sannyasin — an old man, a very old man. He took sannyas thirty years ago; now he is near seventy, He came to me and he said, "I have come to make some inquiries, to know something."

So I asked him, "What do you want to know ?" Suddenly he changed. He said, "No, not to know really — just to meet you, because whatsoever can be known I have known already."

For thirty years he has been imagining, desiring — desiring bliss, Divine experiences, and now, at this late age, he has become weak and death is near. Now he is creating hallucina-tions that he has experienced. So I told him, "If you have experienced, then keep silent. Be here with me for a few moments because then there is no need to talk."

Then he became restless. He said, "Okay ! Then suppose that I have not experienced. Then tell me something." So I told him that there is no possibility with me to suppose anything. "Either you have known or you have not known," I said. "So be clear about it. If you have known, then keep quiet. Be here for a few moments and then go. If you have not known, then be clear. Then tell me so."

Then he was puzzled. He had come to inquire about some methods. Then he said, "Really, I have not experienced, but I have been thinking so much about 'Aham Brahmasmi — I am the Brahman' that sometimes I forget that I have only been thinking. I have repeated it so much, day and night for thirty years continuously, that sometimes I completely forget that I have not known this. It is just a borrowed saying."

It is difficult to remember what is knowledge and what is experience. They get confused; they get mingled and mixed. And it is very easy to feel that your knowledge has become your experience. The human mind is so deceptive, so cunning, that that is possible. That is another reason why Shiva has remained silent about the experience. He will not say anything about it. He goes on talking about methods, remaining completely silent about the result. You cannot be deceived by him.

That is one of the reasons why this book, one of the most significant of books, has remained altogether unknown. This "Vigyana Bhairava Tantra" is one of the most significant books in the world. No Bible, no Veda, no Gita is so significant, but it has remained completely unknown. The reason? It contains only simple methods without any possibility for your greed to cling to the result.

The mind wants to cling to the result. The mind is not interested in the method: it is interested in the end result. And if you can bypass the method and reach the result, the mind will be extremely happy.

Someone was asking me, "Why so many methods? Kabir has said "'Sahaj Samadhi bhali — be spontaneous'. Spontaneous ecstasy is good, so there is no need of methods." I told him, "If you have achieved "Sahaj Samadhi" — spontaneous ecstasy, then, of course, no method is useful. There is no need. Why have you come here ?" He said, "I have not achieved yet, but I feel that 'Sahaj — the spontaneous' — is better."

"But why do you feel that the spontaneous is better ?" I said. Because no method is suggested, the mind feels good that you have nothing to do — and without doing, you can have EVERY-THING !"

Because of this Zen has become a craze in the West, because Zen says achieve it effortlessly; there is no need of effort. Zen is right: there is no need for an effort. But, remember, to achieve this point of no-effort you will need a long, long effort. To achieve a point where no effort is needed, to achieve a point where you can remain in non-doing, a long effort will be needed. But the superficial conclusion that Zen says no effort is needed has become very appealing in the West. If no effort is needed then the mind says this is the right thing, because you can do it without doing anything. But no one can do it.

Suzuki, who made Zen known in the West, has done a service and also a disservice. And in the long run, the disservice will remain for a longer period. He was a very authentic man, one of the most authentic men of this century, and for his whole life he struggled to carry the message of Zen to the West. And alone, with his own effort, he made it known in the West. And now there is a craze. There are Zen friends all over the West. Nothing appeals like Zen now.

But the point is missed. The appeal has come only because Zen says no method is needed, no effort is needed. You do not have to do anything: spontaneously "it" flowers.

It is right — but you are not spontaneous, so it will never flower in you. "To be spontaneous . . ." It looks absurd and contradictory because for you to be spontaneous many methods are needed to purify you, to make you innocent, so that you CAN BE spontaneous. Otherwise you cannot be spontaneous to anything.

This "Vigyana Bhairava Tantra" was translated into English by Paul Reps. He has written a very beautiful book: "Zen Flesh, Zen Bones," and just in the appendix he included this book

"Vigyana Bhairava Tantra". The whole book is concerned with Zen. Just in the appendix he added this book also, the 112 methods, and he called it a pre-Zen writing. Many Zen followers didn't like this because they said Zen says no effort is needed, and this book is concerned only with effort. This book is concerned only with methods, and Zen says no method, no effort is needed. So it is anti-Zen, not pre-Zen.

Superficially they are right. Deeply they are not, because to achieve a spontaneous being one has to travel a long way. One of Gurdjieff's disciples, Ouspensky, used to say, whenever someone would come to him to ask about the path, "We don't know anything about the path. We only teach about some footpaths which lead to the path. The path is not known to us." Do not think that you are already on the path. Even the path is far away. From where you are, from that point, even the path is far away. So first you have to reach to the path.

Ouspensky was a very humble man, and it is very difficult to be religious and to be humble — very, very difficult, because once you begin to feel that you know the head goes mad. He would always say, "We don't know anything about the path. It is very far away, and there is no need just now to discuss it." Wherever you are, first you have to create a link, a small bridge, a footpath which will lead you to the path.

Spontaneity — "Sahaj Yoga" — is very far away from you. In the place where you are, you are totally artificial, cultivated and cultured. Nothing is spontaneous — NOTHING, I say, is spontaneous. When nothing is spontaneous in your life, how can religion be spontaneous ? When nothing is spontaneous, even love is not spontaneous. Even love is a bargain, even love is a calculation, even love is an effort. Then nothing can be spontaneous. And then, to explode spontaneously into the Cosmos is impossible.

From the situation you are in, from that situation it is impossible. First, you will have to throw all your artificiality, all your false attitudes, all your cultivated conventions, all your prejudices. Only then will a spontaneous happening be possible.

345

These methods will help you to come to a point from where nothing is needed to be done — just your being is enough. But mind can deceive — and mind easily deceives, because then it can get consolation.

Shiva never talks about any result — just methods. Remember this emphasis. Do something so that a moment may be possible when nothing is needed — when your central being can just dissolve into the Cosmos. But that has to be achieved. Zen's appeal is for the wrong reasons, and the same is true for Krishnamurti because he says no yoga is needed, no method is needed. Really, he says there is no "method" of meditation. He is right.

He is right, but Shiva says these 112 methods of meditation are there, and Shiva is also right. And as far as YOU are concerned, Shiva is more right. And if you have to choose between Krishnamurti and Shiva, then choose Shiva. Krishnamurti is of no use to you. Even this can be said to help you — that Krishnamurti is absolutely wrong: remember, I say TO HELP YOU. And he is harmful. That too I say to help you because if you get into his argument you will not achieve Samadhi. You will achieve only one conclusion — that no method is needed. And that is dangerous. For you method is needed!

There comes a moment when no method is needed, but that moment has not come for you yet. And before that moment, to know something that is ahead is dangerous. That is why Shiva is silent. He will not say anything of the future, of what will happen. He simply sticks to you, to what you are and what is to be done with you. Krishnamurti goes on talking in terms which cannot be understood by you.

The logic can be felt. The logic is right; it is beautiful. It will be good if you can remember the logic of Krishnamurti. He says that if you are doing some method, then who is doing that method? The mind is doing. And how can any method done by mind dissolve mind? Rather, on the contrary, it will strengthen it more: it will strengthen your mind more. It will become a conditioning; it will be false.

346

So meditation is spontaneous; you cannot do anything about it. What can you do about love? Can you practise any method for how to love? If you practise, then your love will be false. It happens: it cannot be practised. If even love cannot be practised, how can prayer be practised? How can meditation be practised?

The logic is exactly, absolutely right — but not for you, because by listening to this logic continuously you will be conditioned by this logic. And those who have been listening to Krishnamurti for forty years are the most conditioned persons I have come across. They say there is no method, and still they are nowhere.

I say, "You have understood there is no method and you do not practise any method, but has the spontaneity flowered in you?" They say, "No!" And if I tell them, "Then practise some method," immediately their conditioning comes in. They say, "There is no method."

They have not been practising any method, and Samadhi has not happened. And if you tell them, "Then try some method," they say there is no method. So they are in a dilemma. They have not moved an inch, and the reason is that they have been told something which was not for them.

It is like teaching a small child about sex. You can go on teaching, but you are telling something which is yet meaningless for the child. And your teaching will be dangerous because you are conditioning his mind. And, it is not his need; he is not concerned with it. He doesn't know what sex means because his glands are still not functioning. His body is still not sexual. His energy has not yet moved biologically to the sex center, and you are talking to him. Because he has ears, do you think that anything can be taught to him? Because he can nod his head, do you think you can teach him anything?

You can teach, and your teaching can become dangerous and harmful. Sex is not an inquiry for him. It has not become a problem for him; he has not reached that point of maturity where sex becomes significant. Wait ! When he begins to inquire, when he matures and when he asks questions, then tell him. And never tell more than he can understand, because that more will become a burden on his head. And the same is with the phenomenon of meditation.

You can be taught only about methods, not about results. That is taking a jump. And without getting a foothold on the method, taking the jump means simply a cerebral affair, a mental affair. And then you will always miss the method.

It is like small children doing arithmetic. They can always go back to the book and can know the answer. The answer is there: at the back of the book, the answers are given. They can look at the question, then they can go to the back and know the answer. And once a child knows the answer, it is very difficult for him to learn the method because there seems no need. When he already knows the answer, there is no need.

And, really, he will do the whole thing in reverse order. Then through any false, pseudo-method, he will arrive at the answer. He knows the real thing, he knows the answer, so he can arrive at the answer by just creating a false method. And this happens so much in religion that it seems, as far as religion is concerned, everyone is just doing what children do.

The answer is not good for you. The question is there, the method is there, and the answer must be reached by you. No one else should give you the answer. The real teachers do not help you to know the answer before the process is done. They simply help you to go through the process. Rather, on the contrary, even if you have known somehow, even if you have stolen some answer from somewhere, they will say this is wrong. It may not be wrong. They will say, "This is wrong. Throw this: it is not needed." They will debar you from knowing the answer before you REALLY come to know it. That is why no answer is given.

Shiva's beloved, Devi, has asked him questions. He is giving simple methods. The question is there, the method is there. The answer is left for you to work out, to live out.

So, remember, centering is the method, not the result. The result is Cosmic, oceanic experience. There is no center then.

The second question: *"You said if one can really love, then love alone is enough and the 112 methods of meditation are not needed. As you have explained real love, I feel really that I love, I believe. But the bliss I encounter in meditation feels to be of quite another dimension than the deep contentment I experience from love, and I cannot imagine being without meditation also. So explain more about how love alone without meditation can be enough."*

Many things will have to be understood. One, if you are really in love, you will not enquire at all about meditation — because love is such a total fulfillment, that it is never felt that something is lacking, that some gap is to be filled, that you need something more. If you feel that something more is needed, the gap is there. If you feel that something more is to be done and experienced, then love is just a feeling, not a reality. I do not doubt your belief: you may believe that you are in love. Your belief is authentic; you are not deceiving anyone. You feel that you are in love, but the symptoms show that you are not.

What are the symptoms of being in love? Three things. First, absolute contentment. Nothing else is needed; not even God is needed. Second, no future. This very moment of love is eternity. No next moment, no future, no tomorrow. Love is a happening in the present. And third, you cease, you are no more. If you still are, then you have still not entered the temple of love.

If these three things happen — if you are not, then who is going to meditate? If there is no future, then all methods become useless because methods are for the future, for a result. And if at this very moment you are content, absolutely content, where is the motivation to do anything?

There is a school of psychologists (and this is one of the most significant trends in modern thinking) that started with Wilhelm Reich. He said that because of the lack of love, every mental disease arises. Because you cannot feel deep love, because you cannot be in it totally, this unfulfilled being craves for fulfillment in multi-dimensions.

When I say that "if you can love, nothing is needed", I do not mean that then love is enough. I mean that once you love deeply love becomes a door — just like any meditation.

What is meditation going to do? These three things: it will create contentment, it will allow you to remain in the present — help you to remain in the present, and it will destroy your ego. These three things meditation is going to do — with any method. So you can say it this way: love is the natural method. If the natural method has been missed, then other artificial methods have to be supplied.

But one can feel that one is in love; then these three things will become criteria for him. He will think that these should be made the touchstones, the measures. He will observe whether these three things are happening. If they are not happening, then love can be many other things, but not love. And love is a great phenomenon: it CAN BE many things. It can be lust; it can be simple sex; it can be just a possessive tendency; it can be just an occupation because you cannot be alone, and you need someone because you are afraid and you need security. The presence of the other helps you to be secure. Or, it may be just a sexual relationship.

Energy needs outlets. Energy goes on accumulating, then it becomes a burden: you have to throw it and release it. So your love may be just a release. Love can be many things and love is many things. And, ordinarily, love is many things except LOVE.

To me love is meditation. So try this: with your lover be in meditation. Whenever you lover or beloved is present, be in deep meditation. Make this presence of each other a meditative state.

Ordinarily, you are doing the very opposite. Whenever lovers are together, they are fighting. When they are separated then they are thinking of each other, and when they are together they are fighting. When they are separated again, then again they are thinking about each other. When they are put together, again the fight starts. This is not love!

So I will suggest some points: Make the presence of your beloved or lover a meditative state. Be silent. Remain close, but be silent. Use each other's presence to drop the mind; do not think. If you are thinking while your lover is with you, then you are not with your lover. How can you be? You are both there, but miles apart. You are thinking your thoughts, your lover is thinking his thoughts. You just appear to be near, but you are not — because when two minds are thinking, they are poles apart.

Real love means cessation of thinking. In the presence of your beloved or lover, cease completely to think. Then only are you near. Then suddenly you are one. Then bodies cannot separate you. Then deep down within the body, someone has broken the barrier. The silence breaks the barrier: that is one thing.

Make your relationship a sacred phenomenon. When you are really in love, the object of love becomes Divine. If it is not, then know well it is not a love relationship: it is impossible. A love relationship is not a profane relationship. But have you ever felt any reverence for your beloved? You may have felt many other things, but never reverence.

It seems inconceivable, but India has tried many, many ways. That is why India has been insisting that this love relationship between man and woman should be a sacred phenomenon, not a worldly relationship. The lover, the beloved, they become Divine. You cannot look in any other way.

I wonder, have you ever felt any reverence for your wife? The very thing seems irrelevant — reverence for a wife? There is no question. You can feel condemnation, you can feel everything — but never reverence. The relationship is just worldly; you are using each other. The wife may say that she respects her husband, but I have not seen a single wife who really respects. Traditionally, because it has been a convention to respect the husband, the wife goes on saying she respects, and so she will not even utter his name. Not because of respect, because she can utter anything: but she will not utter his name just TRADITIONALLY.

Reverence is the second thing. In the presence of your beloved or lover, feel reverence. If you cannot see the Divine in your beloved or lover, you cannot see Him anywhere else. How can you see Him in a tree where no relationship exists ? When no deep intimacy prevails, how can you see Him in a rock or a tree ? They are unrelated. If you cannot see Him in the person you love, if God is not felt there, He cannot be felt anywhere else. And if He can be felt there, sooner or later you will feel Him everywhere — because once the door is thrown open, once you have a glimpse of the Divine in any person, then you cannot forget that glimpse. And because of that, then everything becomes a door. That is why I say love itself is a meditation.

So do not think in contrast — whether to love or to meditate. That was not my meaning. Do not try to choose whether to love or to meditate. Love meditatively. Or, meditate lovingly. Do not create any division. Love is a very natural phenomenon, and it can be used as a vehicle. And tantra has used it as a vehicle — not only love: even sex. Tantra has used it as a vehicle.

Tantra says that in a deep sex act you can meditate so easily that in any other state of mind it will never be as easy — because this is a natural, biological ecstasy. But whatsoever is known by "sex act" is in a very perverted form. So whenever such things are said, you feel uneasy because whatsoever you have known in the name of "sex" is not sex. It is just a shadow, because the whole society has cultivated your mind against sex.

Everyone is a suppressed person, so natural sex is impossible. And whenever you are in a sex act, a deep guilt feeling is always present there. That guilt feeling becomes a barrier, and one of the greatest opportunities is lost. You could have used it to go deep down into yourself.

Tantra says in the sex act be meditative. Feel the whole phenomenon as holy; do not feel guilty. Rather, feel blessed that nature has given you one source through which you can go deep into ecstasy immediately. And then, be totally free in it. Do not repress; do not resist. Let the sexual communion take hold of you. Forget yourself; throw all your inhibitions. Be absolutely natural, and then you will feel a deep music in the body.

When both bodies become one harmony, then you will forget completely that you are — and, still, you will be. Then you will forget the "I": there will be no "I", just Existence playing with Existence, one being with another. And the two will become one. There will be no thinking; future will cease and you will be in the present this very moment. Without any guilt, without any inhibition, make it a meditation. And then sex is transformed. Then sex itself becomes a door.

And if sex becomes a door, by and by sex ceases to be sexual. And a moment comes when sex has gone: only the perfume has remained. That perfume is love. And later on, even that perfume disappears, and then that which remains is Samadhi.

Tantra says nothing has to be taken as an enemy: every energy is friendly; one has just to know how to use it. So do not make any choice. Transform your love into meditation and transform your meditation into love. Then soon you will forget the word, and you will know the real thing which is not the word. The word "love" is not love, and the word "meditation" is not meditation, and the word "God" is not "God". These are only words. And if you can penetrate in, then God — meditation — love: they all become one.

One more question: *"What are the reasons for man's insensitivity and how to remove them?"*

The child is born. The child is helpless. The human child particularly is totally helpless. He has to depend on others to be alive, to remain alive. This dependence is a bargain. The child has to give many things in this bargain, and sensitivity is one. The child is sensitive; his whole body is sensitive. But he is helpless: he cannot be independent. He has to depend on parents, on family, on society. He will have to be dependent. Because of this dependence and helplessness, the parents, the society, go on forcing things on the child, and he has to yield.

Otherwise he cannot remain alive: he will die. So he has to give many things in this bargain.

The first very deep and significant thing is sensitivity: he has to leave it. Why? Because the more the child is sensitive, the more he is in trouble, the more he is vulnerable. A slight sensation, and he begins to cry. The cry has to be stopped by the parents, and they cannot do anything. But if the child goes on feeling every detail of sensation, the child will become a nuisance. And children do become nuisances, so parents have to curtail their sensitivity. The child has to learn resistance, the child has to learn control. And by and by the child has to divide his mind into two. So there are many sensations which he just stops feeling because they are "not good". He is punished for them.

The child's whole body is erotic. He can enjoy his fingers; he can enjoy his body. The whole body is erotic. He goes on exploring his own body; it is a great phenomenon for him. But the moment comes in his exploration when the child gets to the genitalia. Then it becomes a problem because the father and mother are all repressed. The moment the child (boy or girl) touches the genitalia, the parents become uneasy.

This is to be observed deeply. Their behaviour suddenly changes, and the child notes it. Something wrong has happened. They start crying, "Don't touch!" Then the child starts feeling that something is wrong with the genitalia. He has to suppress. And the genital is the most sensitive part of your body, the most sensitive, the most alive part of your body, the most delicate. Once the genitalia are not allowed to be touched and enjoyed, you have killed the very source of sensitivity. Then the child will become insensitive. The more he will grow, the more he will be insensitive.

So first there is a bargain — necessary, but evil. And the moment one begins to understand, this bargain has to be thrown and you have to regain your sensitivity. The second reason for this bargain is because of security.

I was with a friend for many years; I lived in his bungalow. From the very first day I observed that he would not look at his servants. He was a rich man, but he would never look at his servants, he would never look at his children. He would come running into the bungalow, then he would go running from his bungalow to his car. So I asked him, "What is the matter?"

He said, "If you look at your servants they start feeling friendly, and then they start asking about money and this and that. If you talk with your children, then you are not the master. Then you cannot control them."

So he created a facade of insensitivity around him. He was afraid that if he talked with a servant, if he should feel that he was ill, if he sympathized, then he would have to give some money or some help.

Everyone learns sooner or later that to be sensitive is to be vulnerable to many things. You pull yourself in, you create a barrier around you that is a safeguard — a safety measure. Then you can go on through the streets. Beggars are begging and there are dirty ugly slums, but you do not feel anything, you do not see really. In this ugly society, one has to create a barrier around himself, a wall — a subtle, transparent wall — behind which he can hide. Otherwise, one is vulnerable, and it will be very difficult to live.

That is why insensitivity sets in. It helps you to be in this ugly world without being disturbed, but then at a cost — and the cost is very much. You are at ease in this world without being disturbed, but then you cannot enter into the Divine, into the Total, into the Whole. You cannot enter the other world. If for this world insensitivity is good and for that world sensitivity is good, that creates the problem. If you are really interested in entering that world, you will have to create sensitivity. You will have to throw all these walls, these securities.

Of course, you will become vulnerable. You will feel much suffering, but that suffering is nothing in comparison to the bliss you can reach through sensitivity. The more sensitive you become, the more you will feel compassion. But you will suffer because all around you there is hell. You are closed: that is why you cannot feel it. Once you become open, you will be open to both — to the hell of this world and the heaven of that world. You will become open to both! And it is impossible to remain closed at one point and open at another because, really, either you are closed or you are open. If you are closed, you are closed for both. If you are open, you will be open for both. So remember this: a Buddha is filled with bliss, but also filled with suffering.

That suffering is not of his own. It is for others. He is in deep bliss, but he suffers for others. And Mahayana Buddhists say that when Buddha reached to the door of Nirvana, the gate-keeper opened the door (this is a myth, and very beautiful), the doorkeeper opened the door, but Buddha refused to enter. The doorkeeper said, "Why are you not coming? For millennia we have been waiting for you. Every day the news comes that Buddha is coming, Buddha is coming. The whole heaven is waiting for you. Enter! You are welcome!"

Buddha said, "I cannot enter unless everyone else has entered before me. I will wait! Unless every single human being has entered, heaven is not for me."

Buddha has a suffering for others. As for himself, he is now deep in bliss. See the parallel? You are deep in suffering, and you go on feeling that everyone else is enjoying life. Quite the contrary happens to a Buddha. He is now in deep bliss, and he knows that everyone else is suffering.

These methods are the methods to remove this insensitivity. We will discuss more about HOW to remove it.

Enough.

15
Toward The Untouched Inner Reality

November 18, 1972, Bombay, India

SUTRAS:

22. Let attention be at a place where you are seeing some past happening, and even your form, having lost its present characteristics, is transformed.

23. Feel an object before you. Feel the absence of all other objects but this one. Then, leaving aside the. object-feeling and the absence-feeling, Realize.

24. When a mood against someone or for someone arises, do not place it on the person in question, but remain centered.

One of the great tantrics of this age, George Gurdjieff, thinks that identification is the only sin — and the next sutra, the tenth sutra on centering, which we are going to penetrate tonight, is concerned with identification. So first be crystal clear on what identification means. You were a child once; now you are not. Someone becomes young, someone becomes old, and childhood becomes a past thing. Youth has gone, but still you are identified with your childhood. You cannot see it as happening to someone else; you cannot be a witness to it. Whenever you see your childhood, you are not aloof from it: you are one with it. Whenever someone remembers his youth, he is one with it.

Really, now it is just a dream. And if you can see your childhood as a dream — as a film passing before you and you are not identified with it, you are just a witness, you will achieve a very subtle insight into yourself. If you see your past as a film, as a dream (you are not part of it: you are just out of it — and really you are), then many things will happen. If you are thinking about your childhood, you are not in it; you cannot be. The childhood is just a memory — just a past memory. You are remaining aloof and looking at it. You are different: you are a witness. If you can feel this witnessing and then see your childhood as a film on a screen, many things will happen.

One: if childhood has become just a dream which you can see, then whatsoever you are just now will become a dream the next day. If you are young, then your youth will become a dream. If you are old, then your old age also will become a dream. One day you were a child; now the childhood has become just a dream and you can observe it.

It is good to start with the past: observe the past and disidentify yourself from it; become a witness. Then observe the future — whatsoever you imagine about the future, and be a witness to that also. Then you can observe your present very easily, because then you know whatsoever is present just now was future yesterday, and tomorrow it will become the past. But your witness is never past, never future. Your witnessing consciousness is eternal; it is not part of time. That is why everything that happens in time becomes a dream.

Remember this also: whenever you are dreaming something in the night you become identified with it, and you can never remember in your dream that this is a dream. Only in the morning, when you have awakened from the dream, can you remember that that was a dream and not a reality. Why? Because then you are aloof, not in it. Then there is a gap. Some space is there, and you can see that it was a dream.

But what is your whole past? The gap is there, the space is there. Try to see it as a dream. Now it is a dream, now it is nothing more than a dream, because as dream becomes memory your past has become just a memory. You cannot prove really that whatsoever you think was your childhood was real or just a dream. It is difficult to prove. It may have been just a dream, it may have been real. The memory cannot say whether it was real or a dream. Psychologists say old men occasionally get confused between what they have dreamed and what was real.

Children always get confused. In the morning, small children cannot differentiate. Whatsoever they have seen in the dream was not real, but they may weep for a toy destroyed in the dream. And you also, for a few moments after sleep is broken, are still affected by your dream. If someone was murdering you in the dream, even though your sleep is broken and you are wide awake, your heart still beats fast, your blood circulation is fast, you may be still perspiring and a subtle fear is still there hovering around you. Now you are awake and the dream has passed, but you will take a few minutes to feel that it was simply a dream and nothing else. When you can feel that it was a dream, then you are out of it and there is no fear.

If you can feel that the past was just a dream (you are not to project this and force the idea that the past was just a dream: it is a consequence); if you can observe this; if you can be aware of it without getting involved in it, without being identified with it; if you can stand aloof and look at it; it will become a dream. Anything that you can look at as a witness is a dream.

That is why Shankara and Nagarjuna could say that this world is just a dream. Not that it is a dream: they were not fools, not simpletons saying this world actually is a dream. They meant by saying this that they have become witnesses. Even to this world which is so actual, they have become witnesses. And once you become a witness of anything, it becomes a dream. That is the reason why the world is called a *"maya"* (an illusion). It is not that it is unreal, but that one can become a witness to it. And once you become a witness, aware — fully aware, the whole thing drops just like a dream FOR YOU, because the space is there and you are not identified with it. But we go on being identified.

Just a few days before, I was reading Jean Jacques Rousseau's "Confessions". This is a rare book. It is really the first book in world literature in which someone bares himself totally naked. Whatsoever sins he has committed, whatsoever immorality, he opens himself totally naked. But if you read the "Confessions" of Rousseau you are bound to feel that he is enjoying it: he feels very much elated. Talking about his sins, talking about his immoralities, he feels elated. It seems as if he is enjoying it with much relish. In the beginning, in the introduction, Rousseau says, "When the last day of judgement will come, I will say to God, to the Almighty, you need not bother about me. Read this book and you will know everything."

No one before him has ever confessed so truthfully. And at the end of the book he says, "Almighty God, Eternal God, fulfill my only one desire. I have confessed everything; now let a big crowd gather to listen to my confessions."

So it is rightly suspected that he may have confessed those sins also which he has not committed. He feels so elated, and he is enjoying the whole thing. He has become identified. And there is only one sin which he has not admitted to — the sin of being identified. With whatsoever sin he has committed or not committed, he is identified — and that is the only sin for those who know deeply how the human mind functions.

When for the first time he read his confessions amidst a small group of intellectuals, he was thinking that something earth-shaking would happen because he was the first man to confess so truthfully, as he said. The intellectuals listened, and they became more and more bored. Rousseau felt very uneasy because he was thinking something miraculous was going to happen. When he ended, they all felt relieved, but no one said anything. There was a complete silence for a few moments. Rousseau's heart was shattered. He was thinking that he had created a very revolutionary thing, earthshaking, historical, and there was simply silence. Everyone was just thinking about how to get away from there.

Who is interested in your sins except yourself? No one is interested in your virtues, no one is interested in your sins. Man is such that be becomes elated, he becomes strengthened in his ego, by his virtues and by his sins also. After writing "Confessions", Rousseau began to think himself a sage, a saint, because he had confessed. But the basic sin remained. The basic sin is being identified with happenings in time. Whatsoever happens in time is dreamlike, and unless you get unattached from it, not identified with it, you will never know what bliss is.

Identification is misery, non-identification is bliss. This tenth technique is concerned with identification.

The tenth sutra: *"Let attention be at a place where you are seeing some past happening, and even your form, having lost its present characteristics, is transformed."*

You are remembering your past — any happening: your child-hood, your love affairs, the death of your father or mother, any-thing. Look at it, but do not get involved in it. Remember it as if you are remembering someone else's life. And when this happening is being filmed again, is on the screen again, be attentive, aware, a witness, remaining aloof. Your past form will be there in the film, in the story.

If you are remembering your love affair, your first love affair, you will be there with your beloved: your PAST FORM will be there with your beloved. You cannot remember otherwise. Be detached from your past form also. Look at the whole phenomenon as if someone else were loving someone else, as if the whole thing doesn't belong to you. You are just a witness, an observer.

This is a very, very basic technique. It has been used much, particularly by Buddha. There are many forms of this technique. You can find your own way of approaching this. For example, when you are just falling into sleep at night, just ready to fall into sleep, go backwards through the memories of the whole day — BACKWARDS. Do not start from the morning. Start right from where you are, just on the bed — the last item, and then go back. Then go back by and by, step by step, just to the first experience in the morning when you first became awake. Go back, and remember continuously that you are not getting involved.

For example, in the afternoon someone insulted you. See your-self, the form of yourself, being insulted by someone — but you remain just an observer. Do not get involved; do not get angry again. If you get angry again, then you are identified. Then you have missed the point of meditation. Do not get angry. He is not insulting you. He is insulting the form that was in the afternoon. That form has gone now.

You are just like a river flowing: the forms are flowing. In the childhood you had one form, now you do not have that form. That form has gone. River-like, you are changing continuously. So when in the night you are meditating backwards on the happenings of the day, just remember that you are a witness: do not get angry. Someone was praising you: do not get elated. Just look at the whole thing as if you are looking indifferently at a film. And backwards is very helpful — particularly for those who have any trouble with sleep.

If you have any trouble with sleep, insomnia, sleeplessness, if you find it difficult to fall into sleep, this will help deeply. Why ? Because this is an unwinding of the mind. When you go back you are unwinding the mind. In the morning you start winding, and the mind becomes tangled in many things, in many places. Unfinished and incomplete, many things will remain on the mind, and there is no time to let them settle at the very moment that they happen.

So in the night go back. This is an unwinding process. And when you will be getting back to the morning when you were just on your bed, to the first thing in the morning, you will again have the same fresh mind that you had in the morning. And then you can fall asleep like a very small child.

You can use this technique of going back for your whole life also. Mahavir used this technique of going back very much. And now there is a movement in America called "Dianetics". They are using this method and finding it very, very useful. This movement, Dianetics, says that all your diseases are just hangovers of the past. And they are right. If you can go backwards and unwind your whole life, with that unwinding many diseases will disappear completely. And this has been proven from so many successful incidents. There are so many successful cases now.

So many persons suffer from a particular disease, and nothing physiological, nothing medical helps; the disease continues. The disease seems to be psychological. What to do about it ? To say to someone that his disease is psychological is no help. Rather, it may prove harmful because no one feels good when you say his disease is psychological. What can he do then ? He feels he is helpless.

This going backwards is a miraculous method. If you go back slowly — slowly unwinding the mind to the first moment when this disease happened, if by and by you go back to when for the first time you were attacked by this disease, if you can unwind to that moment, you will come to know that this disease is basically a complex of certain other things, certain psychological things. By going back those things will bubble up.

If you pass through that moment when the disease first attacked you, suddenly you will become aware of what psychological factors contributed to it. And you are not to do anything: you are just to be aware of those psychological factors and go on backwards. Many diseases simply disappear from you because the complex is broken. When you have become aware of the complex, then there is no need of it. You are cleaned of it — purged.

This is a deep catharsis. And if you can do it daily, you will feel a new health, a new freshness coming to you. And if we can teach children to do it daily, they will never be burdened by their past. They will not need ever to go to the past. They will be always here and now. There won't be any hang up; nothing will be hovering over them from the past.

You can do it daily. It will give you a new insight for going backward through the whole day. The mind would like to start from the morning, remember, but then there is no unwinding. Rather, the whole thing is re-emphasized. If you start from the morning, you are doing a very wrong thing.

There are many so-called teachers in India who suggest to do it — to reflect on the whole day, and they always say to do it again from the morning. That is wrong and harmful because then you are re-emphasizing the whole thing and the trap will be deepened. Never go from the morning to the evening: always go backward. Only then can you clean the whole thing, purge the whole thing. The mind would like to start from the morning because it is easy: the mind knows it and there is no problem. If you start backward, suddenly you will feel you have jumped into the morning and you have started forward again. Do not do that. Be aware; go back.

You can train your mind to go back through other things also. Just go back from a hundred — "99, 98, 97": go back. Repeat from a hundred to one backward. You will feel a difficulty because the mind has a habit to go from one to hundred, never from a hundred to one.

In the same way you have to go backward with this technique. What will happen? Going backward, unwinding the mind, you are a witness. You are seeing things that happened to you, but now they are not happening to you. Now you are just an observer and they are happening on the screen of the mind.

While doing this daily, suddenly one day you will become aware during the day, while working in the market, in your office or anywhere, that you cannot be a witness to events that are happening just now. If you can be a witness later on, and look back at someone who had insulted you without becoming angry about it, why not right now (to what is presently happening)?

Someone is insulting you: what is the difficulty? You can pull yourself apart just now and you can see that someone is insulting you, and still you are different from your body, from your mind, from that which is insulted. You can witness it. If you can be a witness to this, you will not get angry. Then it is impossible. Anger is possible only when you are identified. If you are not identified, anger is impossible. Anger means identification.

This technique says look at any happening of the past: your form will be there. The sutra says "your form", not you. YOU were never there. Always your form is involved: you are never involved. When you insult me, you do not insult ME. You cannot insult me. You can insult only the form. The form which I am is there just here and how for you. You can insult that form and I can detach myself from the form. That is why Hindus have always been insisting on being detached from name and form. You are neither your name nor your form. You are the

Consciousness who knows the form and the name, and the Consciousness is different — totally different.

But it is difficult. So start with the past. Then it is easy, because now, with the past, there is no urgency. Someone insulted you twenty years back, so there is no urgency in it. The man may have died and everything is finished. It is just a dead affair, just dead from the past. It is easy to be aware of it, but once you can become aware there is no difficulty in doing the same with what is happening just here and now.

But to start from here and now is difficult. The problem is so urgent and it is so near that there is no space to move. It is difficult to create space and move away from the incident. That is why the sutra says "start with the past". Look at your own form, detached, standing aloof, indifferent, and be transformed through this.

You will be transformed through it because it is a deep cleaning, an unwinding. Then you can know that your body, your mind, your existence in time, are not your basic reality. The substantial reality is different. Things come and go upon it without touching it in the least. You remain innocent, untouched; you remain virgin. The whole thing passes, the whole life passes — good and bad, success and failure, praise and blame — everything passes. Disease and health, youth and old age, birth and death — everything passes, and you are untouched by it.

But how to know this untouched reality within you? That is the purpose of this technique. Start with the past. There is a gap when you can look at your past; the perspective is possible. Or, look at the future. But to look at the future is difficult. Only for a few persons, observing the future is not difficult — for poets, for people with imagination who can look in the future as if they are looking at reality. But ordinarily the past is good to use: you can look in the past. For young men it may be good to look into the future: it is easier for them to look in the future because youth is future oriented.

For old men there is no future except death. They cannot look in the future; they are afraid. That is why old men always start thinking about the past. They always go on again and again in their memories, but they commit the same mistake. They start from the past toward their present state of being. That is wrong. They should go backward.

If they can go backward, many times, by and by, they will feel that their whole past is washed away from them. And then a person can die without the past clinging to him. If you can die without the past clinging to you, you will die consciously; you will die fully aware. Then death will not be a death to you: rather, it will be a meeting with the deathless.

Clean the whole consciousness of the depth of the past, and your very being will be transofrmed through it. Try this. This method is not very difficult. Only persistent effort is needed; there is no inherent difficulty in the method. It is simple, and you can start with your day. Just tonight, on your bed, go backward, and you will feel very beautiful, you will feel very blissful. And then the whole day will have passed. But do not be in a hurry. Pass it slowly so that nothing is missed. It is a very strange feeling because many things will come up before your eyes. You have really missed while passing through the day because you were too much engaged. But the mind goes on collecting even when you are unaware.

You were passing through a street. Someone was singing, but you might not have paid any attention. You might not have even been aware that you have heard the sound just passing in the street. But the mind has heard and recorded it. Now that will cling; that will become a burden to you unnecessarily. So go back, but go very slowly, VERY slowly, as if a film is being shown to you in very slow motion. Go, and see the details, and then your one day will look very, very long. It is really, because for the mind there has been so much information, and the mind has recorded everything. Now go back.

By and by you will become capable of knowing everything that has been recorded. And once you can go back, it is just like a tape recorder: it is washed away. And by the time you will reach the morning, you will fall asleep — and the quality of the sleep will be different: it will be meditative. Then, again, in the morning when you feel that you have awakened, do not open your eyes immediately. Go backward into the night.

It will be difficult in the beginning. You may go a little. Some part, some fragment of a dream which you were just dreaming before the sleep was broken, may come to your mind. But by and by, with gradual effort, you will be able to penetrate more and more and more, and after a three-month period you will be capable of moving backward to the point when you fell asleep. And if you can go backward deep within your sleep, your quality of sleep and waking will change completely because then you cannot dream; dreaming will have become futile. If you can go back in the day and in the night, dreaming is not needed.

Really, now psychologists say dreaming is an unwinding. If you yourself have done it, then there is no need. All that has been hanging in the mind, all that has remained unfulfilled, incomplete, tries to complete itself in the dream.

You were passing and you have seen something — a beautiful house — and a subtle desire arose in you to possess it. But you were going to your office and that was no time for daydreaming, so you just passed by. You did not even notice that the mind had created a desire to possess this house. But now that desire is hanging there suspended, and if it cannot be removed it will be difficult to sleep.

Difficulties in sleep basically mean only one thing: that your day is still hanging over you and you cannot be relieved of it. You are clinging to it. Then in the night you will see a dream that you have become the owner of this house: now you are living in this house. The moment that this dream comes to you, your mind is relieved.

So ordinarily, people think that dreams are disturbances of the sleep. That is absolutely wrong. Dreams are not disturbances of your sleep. They are not disturbing your sleep: they are really helpers. Without them you could not sleep at all. As you are, you cannot sleep without dreams because your dreams are helping to complete things which have remained incomplete.

And there are things which cannot be completed. Your mind goes on desiring absurd desires. They cannot be completed in reality, so what to do? Those incomplete desires go on in you, and they keep you hoping, they keep you thinking. So what to do? You have seen a beautiful woman, and you were attracted to her. Now the desire has arisen to possess her. It may not be possible. The woman may not even look at you. So what to do? The dream will help you.

In dream you can possess the woman, and then the mind is relieved. As far as the mind is concerned, there is no difference between dream and reality — as far as MIND is concerned. What is the difference? Loving a woman in reality and loving a woman in dream, what is the difference for the mind? There is no difference — or this may be the difference: that the dream phenomenon may be more beautiful because then the woman will not disturb. It is your dream and you can do anything, and the woman will not create any problems for you. The other is absent completely. You are alone. There is no barrier, so you can do whatsoever you like.

There is no difference for the mind; mind cannot make any distinction between what is dream and what is reality. For example, if you could be put in a coma for one whole year, and you dream on and on, for one year you will completely not be able to feel in any way that whatsoever you are seeing is a dream. It will be real, and the dream will continue for one year.

Psychologists say if you can put a man in a coma for a hundred years, he will dream for a hundred years, not for a single moment suspecting that whatsoever he is doing is just a dream. And if he dies he will never know that his life was just a dream, that it was never real. For the mind there is no difference: the reality and the dream are both the same. So mind can unwind itself in dream.

If you do this technique, then there will be no need for dreams. The quality of your sleep will be changed totally because without dreams you fall to the very bottom of your being, and without dreams you will be aware in your sleep.

That is what Krishna says in the Gita — that while everyone is deeply asleep, the yogi is not: the yogi is awake. That doesn't mean that the yogi is not sleeping: he is also sleeping. But the quality of the sleep is different. Your sleep is just like a drugged unconsciousness. A yogi's sleep is a deep relaxation with no unconsciousness. His whole body is relaxed; every fiber and cell of his whole body is relaxed with no tension left. But he is fully aware of the whole phenomenon.

Try this technique. Start from tonight, try it, and then do it in the morning also. And when you feel that you are attuned to the technique, that you can do it, after one week try it for your whole past. Just take one day off. Go to some lonely place. It will be good if you fast — fast and be silent. Lie down on some lonely beach or under some tree, and just move toward your past from this point: you are lying on the beach feeling the sand and the sun, and now move backward. Go on penetrating, penetrating, penetrating, and find out the last thing that you can remember.

You will be surprised. Ordinarily you cannot remember much, and you cannot pass the barrier of four or five years of age. Those who have a very good memory may go back to the age barrier of three years, but then, suddenly, a block comes and everything goes dark. But if you try with this technique, by and by you will break the barrier, and very easily you can come to remember the first day you were born. And that is a revelation.

And back again to your sun and beach, you will be a different man. If you make more effort, you can penetrate to the womb. And you have memories of the womb — nine months of memories with your mother. That nine-month period is also recorded in the mind. When your mother was depressed, you have recorded it because you felt depressed. You were so connected with the mother, so united, so one, that whatsoever would happen to your mother was happening to you. When she was angry, you were angry. When she was happy, you were happy. When she was praised, you felt praised. When she was ill, you felt the pain, the suffering, everything.

If you can penetrate to the womb, now you are on the right track. And then, by and by, you can penetrate more and you can remember the first moment when you entered the womb.

Only because of this remembrance, Mahavir and Buddha could say that there are past lives, rebirth. Rebirth is not really a principle. It is just a deep psychological experience. And if you can remember the first moment you entered the womb of your mother, then you can penetrate more and you can remember the death of your past life. And once you touch that point, then the method is in your hands; then you can move very easily to all your past lives.

And this is an experience, and the result is phenomenal, because then you know that through many, many lives you have lived the same nonsense that you are living now. You have been doing this whole nonsense so many times repeatedly. The pattern is the same, the format is the same; only the details differ. You loved some other woman, now you love this woman. You gathered money: the coins were of one kind; now the coins are different. But the whole pattern is the same; it is repetitive.

Once you can see that for many, many lives you have lived the same nonsense, how stupid has been this whole vicious circle, suddenly you are awakened and the whole thing becomes a dream. You are thrown away from it, and now do not want to repeat the same in the future.

Desire stops because desire is nothing but the past being projected in the future. Desire is nothing but your past experience in search of another repetition again; desire means just an old experience that you want to repeat again — nothing else. And you cannot leave desire unless you become aware of this whole phenomenon. How can you leave it ? The past is there as a great barrier, a rock-like barrier. It is upon your head; it is pushing you toward the future. Desires are created by the past and projected into the future. If you can know the past as a dream, all desires become impotent. They fall down, they just wither away — and the future disappears. In that disappearance of past and future, you are transformed.

The eleventh technique: *"Feel an object before you. Feel the absence of all other objects but this one. Then leaving aside the object-feeling and the absence-feeling, Realize."*

Feel an object before you — any object: for example, a rose flower. Anything will do. "Feel an object before you": first "feel it". Seeing won't do: feel it. You see a rose flower, but your heart is not stilled. You are not feeling it: otherwise you may start weeping and crying; otherwise you may start laughing and dancing. You are not feeling it: you are just seeing it. And even that seeing may not be complete, because you never see completely. The past, the memory, says that this is a rose, and you pass on. You have not seen it really. The mind says that this is a rose. You "know" everything about it, as you have known roses, so "what about it?" So you pass on. Just a glimpse is enough to revive the memory of your past experience of roses, and you pass on. Even seeing is not complete.

Remain with the rose. See it, then feel it. What to do to feel it? Smell it, touch it, let it become a deep bodily experience. First close your eyes, and let the rose touch your whole face. Feel it. Put it on the eyes; let the eyes touch it; smell it. Put it against the heart; be silent with it; give a feeling to the rose. Forget everything; forget the whole world. Feel an object before you and feel the absence of all other objects — because if your mind is still thinking of other things, then this feeling will not penetrate deeply. Forget all other roses, forget all other persons, forget everything. Just let this rose remain there. Only the rose, the rose, the rose ! Forget everything else; let this rose envelope you completely. You are drowned in the rose.

This will be difficult because we are not so sensitive. But for women it will not be so difficult: they can feel it more easily. For men it may be a little bit more difficult unless they have a very developed aesthetic sense like a poet or a painter or a musician: they can feel things. But try. Children can do it very easily.

I was teaching this method to the son of one of my friends. He could feel very easily. When I gave him a rose flower, and

I told him all that I have told to you, he did it, and he enjoyed it deeply. And then I asked him, "How are you feeling?" He said, "I have become a rose flower: that is the feeling. I have become a rose flower." Children can do it very easily, but we never train them. Otherwise they could be the best meditators.

Forget all other objects completely. "Feel the absence of all other objects but this one. This is what happens in love. If you are in love with someone, you forget the whole world. If you are still remembering the world, then know well that this is not love. You have forgotten the whole world; only the beloved or the lover remains. That is why I say love is a meditation. You can use this technique also as a love technique: forget everything else.

Just a few days ago, a friend came to me with his wife. His wife was complaining about a certain thing; that is why she had come. The friend said, "I have been meditating for a year and now I am deep in it. And while I meditate I have found it helpful when a peak comes to my meditation to suddenly cry, 'Rajneesh, Rajneesh, Rajneesh.' It helps me, but now a strange thing has happened. When I am making love to my wife, when I come to a sexual peak, I start crying, 'Rajneesh, Rajneesh, Rajneesh.' Because of this my wife is very much disturbed, and she says, 'Are you making love with me, are you meditating, or what are you doing? And why does this Rajneesh come in?' "

The man said to me, "It is now very difficult because if I do not cry, 'Rajneesh, Rajneesh,' I cannot achieve a peak. And if I cry, my wife is very much disturbed. She starts crying and weeping and making a scene. So what to do? Thus, I have brought my wife." Of course, his wife's complaint is right because she does not like for someone else to be present between them. That is why love needs privacy — absolute privacy. The privacy is meaningful just to forget all else.

In Europe and America, now they are working with group sex. That is nonsense — many couples making love in one room. It is absolute nonsense because then love can never go very deep. It will become just a sex orgy. The presence of others becomes a barrier. Then it cannot be meditative. With any object, if you can forget the whole world you are in a deep love — with a rose or with a stone or with anything. But the condition is to feel the presence of this object and feel the absence of all else. Let this object be the only existential thing in your consciousness. It will be easy if you try with some object you are naturally in love with.

It would be difficult for you to put a stone, a rock, before you, and forget the whole world. It would be difficult, but Zen Masters have done it. They have rock gardens for meditation. No flowers, no trees, nothing — just rocks and sand. And they meditate on a rock because, they say, if you can have a deep love relationship with a rock, then no man can create a barrier for you. And men are like rocks. If you can love a rock, then you can love a man. Then there is no problem: they are like rocks — even more stony. It is difficult to break them and penetrate them.

But choose some object you naturally love, and then forget the whole world. Relish the presence, taste the presence, feel it, go deep in it and let it go deep in you. "Then, leaving aside the object . . ." And then comes the most difficult part of this technique. You have left all other objects, and only one object has remained. You have forgotten all: only one has remained.

Now, "leaving aside the object feeling . . ." Now leave aside the feeling that you have for this object. "Leaving aside the object-feeling and the absence-feeling" — of other objects. Now there are only two things; everything else is absent. Now leave that absence also. Only this rose, this face, this woman, this man, this rock, is present. Leave this also, and leave the feeling as well. Suddenly you fall into an absolute vacuum and nothing remains. And Shiva says, "Realize." Realize this vacuum, this nothingness. This is your nature, this is pure Being.

It will be difficult to approach nothingness directly — very difficult and arduous. So it is easy to pass through one object as a vehicle. First put one object in the mind, and feel it so totally that you need not remember anything else. Your whole consciousness is filled with this one object. Then leave this also; forget this also.

You fall into an abyss. Now nothing remains — no object: only your subjectivity is there — pure, uncontaminated, unoccupied. This pure Being, this pure Consciousness, is your nature. But do it in steps; do not try the whole technique. First create one object-feeling. For a few days only do this part; do not do the whole technique.

First, for a few days or for a few weeks, just do one part — the first part. Create an object-feeling; be filled with the object. And use one object: do not go on changing objects, because with every object you will have to make the same effort again. If you have chosen one rose flower, then go on using a rose flower every day. Be filled with it so that one day you can say, "Now I am the flower." Then the first part is fulfilled. When only the flower is there and all else is forgotten, then relish this idea for a few days. It is beautiful in itself — very, very beautiful, vital, powerful in itself.

Just feel it for a few days — and then, when you are attuned to it and it has become easy, then you need not struggle. Then the flower comes there suddenly: the whole world is forgotten and only the flower remains.

Then try the second part: close your eyes and forget the flower also. If you have done the first, the second will not be difficult — remember. But if you try the whole technique in one sitting, the second will be impossible — because if you can do the first, if you can forget the whole world for one flower, you can forget the flower also for nothingness. So the second part will come, but first you have to struggle for it. But the mind is very tricky. The mind will always say try the whole thing, and then you will not succeed. Then the mind will say, "It is not useful or it is not for me." Try it in parts if you want to succeed. Let the first part be complete, and then do the second. Then the object is not there and only your consciousness remains just like a light, a flame without anything around it.

You have a lamp and the lamp's light falls on many objects. Visualize it. In your room there are many, many objects. If you bring one lamp into the darkness of the room, all the objects are lighted. The lamp radiates light on every object so that you can see. Now remain with an object; let there be one object. The lamp is the same, but now only one object is there in its light. Now remove that object also: now light remains without any object.

The same happens with your consciousness. You are a flame, a light. The whole world is your object. You leave the whole world, and you choose one object for your concentration. Your flame remains the same, but now it is not occupied with multi-objects. It is occupied with only one. And then drop that object also. Suddenly there is simply light — consciousness. It is not falling on anything. This Buddha has called "Nirvana"; this Mahavir has called "Kaivalya" — the total aloneness. The Upanishads have called it the experience of the Brahman, or the Atman. Shiva says that if you can do this single technique, you will Realize the Supreme.

The twelfth technique: *"When a mood against someone or for someone arises, do not place it on the person in question, but remain centered."*

If hate arises for someone or against someone, or love arises for someone, what do we do? We project it on the person. If you feel hate toward me, you forget yourself completely in your hate; only I become your object. If you feel love toward me, you forget yourself completely; only I become the object. You project your love or hate or whatsoever upon me. You forget completely the inner center of your being; the other becomes the center. This sutra says when hate arises or love arises or any mood for or against anyone. "Do not project it on the person in question." Remember, you are the source of it.

I love you. The ordinary feeling is that you are the source of my love. That is not really so. I am the source. You are just a screen on which I project my love. You are just a screen; I project my love on you and I say that you are the source of my love. This is not fact. This is fiction. I draw my love energy and project it onto you. In that love energy projected onto you, you become lovely. You may not be lovely to someone else. You may be absolutely repulsive to someone else. Why? If you are the source of love, then everyone must feel loving toward you. But you are not the source. I project love, then you become lovely; someone projects hate, then you become repulsive. And someone else doesn't project anything: he is indifferent; he may not even have looked at you. What is happening? We are projecting our own moods upon others.

That is why if you are on your honeymoon, the moon looks beautiful, miraculous, wonderful. It seems that the whole world is different. And on the same night, just for your neighbour, this miraculous night may not be in existence at all. His child has died; then the same moon is just sad, intolerable. But for you it is enchanting, fascinating; it is maddening. Why? Is the moon the source or is the moon just a screen and you are projecting yourself?

This sutra says, "When a mood against or for someone arises, do not place it on the person in question," (or on the object in question). Remain centered. Remember that you are the source, so do not move to the other: move to the source. When you feel hate, do not go to the object. Go to the point from where the hate is coming. Go not to the person to whom it is going, but to the center from where it is coming. Move to the center; go within; use your hate or love or anger or anything as a journey toward your inner center to the source. Move to the source and remain centered there.

Try it! This is a very, very scientific psychological technique. Someone has insulted you; anger suddenly erupts; you are feverish. Anger is flowing toward the person who has insulted you. Now, you will project this whole anger on to him. He has not done anything. If he has insulted you, what has he done? He has just pricked you, he has helped your anger to arise — but the anger is yours. If he goes to a Buddha and insults him, he will not be able to create any anger in him. Or if he goes to

Jesus, Jesus will give him the other cheek. Or if he goes to Bodhidharma, he will roar with laughter. So it depends.

The other is not the source. The source is always within you. The other is hitting the source, but if there is no anger within you it cannot come out. If you hit a Buddha, only compassion will come out because only compassion is there. Anger will not come out because anger is not there. If you throw a bucket into a dry well, nothing comes out. In a water-filled well, you throw a bucket and water comes out, but the water is from the well. The bucket only helps to bring it out. So one who is insulting you is just throwing a bucket in you, and then the bucket will come out filled with the anger, hate, or fire that was within you. You are the source, remember.

For this technique, remember that you are the source of everything that you go on projecting onto others: always remember this. And whenever there is a mood against or for, immediately move within and go to the source from where this hate is coming. Remain centered there; do not move to the object. Someone has given you a chance to be aware of your own anger: thank him immediately and forget him. Close your eyes, move within, and now look at the source from where this love or anger is coming. From where ? Go within; move within: you will find the source there because the anger is coming from your source.

Hate or love or anything is coming from your source. And it is easy to go to the source at the moment you are angry or in love or in hate, because then you are hot. It is easy to move in then. The wire is hot and you can take it in. You can move inward with that hotness. And when you reach a cool point within, you will suddenly Realize a different dimension, a different world opening before you. Use anger, use hate, use love, to go within.

We use it always to move to the other, and we feel very much frustrated if no one is there to project upon. Then we go on projecting even on inanimate objects. I have seen persons being angry at their shoes, throwing them in anger. What are they doing? I have seen angry persons pushing a door in anger, throwing their anger on the door, abusing the door, using dirty language against the door. What are they doing?

I will end with one Zen insight about this. One of the greatest of Zen Masters, Lin-chi, used to say, "While I was young I was very fascinated by boating. I had one small boat, and I would go in the lake alone. For hours together I would remain there.

"One day it happened that with closed eyes I was on my boat meditating on the beautiful night. One empty boat came flowing downstream and struck my boat. My eyes were closed, so I thought, 'Someone is here with his boat, and he has struck my boat.' Anger arose. I opened my eyes and I was just going to say something to that man in anger. Then I realized that the boat was empty. Then there was no way to move. To whom could I express the anger? The boat was empty. It was just flowing downstream, and it had come and struck my boat."

So there was nothing to do. There was no possibility to project the anger on an empty boat.

So Lin-chi said, "I closed my eyes. The anger was there — but finding no way out, I closed my eyes and just floated backward with the anger. And that empty boat became my Realization. I came to a point within myself in that silent night. That empty boat was my Guru. And now, if someone comes in a boat and insults me, I laugh and I say this boat is also empty. I close my eyes and I go within."

Use this technique. It may work miracles for you.

16
Beyond The "Sin"
Of Unconsciousness

November 19, 1972, Bombay, India

QUESTIONS:

1. How to practise not placing our moods on others without suppressing ourselves?

2. Why are psychoanalysts in the West not very successful with the "unwinding" technique?

3. Isn't it true that no method is powerful unless one is initiated into it?

4. If identification is "the only sin", why do many techniques use it and say "become one" with a thing?

The first question: *"The last technique you discussed yesterday said that when a mood against someone or for someone arises, not to place it on the person in question but to remain centered. But when we experiment with this technique on our anger, hatred, etc. we feel that we are suppressing our emotions and it becomes a suppressed complex. So please clarify how to be free from these suppressed complexes while practising the above technique."*

Expression and suppression are two aspects of one coin. They are contradictory, but basically they are not different. In expression and in suppression, in both, the other is the center.

I am angry: I suppress the anger. I was going to express anger against you; now I suppress the anger against you. But the anger goes on being projected onto you whether expressed or suppressed.

This technique is not for suppression. This technique changes the very base of expression and suppression both. This technique says do not project it on the other: you are the source. Whether you express it or suppress it, you are the source. The emphasis is neither on expression nor on suppression. The emphasis is on knowing from where this anger arises. You have to move to the center, the source from where anger, hate and love arise. When you suppress, you are not moving to the center You are struggling with the expression.

Anger has arisen in me. Ordinarily, I can do two things — express it on someone or repress it. But in both the cases I am concerned with the other and I am concerned with the energy of anger that has come to the surface — not with the source.

This technique is to forget the other completely. Just look at your energy of anger arising and move deep down to find the source within yourself, from where it is coming. And the moment you find the source, remain centered in it. Do not do anything with anger — remember. In expression you are doing something with anger; in suppression also you are doing something with anger. Do not do anything with anger; do not touch it. Just use it as a path. Just go deep down into it to know from where this has arisen. And the moment you will find the source, it is very easy to be centered there. Anger has to be used, really, as a path to find the source. Any emotion can be used.

When you suppress, you are not going to find the source: you are just struggling with energy that has come up and wants to be expressed. You can suppress it, but it will be expressed sooner or later because you cannot struggle with the energy that has come up. It has to be expressed. So you may not express it upon "A", but then you will express it upon "B" or "C". Whenever you find someone who is weaker than you, you will express the energy. And unless you express it you will feel burdened, tense, heavy and ill at ease.

So it will be expressed. You cannot suppress it continuously. From somewhere it will leak out, because if it is not going to leak out you will be constantly worried by it. So suppression is really nothing but postponing expression. You will simply postpone.

You are angry at your boss; you cannot express it. It is not "economical". You will have to push it down, so you just wait until you can express it upon your wife or upon your child or somewhere — upon your servant. And the moment you reach your home you will express it. You will find causes, of course, because man is a rationalizing animal. He will rationalize; he will find something — something very trivial. But now that will become very meaningful because you have something to express.

Suppression is nothing but postponing. You can postpone for months, for years. And those who know say that you can postpone for lives also, but it will have to be expressed. This technique is not concerned at all with suppression or expression — no! This technique uses your mood, your energy, as a path for you to go deep down within yourself.

Gurdjieff used to create situations in which he would force anger upon you, or hatred, or any other mood, and that was a created phenomenon. You would not be aware.

Gurdjieff would be sitting with his disciples and you enter. You are not aware of what is going to be there, but they are ready to create anger in you: they will behave in such a way. Someone will say something, and the whole group will behave so insultingly you will become furious. Suddenly anger will come up; you are aflame. And when Gurdjieff would see that now a point has come from where you can go deep down or you can go out, when the peak has come within you and you are just going to explode, then he would say, "Close your eyes, and now be aware of your anger and go back."

Only then would you realize that the situation was a created one. No one was interested in insulting you. That was just a drama, a psychodrama. But the anger has arisen. And even if you come to know that it was simply a drama, the energy cannot suddenly go down. It will take time. Now you can move down with the falling energy to the source. This energy will just help you to go down from where it has come; you can connect now with the original source. And this is one of the most successful methods of meditation.

Create any mood — but there is no need because the whole day moods are there. Use any mood to meditate. Then you have forgotten the other completely, and you are not suppressing anything. You are just moving down with some energy which has come up. Every energy comes from the source, so right now the path is warm and you can use that path to go back. And the moment you reach to the original source, the energy will subside into the original source. It is not suppression: the energy has gone back to the original source. And when you become capable of reuniting your energy with your original source, you have become the master of your body, your mind, your energy. You have become the master! Now you will not dissipate your energy.

Once you can know how the energy falls back with you to the center, there is no need of any suppression and there is no need of any expression. Right now you are not angry. I say something: you become angry. From where is this energy coming? A moment before you were not angry, but the energy was in you. If this energy can fall back again to the source, you will again be the same as you were a moment before.

Remember this: energy is neither anger nor love nor hate. Energy is simply energy — neutral. The same energy becomes anger; the same energy becomes sex; the same energy becomes love; the same energy becomes hate. These are all forms of the same energy. You give the form, your mind gives the form, and energy moves into it.

So, remember, if you love deeply, you will not have much energy to be angry. If you do not love at all, then you will have much energy to be angry, and you will go on finding situations in which to be angry. If your energy is expressed through sex, you will be less violent. If your energy is not expressed through sex, you will be more violent. That is why militaries will never allow sex relationships for the soldiers. If it is allowed, the militaries become absolutely impotent to fight.

That is why whenever civilization comes to a peak, it cannot fight. So always, more cultured and more civilized societies are run over and defeated by lesser civilizations — always, because a more developed society cares about its individuals' every need, and sex is included. So when a society is really established, affluent, everybody's sexual need is fulfilled — but when the sexual need is fulfilled you cannot fight. You can fight very easily if the sexual need is not fulfilled. So if you want a world of peace, more freedom for sex will be needed. If you want a world of warring, fighting, then deny sex, suppress sex; create anti-sexual attitudes.

This is a very paradoxical thing: the so-called saints and sages go on talking about peace, and they go on talking against sex also. They go on creating an anti-sex atmosphere, and at the same time they go on saying that the world needs peace, not war. This is absurd. Hippies are more correct. Their slogan is right: "Make love; do not make war." That is right. If you can make love more, really you CANNOT make war.

That is why the so-called sannyasins who have suppressed sex will always be violent, angry — angry about nothing: just angry, just violent, bubbling to explode. Their whole energy is moving unexpressed. Unless the energy falls down to the source, no *brahmacharya* — no real celibacy, is possible. You can suppress sex: then it will become violence. If sex energy moves down to the center, you will be just like a child.

The child has sex energy — more than you, but it is still in the source. It has not moved to the body yet. It will move. When the body will be ready and the glands will be ready and the body will be mature, the energy will move. Why does a child look so innocent? The energy is at the source; it has not moved. Again the same thing happens when someone becomes Enlightened: the whole energy moves to the source, and the person becomes childlike. That is what Jesus means when he says that "Only those who are like children will be able to enter into my Kingdom of God".

What does it mean? Scientifically it means your whole energy has moved back to the source. If you express, it has moved out. And when it is expressed, you are creating a habit for the energy to move out, to leak out. If you suppress, then the energy has not moved to the source, it has not moved out: it is suspended. And a suspended energy is a burden.

That is why, if you really express anger, you feel relief. If you go through sex, you feel relief. If you destroy something, your hate is released and you feel relief. Why is this relief felt?

THE BOOK OF THE SECRETS

Because suspended energy is burdensome, heavy. Your mind is cloudy with it. You have to throw it out or allow it to move back to the original source: these are the only two things.

If it goes back to the source, it becomes formless. In the source energy is formless. For example, this electricity is formless. When it moves into a fan, it takes one kind of form. When it moves into a bulb, it takes a different form. You can use it in a thousand ways. The energy is the same. The form is given by the mechanism through which it moves.

Anger is a mechanism; sex is a mechanism; love is a mechanism; hate is a mechanism. When energy moves into the channel of hate, it becomes hate. If the same energy moves into love, it becomes love. And when it moves into the source, it is formless energy — pure energy. It is neither hate nor love nor anger nor sex: simply energy. Then it is innocent, because formlessness is absolute innocence. That is why Buddha looks so innocent — childlike. The energy has moved to the source.

Do not express, because you are wasting your energy and helping the other also to waste his. Do not suppress, because then you are creating a suspended phenomenon which will have to be released. Then what to do?

This technique says do not do anything with the mood itself. Just go back to the source from where the mood is coming. And while the mood is hot, the path is clear, visible inside. You can move to it. Use moods for meditation. The result is miraculous, unbelievable. And once you find the key that shows you how to pour the energy back to the source, you will have a different quality of personality. Then you will not be dissipating anything. Then it will look stupid.

Buddha has said that whenever you are angry against someone, you are punishing yourself for the misdeed of the other. He has insulted you: that is his deed. And you are punishing yourself by being angry; you are dissipating your energy.

This is stupid, but then, by listening to Buddha, Mahavir, Jesus, we start repressing: we start suppressing our energy; then we think that it is not good — that it is stupid to be angry.

So what to do ? "Suppress" the anger. "Do not" be angry. "Pull yourself in; close yourself." Fight with your anger and "suppress it". But then you will be sitting on something which will explode any moment. You are sitting on a Vesuvius: any moment it will explode.

You go on collecting: the whole day's anger is collected; the whole month's anger is collected; the whole year's anger, and the anger of your whole life, and then the anger of many lives, is collected. That is there; it can explode at any moment. Then you become very afraid of being alive even, because any moment anything can go in and you explode. You become afraid. Every moment is an inner struggle.

Psychologists say it is better to express than to suppress, but religion cannot say this. Religion says both are stupid. In expression you are harming the other and also yourself. In suppression you are harming yourself, and you will harm someone else someday. Move to the source so that the energy falls back to the source and becomes formless. Then you will feel very powerful without being angry. Then you will feel energy — vital energy: you will be alive. You will have an intense life without forms. Anyone will be impressed just by your presence. You need not dominate anyone: just your presence, and they will feel that some powerful source has come.

Whenever someone goes to a Buddha or to a Krishna, suddenly his energy feels a change of climate because of such a powerful source. The moment you move near, you are magnetized. No one is magnetizing you; no one is trying anything. There is just the presence. You may feel that someone has hypnotized you, but no one is hynotizing. The presence of a Buddha whose energy has become formless, whose energy has gone to the source, who is centered at his source, the very presence, is hypnotizing. It becomes charismatic.

Buddha became Enlightened. Before his Enlightenment he had five disciples — BEFORE. They were ascetics — and when Buddha himself was a great ascetic, torturing his body in many, many ways, inventing new and more sadistic techniques to torture himself, those five were his ardent followers. Then Buddha felt that this was wholly, absolutely absurd. Just by torturing one's body one is not going to Realize oneself. When he realized this, he left ascetic ways. Those five followers left him immediately. They said, "You have fallen down. You are no more an ascetic." They left him.

When Buddha became Enlightened, the first idea that came to his mind was about those five followers. Once they were his followers, so he must go to them. He felt a duty. He must find them and tell them what he has found. So he searched for them, and he travelled in Bihar, from Bodh Gaya to Benares, just to find them. They were at Sarnath. Buddha never came back to Benares again, never came back to Sarnath again, because he came only for those five disciples.

He came to Sarnath. It was evening time, the sun was setting, and those five ascetics were sitting on a hillock. They saw Buddha coming, so they said, "That fallen Gautam Buddha, that Gautam Siddharth who has fallen from the path, is coming. We must not pay any respect to him. We should not pay to him even ordinary respect."

So they closed their eyes. Buddha came nearer and nearer, and those five ascetics began to feel a change — a change of mind. They became uneasy. When Buddha reached just near, suddenly all the five opened their eyes and fell at the feet of Buddha. Buddha said, "But why are you doing this? You decided not to give any respect to me, so why are you doing this?"

They said, "We are not doing. It is happening. What have you gained? You have become a magnetic force. We are just being pulled. What are you doing to us? Have you hypnotized us?" Buddha said, "No! I have done nothing to you, but something has happened in me. All the energies have fallen to the source. So wherever I move, suddenly a magnetic force is felt." That is why those who are against Buddha or Mahavir go on saying for centuries that that man was not good; he was hypnotizing people.

No one is hypnotizing. You become hypnotized: that is another thing. When your energy falls back to the original source, you become a magnetic center. This technique is to create this magnetic center in you.

The second question: *"Yesterday you said that the meditation technique of unwinding the mind is very significant. But in the West hundreds of Freudian and Jungian psychoanalysts and psychiatrists are practising this technique, but they are not getting very significant results in trying to transform the being. What are the reasons and drawbacks for their being unsuccessful?"*

There are many things to be noted. One: Western psychology does not yet believe in the Being of man. It believes only in the mind. Nothing beyond the mind is for Western psychology yet. If there is nothing beyond mind, then whatsoever you do is not going to help man really. At the most it can help man to be normal — at the most!

And what is normal? What is normalcy? Just the "average". If the average man himself is not normal, then being normal means nothing. It simply means you are adjusted with the crowd. So Western psychology is doing only one thing: whenever someone is maladjusted with the crowd, Western methods make that man again adjusted with the crowd. The crowd is not questioned at all; whether the crowd itself is okay is not the question.

For Eastern psychology, the crowd is not the criterion. Remember this distinction: for Eastern psychology the crowd is not the criterion, society is not the criterion. Society itself is ill. Then what is the criterion? For us a Buddha is a criterion. Unless you become Buddha-like, you are ill — not the society.

For Western psychology society is the criterion, because Buddha cannot be a criterion. They do not believe that there is such a thing as the inner Being. If there is no such thing as the inner Being, then there cannot be any Enlightenment. But when the inner Being becomes illumined, then there IS Enlightenment.

So Western psychology is really just therapeutic, just a part of medicine. It tries; it helps you to be readjusted. It is not a transcendence. The Eastern effort is for how to transcend the mind, because for us there are no mental diseases, remember. For us there are no mental diseases. Rather, the mind is the disease. For Western psychology the mind is not the disease. The mind is you: it is not the disease. The mind can be healthy, the mind can be ill.

For us the mind is the disease. The mind can never be healthy. Unless you go beyond mind, you can never be healthy. You can be ill and adjusted or you can be ill and unadjusted, but you can never be healthy. So the normal man is not really healthy. He is just within the boundaries: he is ill within the boundaries. The abnormal person is one who has gone beyond the boundaries, and the difference between the two is only of degrees — of quantity, not of quality.

A madman in a madhouse and you: there is no qualitative difference — only one of degrees. He is a little bit more mad than you; you are within the boundaries. Functionally, you can pull on. He cannot pull on now: he has gone further than you. He has an advanced case, nothing else. You are just on the path, and he has reached.

Western psychology tries to bring him back to the fold, to the herd, to the crowd. It makes him "normal". It is good: as far as it goes, it is good. But for us, unless a man goes beyond mind he is mad, because for us the mind is madness.

So we are trying to unwind the mind just to know that which is beyond it. They also try unwinding methods just to adjust the mind, but the beyond is not there. And remember this: unless you can go beyond yourself, nothing worthwhile happens. Unless something is beyond you which you can reach, life is meaningless.

Certain other things also: for Freud and the Freudians, man is really such a being that cannot be happy. The very being is such for them that man cannot be happy. If you are not unhappy, that is all. Remember, if you are not unhappy, be satisfied: it is enough. You cannot be happy. Why? Because

Freudian psychology says that happiness lies in being instinctual, happiness lies in being like an animal. That man cannot be. Reason goes on continuously interfering. You can lose your reason and become like an animal; then you can be happy. But then you will not be aware of happiness. This is the paradox for them.

If you fall down and become like an animal, you will be happy but you will not be aware. If you try to be aware you cannot be happy, because you cannot become like an animal. And the reason goes on interfering in everything. Man cannot lose reason and also man cannot live with reason: that is the problem. So you cannot be happy according to Freud. At the most, if you are wise, you can arrange your life in such a way that you will not be unhappy. This is a very negative thing.

For Eastern psychology or metaphysics or religion, a positive goal exists. You can be happy. You can be happy! Not only happy: you can be blissful. And Eastern psychology says that if you can feel that you are unhappy, that shows your potentiality, your possibility that you can be happy; otherwise, you cannot feel this being unhappy either.

If a man can see darkness he has eyes, and one who can see darkness can see light. Remember, blind men cannot see darkness. You may have been thinking that blind men live in darkness. Forget it completely. They cannot see darkness, because even to see darkness eyes are needed. If you can feel unhappiness you have eyes, and if you can feel unhappiness you can feel happiness. Really, if you cannot feel happiness, there is no possibility of feeling unhappiness. These are polar opposites.

You are capable of being totally happy, but then the mind will not do. Take it in this way: if you fall down and become just a body, you will be happy. Freud also agreed with this: if you fall down and forget your reason completely, if you become like an animal, just a body, you will be happy but you will not know it. With the mind you can know it, but then you cannot be happy because the mind goes on disturbing. The body can be happy, but the mind goes on disturbing.

There is another possibility which the East has worked out: go beyond. Freud says if you fall down and become an animal, you will be happy but you will not know it. If you are in the mind you can know, but you cannot be happy. Eastern search says that if you go beyond mind you will be happy and also aware: that is a third point — of the beyond.

So these are three points. Man is in the middle. Below is the animal existence. Go to a forest and look at animals: they may not be aware that they are happy, but you will feel that they are happy. Go to the beach in the morning, or go to a garden in the morning and listen to the singing of the birds. They may not know it, but you will feel they are happy. You have never been singing like that. Look deep down in their eyes: they are so unclouded and innocent. They are happy, but you are not happy.

Fall down and become a body only: then you will be happy. Or, go beyond and become the spirit or become the Being, and you will be happy. But in the middle you will be always tense because mind is really not the end. It is just a rope stretched between two realities — body and soul.

So you are just on the rope like a *nata* (a tightrope walker). A tightrope walker cannot be at ease. Either he must go back or he must go forward, but he must not remain on the rope. He must get down from the rope, and there are two possibilities: he can go backward, or he can go forward and beyond. Mind is a rope, and to live with the mind is a tightrope walking. You are bound to be unbalanced, uneasy. Every moment there is anxiety, anguish. The mind's life is tension. That is why Western psychology succeeds in making you normal, but fails to make you a self-actualized person.

But there are new trends, and they are thinking. And the East is now penetrating the West very deeply. Really, that is the East's way to conquer. The West conquered the East: the way was very gross. The East has its own ways of conquering — very subtle ways, silent ways. Now the East is penetrating the Western mind deeply. Without any violence, without any visible conflict, the East is penetrating the West very deeply. And sooner or later, Western psychology will have to evolve concepts about transcending — about how to transcend the mind.

Unwinding can be helpful in both the ways. If you are just trying to create a normal mind, unwinding will be helpful. But then your goal is not transcendence. If your goal is transcendence, then too unwinding can be helpful. All these techniques can be used for ordinary mental peace also, and all these techniques can be used for a real silence which is not of the mind.

There are two types of silence — one of the mind in which the mind is silent, and another silence when the mind is no more. That silence, when the mind is no more, is altogether different from mental peace. The mind is there, only not very mad. The madness is slowed down — that is all.

Western psychology must become a metaphysics: only then can man transcend. It must become a philosophy also, and ultimately it must become religion. Only then can man be helped to transcend.

The third question: *"You have been explaining many meditation methods to us. However, isn't it true that no method can be all that powerful unless one is initiated into it?"*

A method becomes qualitatively different when you are initiated into it. I am talking about the methods: you can use them. Once you know the scientific background and the way, the know-how, you can use it. But initiation makes it qualitatively different. If I initiate you into a particular method it will be a different thing, because many things are implied in initiation.

When I talk about a method and I explain it to you, you can use it on your own. The method is explained to you, but whether it will suit you or not, how it will work upon you, what type of person you are, is not discussed. It is not possible.

In initiation, you are more important than the technique. When the Master initiates you, he observes you. He finds out what is your type, he finds out how much you have worked through in your past lives, where you are right at this moment, at what center you are functioning right now, and then he decides about the method: he chooses the method. It is an individual approach. Method is not important: YOU are important. YOU are being studied and observed and analyzed. Your past lives, your consciousness, your mind, your body, they are dissected. You are felt deeply in terms of where you are because the journey begins from that point — the point where you are just now. Any method will not do.

Then the Master chooses a particular method for you, and if he feels that this particular method has to be changed for you, that minute alterations or some additions are needed, he adds, he deletes, he makes the method fit for you. And then he gives the initiation; then he gives the method to you. That is why it is insisted that whenever you are initiated in a method, you are not to talk about it. It has to be secret because it is individual. If you tell it to someone else, it may not be helpful or it may even be harmful.

It has to be kept secret. Unless you achieve and your Master says now you can initiate others, it should not be talked about at all — not uttered, not even to your husband or your wife or your friend. No, it is absolutely secret because it is dangerous. It is very powerful. It has been chosen and made for you. It will work for you, but it is not for any other individual in the world. Really, each individual is so unique that he needs a different method, and with a slight difference a method can become suitable for him.

What I am talking about — these 112 methods — they are generalized methods. They are 112 generalized methods, all the methods which have been used. This is a general form so that you become acquainted. You can try. If something suits you, you can go on. But this is not initiation into a method. Initiation is a personal, individual affair between the Master and the disciple. It is a secret transmission. Then, not only this: many other things are implied in initiation. Then the Master chooses a right moment when he will give the method to you so that it goes deep into the unconscious.

While I am talking, your conscious mind is listening. You will forget. When I have talked about 112 methods, you will not even be able to rename them again — the 112. You will forget many completely. You will be able to remember a few, and then you will be mixed up and confused. What is what you will not know.

The Master has to choose a right moment when your unconscious is open, and then he gives you the method. Then it goes deep down into the unconscious. So many times initiation is given in sleep, not when you are conscious. Many times initiation is given to you in a deep hypnotic trance, when your conscious mind is completely asleep and your unconscious mind is open.

That is why surrender is so much needed in initiation. Unless you surrender initiation cannot be given, because unless you surrender your conscious mind is always alert and on watch. When you surrender, your conscious mind can then be relieved of its duty and your unconscious mind can come directly in contact with the Master.

A right moment has to be chosen, and then you have to be prepared for initiation. It may take months to prepare you: there has to be the right food, the right sleep, and everything has to come to a tranquil point. Only then can you be initiated, so initiation is a long process, an individual process. Unless someone is ready to surrender totally, initiation is not possible.

So I am not initiating you into these methods. I am just making you acquainted with these methods. If someone feels that some method hits him deeply and he feels that he should be initiated in that method, I can initiate him into that method. But then it is going to be a long process. Then your individuality has to be completely known. You have to become totally naked so that nothing remains hidden. And then, THEN things become very easy — because when a right method is given to a right person at a right moment, it works immediately.

Sometimes it happens that while initiating the disciple, the disciple becomes Enlightened: just the initiation becomes the

THE BOOK OF THE SECRETS

Enlightenment. Then the method becomes alive — when it is given by a Master privately, individually. Whatsoever I am doing now is not initiation, remember this. This is a scientific approach just to revive the 112 methods — to make them known.

If someone is interested, he can be initiated. And when you are really interested you will seek initiation, because working alone on the method is a very long affair. It may take lives, it may take years, and you may not be able to' sustain so long a period. Through initiation it becomes very easy, and then the method becomes a transmission. Then through the method the Teacher starts working in you. Initiation is a living relationship with the Master, and a living relationship, of course, goes deep. It changes you and transforms you.

The next question: *"You quoted George Gurdjieff as saying that identification is the only sin, but in many techniques the process of identification is used. They say, for example, become one with the beloved, become one with the rose flower or become one with the Guru. And, moreover, empathy is supposed to be a meditative and spiritual quality, so the above saying of Gurdjieff's seems to be partially true and useful only for certain techniques."*

No! It is not partially true: it is totally true. But then you will have to understand. Identification is unconscious, but when you use identification in a meditative technique it is conscious.

For example, your name is Ram. Someone insults "Ram": immediately YOU feel insulted because you are identified with the name "Ram". But this is not a conscious thing for you: it is unconscious. Your mind doesn't work in this way: "I am called Ram. Of course, I am not Ram. This is only my name, and everyone is born nameless. This name is given, and it is arbitrary. This man is only insulting my arbitrary name, so am I to be angry or not?" You would never reason it out in this way. If you would reason it out in this way, you would not be angry at all. But suddenly someone insults "Ram" and you are insulted, but this is just an arbitrary name. This identification is unconscious: it is not conscious.

398

When you are identifying with a rose, it is a conscious effort. You are not identified with the rose. You are TRYING to identify yourself with the rose, and you are trying to forget yourself. You are trying to become one with the rose, and you are deeply conscious — aware of the whole process. YOU are doing it. Even if identification is done consciously, it becomes a meditation. And even if you do a certain technique of meditation unconsciously, it is not meditation — remember.

You go on doing your prayer every morning or every night unconsciously, just as a routine affair. While doing it you are not conscious at all of what you are doing. You are not conscious at all of what words you are saying in prayer. You just repeat them like a parrot.

This is not meditation. And if you are taking your bath consciously, it is a meditation. So remember this: whatsoever you are doing consciously, with alertness, fully aware, becomes meditation. Even if you kill someone consciously, while fully conscious, it is meditative.

That is what Krishna was saying to Arjuna: "Do not be afraid. DO NOT be afraid! Kill, murder, fuly conscious, knowing fully that no one is murdered and no one is killed." Arjuna can very easily kill his enemies unconsciously. He could go mad in a rage and kill: that is easy. But Krishna is saying, "Be alert. Be fully conscious. Just become the instrument of Divine hands, and know well that no one is killed, no one can be killed. The inner Being is eternal, immortal. So you are only destroying forms, not that which is behind the forms. So destroy the forms." If Arjuna can be so meditatively aware, then there is no violence. No one is killed, no sin is committed.

I will tell you one anecdote in Nagarjuna's life. Nagarjuna was one of the great Masters India has produced — of the calibre of Buddha and Mahavir and Krishna. And Nagarjuna was a rare genius. Really, on the intellectual level there is no comparison in the whole world. Such a keen and penetrating intellect rarely happens. He was passing through a city — a capital city. He always remained naked. The queen of that kingdom was a believer, a follower — and a lover of Nagarjuna, a devotee. So Nagarjuna came to the palace to ask for food. He had one wooden begging bowl. The queen said, "Give this begging bowl to me. I will cherish it as a gift, and I have another made for you. You can take that."

Nagarjuna said, "Okay!" The other one was golden, and many precious stones were used in it. It was very valuable. Nagarjuna didn't say anything. Ordinarily no sannyasin would take it. He would say, "I cannot touch gold." But Nagarjuna took it. If, really, gold is just mud, then why make any distinction? He took it. Even the queen didn't feel it good. She felt, "Why? He should have said 'No'. Such a great saint! Why has he taken such a valuable thing while he lives naked, without any clothes, without any possessions? Why should he not reject it?"

If Nagarjuna would have rejected, the queen would have insisted, requested, but then she would have felt better. Nagarjuna took it and went away. One thief saw him passing from the city, and the thief thought, "This man cannot have this begging bowl. Someone is bound to steal it or someone is bound to take it away from him. With this nakedness — how can he protect it?" So he followed: the thief followed Nagarjuna.

Nagarjuna was staying outside the town in an old monastery, alone. The monastery was just in ruins. He went in; he heard the footsteps of the man. But he didn't look behind because he thought, "He must be coming for the begging bowl, not for me, because who would come? No one ever comes following me to these ruins."

He went in. The thief stood behind a wall and waited. Nagarjuna, seeing that he was waiting outside, threw the begging bowl out of the door. The thief couldn't understand. What type of man is this? Naked, with such a precious thing, and he has thrown it out.

So he asked Nagarjuna, "Can I come in, Sir? I have to ask a question." Nagajuna said, "I have thrown the bowl out just so that you can come in — to help you to come in, because I am just going to take my afternoon nap. You would have come for the begging bowl, but then there would have been no meeting with me. So come in."

The thief came in. He said, "Such a precious thing and you have thrown it? I am a thief, and you are such a sage that I cannot lie before you. I am a thief." Nagarjuna said, "Do not be worried. Everyone is a thief. You proceed on. Do not waste time about such unnecessary things." The thief said, "Sometimes, looking at persons like you, my mind also longs to know how this state can be attained. I am a thief; it seems impossible for me. But I hope and I pray that someday I will also be capable of throwing such a precious thing. Teach me something. And I go to many sages, and I am a well-known thief, so everyone knows me. They say, "First leave your business, your profession, and only then can you proceed in meditation. That is impossible. I cannot leave it, so I cannot proceed in meditation."

Nagarjuna said, "If someone says first leave theft and then proceed in meditation, then he doesn't know meditation at all — because how is meditation related with theft? There is no relationship. So you go on doing whatsoever you are doing. I will give you a technique; you practise this."

The thief said, "Now it seems we can go together. So I can go on doing my profession? What is the technique? Tell me immediately."

Nagarjuna said, "You just remain aware. When you go to steal something, just be fully conscious and aware. When you are breaking into some house, be fully conscious. When you are breaking into a treasury, be fully conscious. When you are taking something out of the treasury, be fully conscious. Do it consciously. Whatsoever you do is no concern of mine. And come after fifteen days, but do not come if you do not practise. Practise fifteen days, go on doing whatsoever you are doing, but do it fully consciously."

The third day the thief came back and he said, "Fifteen days are too long, and you are a very tricky fellow. You have given such a technique that if I am fully conscious I cannot steal.

401

The last three nights continuously I have been to the palace. I reached the treasury, I opened it. Precious things were before me, but then I became fully conscious. And the moment I become fully conscious, I became like a Buddha statue. I could not proceed further; my hand would not move. And the whole treasury seemed useless, so I have been going back there again and again. What am I to do? And you said that leaving my profession was not a condition, but your method seems to have a built-in process."

Nagarjuna said, "Do not come to me again. Now you can choose. If you want to go on stealing, forget meditation. If you want meditation, then forget stealing. You can choose." The thief said, "You have put me in a dilemma. For these three days, I have known that I am alive. And when I came back without taking anything from the palace, for the first time I felt that I was a sovereign, not a thief. These three days have been so blissful that now I cannot leave meditation. You have tricked me; now initiate me and make me your disciple. There is no need to go on trying. Three days are enough."

Whatsoever may be the object, if you are conscious it becomes meditation. Try identification "consciously": it becomes meditation. Unconsciously, it is a great sin.

You are all identified with many things: "This is mine, that is mine..." You are identified! "This is my country, this is my nation, this is my national flag..."

If someone throws your national flag, you become furious. What is he doing? And you have no nation and all national flags are myths. It is good to play with them like children; they are toys. But you can murder and be murdered for them, and countries can be created and destroyed for insulting a national flag. And it is just a piece of cloth!

What is happening? You are identified with it. That identification is unconscious. Unconsciousness is sin.

Enough for today.